SHI near Nankin.

CHINESE CIVILIZATION

CHINESE CIVILIZATION

From the Ming Revival to Chairman Mao

YONG YAP & ARTHUR COTTERELL

St. Martin's Press, New York

For Alan

© Yong Yap and Arthur Cotterell 1977

Printed in Great Britain
Library of Congress Catalog Card Number: 77–24816
ISBN: 0–312–13381–2

First published in the United States of America in 1977

The poetry on page 116 and the prose on pages 117 and 118
are reproduced from *Yuan Mei: Eighteenth-
Century Chinese Poet* by Arthur Waley, by kind
permission of Stanford University Press.

Contents

Acknowledgements

The author and publishers would like to thank the following museums, institutions and photographers for permission to reproduce illustrations and for supplying photographs:

Courtesy of the Asian Art Museum of San Francisco, Avery Brundage Collection 112; Bodleian Library 34; British Museum 44–5, 66, 74 above, 77, 84 left and right, 85, 87, 90, *103*, 129, *141* (Michael Holford Library); Camera and Pen International 28, *40*, 48, 51, 52, 55, 56–7, 58, 189; Camera Press 151, 152, 156, 159, 171, 178, 179, 186–7 (photo Sven Simon), *194–5*, 202, 205 (photo Alfred Gregory), 219 (photo Max Hastings), 220 (photo Richard Harrington), 223, 224, 229, 230; Chait Galleries, New York 60, 63; Percival David Foundation of Chinese Art *37*; Mary Evans Picture Library endpaper, 83, 88–9, 91, 99, 124 above and below, 130, 139, 176; Werner Forman Archive 70; from W. and F. Halfpenny, *New Designs for Chinese Temples* (London, 1752) 98; Michael Holford Library (Collection Mr P. D. Krolik, London) 109; Keystone Press Agency 180, 184–5, 191, 206, 209 left and right, 212–13, 216–17; MacQuitty Collection *193*, *196* above and below; from Martin, *Awakening of China* (1902) 146; from J. V. G. Mills, *Ma Huan, Ying-yai Sheng-lan, The Overall Survey of the Ocean's Shores, 1433* (Cambridge University Press) 31; National Palace Museum, Taipei, Taiwan, Republic of China 73, 74 below, 80, 81; from Joseph Needham, *Science and Civilisation in China*, vol. 4 (W. Heffer & Sons Ltd) 21, 25, 26 above and below; Popperfoto 166–7, 169, 199, 200–1; Radio Times Hulton Picture Library 82, 120, 127, 135, 163, 164, 165; from Osvald Sirén, *Gardens of China* (Ronald Press, New York, 1949) 117; Courtesy of the Smithsonian Institution, Freer Gallery of Art, Washington, DC 96, 100–1; Spectrum Colour Library *38–9*; Spink & Son, London, frontispiece, 69, 114, 115; from Thompson, *Illustrations of China and its People* (1873–4) 136–7; Ullstein Bilderdienst, West Berlin 148 above; Victoria and Albert Museum *78* above, 78 below (Michael Holford Library), *104*, 106–7, 111 (Michael Holford Library), 131, *142–3*, *144* above (Michael Holford Library), *144* below; Roger Viollet, Paris 133, 147 above; Weidenfeld and Nicolson Archive 12, 75, 123, 146 below, 148, 174, 186; from W. Perceval Yetts, 'The Legend of Confucius', in *Nine Dragon Screen* (China Society, London, 1965) 16.

Picture research by Anne Horton
Maps by Cartographic Enterprises

Numerals in italics indicate colour illustrations

The author and publishers have taken all possible care to trace and acknowledge the source of illustrations. If any errors have accidentally occurred, the publishers will be happy to correct them in future editions, provided that they receive notification.

Maps

METRIC MEASUREMENTS

Some readers may be less familiar with the metric measurements used throughout this text. The following is a guide to their English equivalents:

1 millimetre	0.04 inch
1 centimetre	0.39 inch
1 metre	3.3 feet (1.1 yards)
1 kilometre	0.6 mile
1 square centimetre	0.155 square inch
1 square metre	11 square feet (1.2 square yards)
1 square kilometre	0.386 square mile
1 hectare	2.5 acres
1 kilogram	2.2 pounds
1 tonne	0.98 ton

Preface

The Yuan Empire of the Mongol invader Kubilai Khan, whose splendour and power so amazed the thirteenth-century Venetian traveller Marco Polo, represented no more than an interval of disruption between the early and the late phases of Chinese civilization. To the successors of the Mongols, the native Ming dynasty, fell the task of restoring the blighted national heritage.

After a discussion of the remarkable and little-known early phase of Chinese history in the Introduction, this book describes the development of civilization in China after the expulsion of the Mongols in 1368. It covers the major artistic and literary achievements of the Ming dynasty and of the eighteenth-century Ch'ien Lung period, European imperialist expansion in East Asia in the nineteenth century and Chinese reaction to it, the final dissolution of the imperial system in 1911–12, and the massive political, social and economic reconstruction of the present-day People's Republic. *Chinese Civilization from the Ming Revival to Chairman Mao* attempts to illustrate for the reader the underlying continuity of a great tradition in a country which once again is re-emerging as a leading influence in world affairs.

Introduction

Not far from the black brick fortifications of ancient Nanking, the first imperial capital of the Ming dynasty, on the southern slope of Purple Mountain, there are two distinguished tombs, where rest the mortal remains of two of the founders of late Chinese civilization. The oldest tomb, the Ming-hsiao-ling, was built at the end of the fourteenth century for the first Ming emperor, Hung-wu, whose concern for restoring the former glories of the Chinese Empire on a firm basis can be still observed in the circuit of twenty kilometres which forms the city walls of Nanking. Approaching this tomb is an avenue lined by splendid, daunting statues of animals and men – elephants, camels, lions, as well as officials from both the civil and military arms of government. Though visitors to the Ming-hsiao-ling, passing along this imperial roadway, have not always been able to resist that powerful desire to attain immortality by scratching their names on the statuary, it is the inscription which Emperor Ming Hung-wu himself had engraved on a great stone that dominates everything. 'Rule like the T'ang and Sung,' the characters proclaim. This injunction to his successors echoed down the ages and later occupants of the dragon throne were often reminded of the duty to past traditions of greatness by anxious scholars and officials. The Chinese have seen the Ming period (1368–1644) as one of recovery from the ravages and misgovernment of the Mongol conquest, which was brought to an end by Emperor Ming Hung-wu and his generals. In 1372 a Ming army under general Hsu Ta had crossed the Gobi desert, sacked Karakorum, and pursued the last Mongol ruler into the fastness of Siberia.

The other tomb, the Chung-shan-ling-mo, set in a forested hillside, is the mausoleum of Dr Sun Yat-sen, the founder of the Chinese Republic. By siting this mausoleum, which is reached by a climb of nearly four hundred steps via intermediate pavilions, in the vicinity of the Ming tomb its builders were making an historical judgment of the first importance. Whereas Chu Yuan-chang, the peasant monk who became Emperor Ming Hung-wu, restored the Chinese imperium and inaugurated the late phase of Chinese civilization, half a millennium later an equally humble man, a Chinese emigrant to Hawaii, Dr Sun Yat-sen, drew upon his Western experience and education to convert the agitation against the declining Ch'ing dynasty (1644–1911) into a modern political movement, so bringing to a close the imperial era: he became the provisional president of the Republic. Both men shaped the course of later Chinese history. Our perspective, however, on the events that have flowed from the incident on 9 October 1911, when a bomb accidentally exploded in the office of the main revolutionary organization in Hankow and precipitated

Water-powered blowing-engine for blast furnaces and forges as depicted in the *Nung Shu* (*Treatise on Agriculture*), published in 1313.

an anti-Manchu revolution that forced the last Ch'ing emperor to abdicate within five months, is less certain and perhaps more open to question because the interpretation of contemporary events remains more a matter of debate. As in the case of Emperor Ming Hung-wu, the advice of Dr Sun to posterity is inscribed on the walls of his mausoleum: they are his three principles of nationalism, the people's livelihood and democracy. The contrast between the outlook of these two founding ancestors, the former of the restored Empire and the latter of the modern Republic, is underlined by the materials used for the construction of their tombs. Despite its recall of ancient imperial tombs and its traditional roof of coloured tiles, the overwhelming impression of the Chung-shan-ling-mo on the visitor is the sudden arrival of the present: brick and stone have been replaced by concrete.

When Emperor Ming Hung-wu chose the T'ang dynasty (618–906) and the Two Sungs (960–1279) as models for his successors to emulate he had in mind the achievements of the Empire in reunification after intervals of confusion and foreign invasion. The T'ang rulers had succeeded in holding together the largest and most populous state in the world, thereby making China an exception in the pre-modern world to the rule that political units of such magnitude are unable to survive over long periods of time. More than fifty-three million people inhabited provinces that stretched from the Great Wall in the north to Annam in the south, a distance of nine thousand kilometres, and from Tibet in the west to the Pacific in the east, another five thousand kilometres. In addition, Chinese authority extended into Central Asia, 'the Western Regions', as far as the Aral Sea. But this western extension was not an innovation of T'ang foreign policy: Chinese arms first reached Central Asia during the reign of Emperor Han Wu-ti (140–87 BC), a ruler determined to deal with the nomad menace, then the Hsiung Nu or the Huns, even if it took a three-thousand-kilometre march to obtain Ferghana horses as mounts for his own cavalry. Inherited, too, from the Han Empire (202 BC–AD 220) was the chief institution devised to run the imperial system, the civil service. Though the origins of state bureaucracy lie in the late feudal period (722–221 BC), when rival princes sought to attract to their service scholar statesmen and officials, it was only after the establishment of a unified empire that the Confucian conception of the loyal civil servant became the social ideal. Confucius (551–479 BC) failed to attain ministerial office during his own lifetime, and experienced the coldness of neglect, but his teachings had such an immense influence on China from the Han Empire onwards that he has been dubbed the 'uncrowned Emperor'. What this pragmatic philosopher sought was the opening up of public administration to the able and virtuous, those who knew of the duty of minister to prince and the relationship of son to father. The *carrière ouverte aux talents* became a reality in the T'ang transformation of the examination system of the Han, the *k'o-chu*, into the standard means of recruitment to the civil service. This arrangement was perfected during the Northern Sung dynasty (960–1126), when there were in the capital government-sponsored universities and colleges to prepare candidates for the entrance examinations and in the provinces grants of land were made to encourage local scholarship and sustain the widespread movement for popular education.

Feudalism had been dealt its death-blow by Ch'in Shih Huang-ti, 'the

First Emperor', in the original unification of China, eight hundred years before the T'ang. The short-lived Ch'in dynasty (221–207 BC) was a turning point in early Chinese civilization because of the effectiveness of centralization and the reduction of all 'in a uniform manner'. Through extreme measures and the heavy burdens he placed on the people, such as the construction of the Great Wall, Ch'in Shih Huang-ti provoked a popular revolt that swept away his house and branded him as a ruthless tyrant; yet in the moment of Ch'in's humiliation all attempts to re-establish feudal authority failed. From the outset the Han Empire was a compromise that reflected these uncertain political conditions which were only resolved in the vast social and economic revolution of the Former Han (220 BC–9 AD). The first Han emperor, Kao-tsu, was the other successful peasant claimant to the dragon throne in Chinese history. Retaining the administrative structure of the Ch'in Empire, his house came to rely on scholar officials of Confucian persuasion. The *shih* – the gentry, knights and scholars – were the most senior of the four estates below the feudal hierarchy, whose families had been uprooted and dispersed by Ch'in Shih Huang-ti. Such younger sons of noble families, educated but without rank, were obliged to rely on their own exertions, finding their way to status and wealth by service in what were the beginnings of a secretariat for central administration. Seeking firm support for his regime, Emperor Han Kao-tsu favoured an alliance between the *shih* and the *nung*, the peasant-farmers, in order to ensure administrative order and agricultural prosperity. The use of corvée, the set number of labour days owed to the government by the *nung*, was relaxed with the discontinuation of grandiose projects like the Great Wall, and the civilian arm of government was allowed to gain the initiative in the imperial executive.

The four estates of Chinese society, in order of precedence, were *shih*, the scholar gentry; *nung*, the peasant-farmers; *kung*, the artisans; and *shang*, the merchants. The low social position of the merchants, a consequence of princely interest in such economic activities as metallurgy and hydraulic conservancy works from feudal times, was confirmed by the Confucian distaste for business and imperial intervention in means of production and distribution during the reign of Emperor Han Wu-ti. In 120–19 BC an imperial monopoly was declared over the iron and salt industries, while the *p'ing chang*, or 'levelling system', was set up in 110 BC in order not only to prevent any cornering of the food market by the *shang*, but also to fill the treasury coffers. The 'ever normal' granary served to limit speculation: provincial officials were ordered to establish public granaries, to buy grain when prices were low, and to sell in times of shortage. These policies of nationalization recur with modifications throughout Chinese history – a Fermented Beverages Authority came into existence at the end of the Former Han and the T'ang added tea to the list of industries under imperial control. Nationalization was part of the throne's attempt to protect the *nung*, upon whose diligent toil the Empire rested. More directly the later 'equal field' system, which entailed the periodic redistribution of land to the poorest peasant-farmers, sought to preserve the agricultural basis of the economy. Emperor Han Wu-ti had decreed in 119 BC that merchants could not own land, but such regulations were generally found unenforceable. The blocking of all avenues of social advancement to the *shang* was much more effective because it prevented the

漢以臣皆墨城諸弟各三孔治
往服墨北子廬年子任
從心北泗而於絰子別
弟喪去墓去塚皆魯
子及魯上家上服城
及六凡而哀而心北
家年六去推心喪泗

sons of successful businessmen from becoming officials. A poor scholar without an official position would prefer farming to trade as a means of livelihood, lest he spoil any future opportunity of a civil service career.

The administrative system, therefore, played a vital part in preserving the Empire: it proved to be one of the most stable frameworks for social order ever developed. Into its offices were recruited the learned, the *shih*, whose scale of values differed profoundly from that of the *shang*. Thus the state retained its oversight of the economy and was instrumental in the advance of science and technology. Inventions of major importance, to name a few, were the seismograph by Chang Heng (78–139); paper by Ts'ai Lung, the director of the imperial workshop, in 105; block-printing during the T'ang Empire, movable type being introduced at the beginning of the Two Sungs; and in 31 the introduction of a water-powered metallurgical blowing-engine, an application which led directly to the production of steel. Yet, above all, the perennial concern of government was water control. The founder of the first dynasty, the legendary Hsia (*c.* 2000–1500 BC), was Yu the Great Engineer, who dealt with 'the inundating waters' by opening 'passages for the streams throughout the nine provinces and conducting them to the seas'. The model of public service, Yu spent thirteen years mastering the waters without once returning home to see his wife and family, and brought 'water benefits' to all the people: floods ceased and the fields were irrigated. The close link between hydraulic engineering and politics was connected with the fundamental role of nature in early Chinese civilization, when it was believed that natural phenomena, like flooding, earthquakes or eclipses, were manifestations of supernatural power. The benevolence of Shang Ti, Heaven, was entreated by the sacrifices of the priest-king, whose chief duties were the preservation of a harmonious relationship with the spiritual realm and the organization of practical works in the countryside. This ancient intimacy of man and environment which found expression in the Yin-Yang theory – a view of the

The grave of Confucius, at which his disciples remained in mourning for at least three years. During the Han Empire (202 BC–AD 200) it became a custom for the emperor to offer sacrifices to the philosopher.

universe as a single intricately balanced organism, undergoing continuous alterations through the interaction of the two natural forces of the Yin and the Yang – stemmed from the everyday experience of the farmer of the Yellow River valley, the cradle of Chinese civilization. The loess soil of North China is very fertile when well watered but a sudden deluge, or flooding from rivers, can alter the landscape itself. The Yellow River, sometimes called 'China's Sorrow' because of its tendency to change course, compelled the Chinese to become expert in hydraulic conservancy schemes, whilst the combination of the self-fertilizing capacity of loess when there is sufficient moisture and the capacity for self-renewal of the rich silt deposits in the alluvial plains by flooding or irrigation permitted accelerated development towards civilization. Never passing through a pastoral period, the Chinese people were from early times able to support by agriculture a large population in high densities.

The triumph of Ch'in Shih Huang-ti and the imperial unification of 221 BC was achieved partly through the economic and strategic advantages of the Chengkuo Canal, opened in the year 246 BC. The construction of large-scale hydraulic conservancy schemes was a settled policy on the part of the state of Ch'in. Organizing such public works greatly increased the central authority of the prince, at the expense of the nobility, and a more streamlined state emerged, the predecessor of the bureaucratic system that later comprised the Empire. The Chengkuo Canal transformed present-day Shensi into the first key economic area, an area where agricultural productivity and facilities of transport provided a supply of grain-tribute so superior to that of other areas, that the people who controlled it could control all China. As the Han historian Ssu-ma Ch'ien noted: 'When the canal was finished it irrigated 266,800 hectares of poor land with rich silt. . . . Thus, the interior became a fertile plain without bad years. Ch'in, then, grew rich and strong and finally conquered all the other feudal states'. The corvée provided the manpower required for hydraulic engineering, a vast supply of labour unavailable in primitive collectivist society. In striking contrast to Rome, slavery was never a significant feature in the social development of China. Exactly how many slaves existed at various periods is impossible to calculate from surviving evidence, but all historians are agreed on the relative smallness of this inferior class. In 44 there were one hundred thousand government slaves, the majority of whom were engaged in looking after government-owned livestock. The *shih* frequently complained about their uselessness: they 'idle with folded hands' unlike the hard-working *nung*. The availability of free labour was the result of another advance in technology, the working of iron. 'The ugly metal', as it was called, provided more efficient hoes, ploughshares, picks and axes: it allowed the effective working of the land by a smaller number of peasant-farmers, so reducing the need for feudal bonds. China has been called a hydraulic society, but the rapid strides in iron metallurgy, leading to the production of cast iron in the fourth century BC or seventeen centuries before the West, may have been the chief economic factor that shaped Chinese society, putting to an end the Bronze Age legacy of slavery from the Shang, the first historical dynasty (1500–1207 BC).

Iron weapons, or bronze weapons with iron cores, partially explain the crushing defeats that the armies of Ch'in Shih Huang-ti inflicted on his opponents, since in his possession were the rich deposits of iron ore in present-day Szechuan. Imperial unification was intimately bound up with technical advance, but the ability of a dynasty to endure was also related to the acquiescence of the governed and the means by which they could effect political changes. Another formative influence on the social structure was the crossbow, an offensive weapon used by the conscripted *nung*. Such a powerful weapon being in the hands of the people without a superior armour being available to the ruling class meant that the balance of authority was not fixed and unmoving. The *nung* were not at an overwhelming tactical disadvantage, like the medieval serf pitted against the armoured knight in the West, and the philosopher Mencius (*c.* 390–305 BC), the greatest disciple of Confucius, could reasonably argue the right of the people to take up arms. Whereas Confucius had seen the *shih* as custodians of public morality, even to the extent of outright criticism of the dubious policies of a prince, Mencius elaborated the concept of righteous opposition to unjust government into a democratic theory of justified rebellion against wicked rulers. From the firmness of principle advocated by Confucius derived the Censorate, the mentor of the imperial civil service: from Mencius' notion that the Mandate of Heaven was withdrawn from a corrupt dynasty whenever a successful rebel arose evolved what has been termed the 'Chinese Constitution'. The achievement or loss of the Mandate acted as the safety valve of the centralized Empire. Rebellions, either peasant risings often associated with religious upheavals or bids for the dragon throne by powerful generals, had to demonstrate something more than brute force. It was a lesson that Chu Yuan-chang learned – the consent of the *nung* was as crucial as the co-operation of the *shih*.

A world apart, isolated geographically from the other centres of ancient civilization, the Empire has appeared to some observers as unchanging. In reality there were internal transformations and constant movements of boundaries: these alterations are not always perceived clearly for the reason that they were slow and large-scale. The disintegration of the Han Empire in the period of the Three Kingdoms (221–65) was a symptom of profound changes in economic balance, with new economic areas in Szechuan and the lower Yang-tze valley rivalling the older core area of Shensi, as well as the decline of the imperial model through the growth of powerful families in the provinces. That China recovered from this time of disunity which culminated in the Tartar Partition (317–587), when all the lands to the north of the Yang-tze River watershed passed into the hands of barbarian tribesmen from the steppes, is testimony to the singular resilience and absorptive capacity of its culture. Sinicization of the invaders of North China in 500 led the Toba Wei emperor to issue a decree prohibiting the use of the Tartar language, costume and customs. Everyone had become Chinese. There was nothing like the collapse of Latin culture in the western provinces of the Roman Empire after the invasion by Germanic tribes. On the contrary, the *nung*, steeped in the ancient lore, constituted a huge cultural reservoir not easily drained of Chinese traditions, whilst the *shih*, in sole possession of literacy, administrative ability and knowledge of hydraulic engineering, were essential for the apparatus of state. The T'ang rulers took over and built upon the achievements of the Tartar dynasties, notably the reform of the tax system, the revision of land-tenure and the re-creation of the divisional militia, just as they continued with moderation the water schemes of the semi-barbarian dynasty, the Sui, which reunited the Empire in 589.

Culturally, the T'ang dynasty was an era of renaissance. Emperor T'ang Hsuan-tsung, known during his reign as Ming Huang, 'the Bright Emperor', presided over a splendid court until the disastrous rebellion of An Lu-shan in 755. Poets, painters and musicians thronged the palace; architects were commissioned to enhance the beauty of the capital; and the tragic love of Ming Huang for Yang Kuei-fei, a beautiful concubine, lent a romantic glamour to his early reign. This was the time in which China's finest poets lived. Literary activity was encouraged in some measure by the restoration and development of the civil service examinations. Empress Wu, the only woman to don the yellow robe as sole member of the Chou dynasty (690–705), made poetry a requisite for higher qualifications and official promotion. The Literary Examination opened the way to an official career for Po Chu-i in 800, when his poetical compositions were highly commended. Another contributory factor towards the intellectual ferment of the T'ang was the partial eclipse of the Confucian ethic. Taoism, the ancient antagonist of Confucian philosophy, received the accolade of respectability when its books were declared classics and accepted as subjects worthy of examination. Originally a reaction against the feudal religion of ancient China, the sacrifices prepared by the priest-king for Shang Ti and the deceased ancestors which Confucianism had adapted as an ethical code to suit the social conditions of a stable empire, Taoism developed as an alternative philosophy for the *shih* and the closest thing to an indigenous faith of personal salvation for the *nung*. In the event it was the popular response that became dominant, though the old subversive elements of Taoist doctrine were never entirely lost. Social organization was thought of as a necessary evil, nothing more. 'A thief steals a purse and is hanged,' Chuang-tzu had remarked in the fourth century BC, 'whilst another man steals a state and becomes a prince.' The transformation of Taoism, on the other hand, into a religious faith with an elaborate church and liturgy was caused by competition with Buddhism, the only significant import to the Chinese cultural area before the nineteenth century. By 500 the Indian religion had penetrated all parts of China, but it was during the T'ang Empire that the Buddhist challenge for spiritual hegemony was finally resolved. Although the struggle was fiercely contested and accompanied by scenes of mass fervour, the strength of the rational, sceptical tradition of Confucian philosophy proved decisive. The *sangha*, the Buddhist monk community, was incorporated in the apparatus of state, a Bureau of National Sacrifice being established in 694 to scrutinize the ordination of monks and nuns. The Chinese political tradition that took for granted strong central authority, embodied in the ruler as Son of Heaven, fully reasserted itself in 845 when Emperor T'ang Hui-ch'ang, considering the religious establishment had grown too large, laicized all those in holy orders: 260,500 persons in all. Despite the tendency of the Chinese mind to disbelieve in asceticism and eschew anxiety about the life to come, the impact of Buddhism was profound and a final adjustment only occurred in Neo-Confucianism, the Sung reinterpretation of Confucian thought.

In the Two Sungs we reach the zenith of early Chinese civilization. Fifty years of confusion which followed the fall of the T'ang in 907, a political fragmentation aided by advances in military technology connected with gunpowder, were ended by a northern general, Chao Kuang-yin, who re-united the provinces under the Northern Sung dynasty. When one of his rivals begged for independence, he asked: 'What wrong have your people done to be excluded from the Empire?' It had become inconceivable that any province should seek to isolate itself: the Empire was the Greece and Rome of East Asia, China was the civilized world. And the common script of the Chinese language, unrelated to differences in dialect sound, offered access to the cultural heritage to anyone who had mastered it, thus acting as a contri-butory factor in the age-long unity of the country. Although brought to power by a *coup d'état*, an uncommon start for a lasting dynasty, Chao Kuang-yin was readily accepted because of his reputation for rectitude and learning. His settlement of political difficulties was shrewd: members of the deposed house were spared, the civil service restored to its pre-eminent position, and he retired the military officers who had placed him on the dragon throne. His pacific policy of containment of the nomad peoples, rather than the expansion of borders pursued by the Han and T'ang, gave the Empire the peaceful conditions needed for cultural advance, though foreign invasion was to terminate the Two Sungs and the early phase of Chinese civilization. In 1126 Kin tribesmen overran North China and captured the capital, K'ai Feng. These fierce nomadic people had entered the Great Wall by way of Hopei, the northern part of which had been ceded shortly after the fall of the T'ang. But the Empire rallied under the Southern Sung dynasty (1127–1279) and a frontier almost identical to that created during the Tartar Partition was stabilized. It was the northern boundary of the wet, rice-grow-ing valleys of central and southern China, country unsuited to the military tactics of nomad cavalry.

The loss of the northern provinces was less calamitous than first appeared, since Kiangnan, as the South was now called, contained the key economic area. The southern expansion of the Chinese people is an historical process that has lasted several thousand years, throughout the early phase of Chinese civilization the general tendency was a shift in direction southwards of the economic centre of gravity. Hence the Sung Empire, though at its fullest extent smaller than the T'ang, was more populous and wealthy. There were over one hundred million inhabitants in 1124 and urban growth was a remarkable phenomenon of the period. The annual revenue of the imperial government was twice as much as the T'ang, whilst the incipience of a cash economy based on paper money and credit inaugurated a massive expansion in trade. Marco Polo, a native of industrious Venice, was to be staggered by the size and intensity of commercial activity in the Yuan Empire (1279–1368). Nothing like it could be found in contemporary Europe. Yet the *shang* were unable to make lasting social and political headway against the scholar-bureaucrat. Wang An-shih (1021–86) was the Sung minister responsible for introducing economic reforms capable of regulating the trade boom, rationalizing government expenditure and reviving the rural economy. An example of innovation was his *shih yi fa* or exchange system, a further develop-ment of the *p'ing chang*: it was intended to reduce fluctuations in price and curtail profits on a wide range of goods. A commodity depressed because of

引河搶紅

A canal being dug on the Yellow River near K'ai Feng. This early nineteenth-century sketch indicates the traditional Chinese genius for organizing very large numbers of workers in civil engineering. Friendly competition between gangs was stimulated by prizes such as food and clothing.

over-supply could be exchanged at one of the state marketing agencies for another that was in short supply, if the disposer of the commodity preferred not to receive cash payment or a bill of exchange. Though such policies of state intervention raised the hackles of conservative *shih*, the conduct of politics was carried on in a most civilized manner: ruined officials were either posted to distant provinces or retired, as Wang An-shih was forced to resign in 1076. Indeed, it was this minister's methods that were challenged, rarely his objectives.

China had reached the edge of modern science and was undergoing a minor industrial revolution. Water-powered textile machinery could spin thirty-two spindles at the same time. Transport facilities had improved through the invention of the lock, the double-hulled sailing ship and iron-chain suspension bridges. In 1111 imperial concern for medicine led to the compilation of the *Sheng Chi Tsung Lu (The Imperial Medical Encyclopedia)*, and a watchdog over the pharmaceutics industry was established in the Imperial Drugs Office. The intellectual response to these changing conditions was Neo-Confucianism. As Joseph Needham has said, it was 'an empirical rationalism, a kind of scientific humanism'. The good life, according to Chu Hsi (1130–1200), was attunement to *li*, the pre-established harmony and unity of the universe. 'There is', he said, 'no man in heaven judging sin.' Such a philosophical outlook, as European thinkers of the Enlightenment were impressed to discover, could form the basis of a system of ethics which dispensed with supernatural sanction. Artistically, the Two Sungs witnessed the apotheosis of Chinese painting in the landscape and acted as patrons to a host of famous authors. In Emperor Sung Hui-tsung, painter, calligrapher, poet and landscape gardener, we encounter the cultivated ruler and one of the chief reasons why K'ai Feng is the city in which later *shih* would have preferred to live. It remains an irony of history that Emperor Sung Hui-tsung should have provoked the Kin tribesmen and died their prisoner.

But beyond the Kin, a new, much more ferocious and formidable power arose on the steppes: this was the Mongol horde under Genghiz Khan. Despite having possession of the most advanced weapons in the world – explosive grenades, bombs, rocket-aided arrows, poisonous smokes, the 'fire-spurting lance' or gun, flamethrowers, and even an iron-plated armoured car – the Sung armies were unable to withstand the Mongol onslaught once those ruthless horsemen turned their full attention to conquering the South after the destruction of the Kin (1211–12). Nearly half a century of war was necessary before the last member of the Southern Sung dynasty perished in a sea battle off what is now Hong Kong in 1279. By the conquest of China the Mongols inherited the richest country in the world and acquired a military technology second to none, as the combined forces of Poles and the Teutonic knights found to their cost at the battle of Wahlstadt.

The Mongol invasion was a definite rupture in the pattern of Chinese history. Though sinicized barbarians like Yelu Ch'u-ts'ai were able to mitigate the harsh rule of the Great Khan – dissuading him on one occasion from genocide – the Mongol imperium remained an alien usurpation even after the accession of Kubilai Khan, when present-day Peking replaced Karakorum as the capital. What the Yuan Empire (1279–1368) represents is the greatest clash in world history between the nomadic culture of the steppe and the civilization of intensive agriculture. Evidence of ancient friction between the steppe and the sown can be found in the fact that Ch'in Shih Huang-ti built the Great Wall by linking together walls thrown up by feudal states prior to his reign. Its irregular course only approximates to an absolute frontier; it was 'the product of social emphasis continuously applied along a line of cleavage between two environments'. Not only did imperial policy always seek to protect the *nung* by maintaining a physical barrier but it was also anxious to halt any movement to the north in case the farmers of the northern outposts might abandon agriculture and take up stock raising, so strengthening the nomad economy. The corollary was encouragement of migration southwards with the consequent rise of the Yang-tze River valley as the key economic area.

The Yuan Empire overreached itself in the reign of Kubilai Khan (1260–94) by abortive expeditions of conquest to Japan and Champa, modern South Vietnam and Cambodia. The economy could not endure the strain, North China having been laid waste in the initial Mongol attacks. Impoverishment of whole regions lowered the number of people liable to taxation to

58,837,711, barely half the total of the Two Sungs. As a Yuan civil servant, Marco Polo could express admiration at the Grand Canal, 'which the great khan has caused to be dug, in order that vessels may pass from one great river to another, and from the province of Manji by water, as far as Kanbula, without making any part of the voyage by sea'. To him this grand trunk canal of the Chinese waterways system, the route by which grain from Kiangnan reached the Mongol capital at Peking, was a contemporary feat of engineering unrelated to the hydraulic tradition of Chinese history. He was unaware of the 'water benefits' started by Yu the Great Engineer, just as the full extent of the destructiveness and disruption in the Empire was not evident to him because of the lack of knowledge of the level to which the Chinese civilization had attained prior to the fall of the Southern Sung. In spite of the efforts of Yelu Ch'u-ts'ai the Yuan dynasty preferred to exclude the *shih* from office as far as possible, and became a non-Chinese regime supported by officials of foreign origin. In 1315 the restarting of the examination system came too late to rally any support to the Yuan, against whom popular rebellions, those indicators of impending dynastic change, increased in number and extent from the 1340s. All the conditions were ready for a national rising, save for a leader. That person was found in the former monk, beggar and bandit, Chu Yuan-chang.

1

Ming: the Chinese Recovery
1368–1644

Kubilai was the last khaghan, 'khan of khans', and the first Yuan emperor. Nominally his authority extended over the world empire of the Mongols, the four dominions of China, Chaghadai (Central Asia), Persia and Kipchak (West Asia and Russia), but the lesser khans were so restive that before his death in 1294 the limits of his actual power were East Asia. The transfer of the capital from Mongolia to Hopei and the construction of Kanbula–Ta-t'u on the classical lines of Chinese city planning were witnesses of this fundamental rift within the nomad conquerors. Though the lands adjacent to the Great Wall remained under the control of Kubilai Khan, whose forces supplied by Chinese grain-tribute could remain for longer periods in the field, the political affairs of the steppe became increasingly irrelevant to the Yuan dynasty, now absorbed in the complexities of ruling the Empire. By the reign of Tugh Temur (1328–32) differences between Mongol clans over the conduct of government had opened the way to a partial recovery of influence by Chinese officials in the civil service. Alarmed, Bayan, the Mongol Imperial Chancellor, persuaded Togan Temur (1333–68) to abolish the examination system for a second time, seeking a return to the reign of Kubilai Khan when government posts were strictly allocated. The ethnic order of precedence had been Mongols, foreign allies, northern peoples like the Kin, and, last, Chinese. An apocryphal story relates how the Imperial Chancellor stopped the examinations when he found out that one of his servants was missing. 'As for the Chinese who study books', Bayan said, 'they always deceive people. Formerly I had a groom. For some time I did not see him. When I asked about him, I was told that he had gone as a candidate. I never realized the examinations were taken by these kinds of people.'

If Bayan expected that the abolition of the examination system would be sufficient to hold in check the Chinese subjects of the Yuan emperor, he must have been disappointed in the risings which broke out in Kwantung in 1337 and in Kiangsi the ensuing year. Suspicious of collusion between the *shih* and the rebellious *nung*, he proposed a typically Mongol solution: selective genocide. Chinese with the surnames Chang, Wang, Liu, Li and Chao should be exterminated. Feeling himself not strong enough to dispatch above three quarters of the population, Togan Temur temporized, encouraged Confucian scholars, and exiled Bayan to South China, where he died in 1340. But this emperor, who displayed the characteristic Mongol weakness for drink and the harem, was no match for the rising tide of popular discontent, the inevitable reaction to misrule and corruption. Unrest was widespread in the 1340s, culminating in the rebellion of the 'White Lotus', a secret society

The oldest Chinese picture of a European vessel. Seventeenth century.

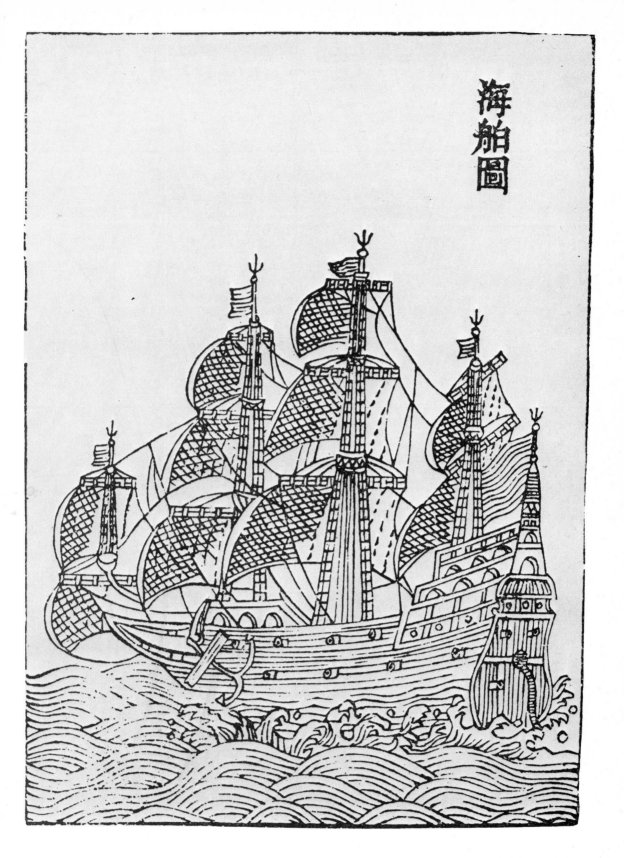

海舶圖

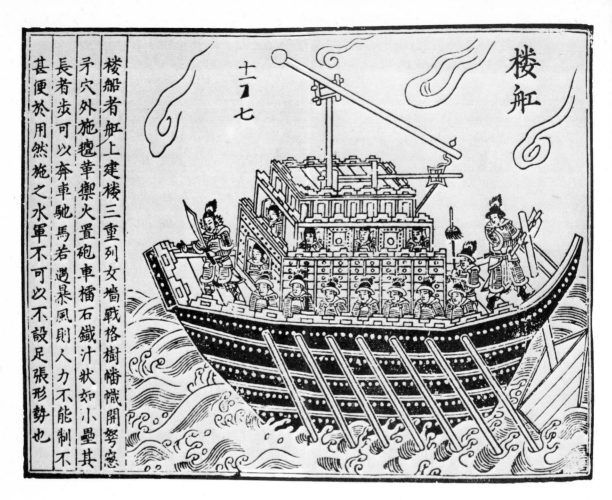

楼舡

楼船者舡上建楼三重列女墙戰格樹幡幟開弩窗
矛穴外施氈革禦火置砲車檑石鐵汁狀如小壘其
長者步可以奔車馳馬若遇暴風則人力不能制不
甚便於用然施之水軍不可以不設足張形勢也

ABOVE A Sung battleship of the eleventh century. The text says that such 'tower ships' have three decks, bulwarks, openings for crossbows and lances, catapults, and a leather skin to prevent fire. They are like a 'city wall'. Their shortcoming was handling in a storm.

LEFT An articulated barge loaded with mines and explosives. Late sixteenth century.

whose doctrines were an amalgam of Taoist and Buddhist cosmology. Centred on the Huai River valley, the rebels halted the grain supply to the capital via the Grand Canal and defeated imperial troops sent against them. Though the area was pacified in 1354, the movement encouraged rebellions and mutinies elsewhere so that the authority of Togan Temur was soon reduced to Kanbula and its environs as well as isolated areas like Yunnan.

The Chinese leaders of the rebel forces could not agree together, and therefore the Yuan dynasty enjoyed a brief breathing space before it faced the combined wrath of the insurgents. The central struggle was for control of the key economic area of the Yang-tze valley. The chief contenders were Chang Shih-ch'eng, who ruled the coastal region around Soochow, Ch'en Yu-liang, whose capital was on the middle course of the Yang-tze at Wu-ch'ang, and between them at Nanking, Chu Yuan-chang. The latter, a famine orphan saved from beggary by a Buddhist monastery, had risen through his own ability to become a bandit chief and then commander of an army. In this three-cornered contest he proved the most able general, the turning-point of the war being the naval campaign of 1363. When Ch'en Yu-liang invested Nan-ch'ang with a force of three hundred thousand men carried in a formidable armada of warships, Chu Yuan-chang was obliged to throw his full strength into the defence of the most important city of Kiangsi. The largest of Ch'en Yu-liang's vessels, we are told, 'was in height several *chang*. The outside was painted in red lacquer. From top to bottom there were three decks. On the decks were erected tents for the riding horses. Below were placed several tens of oars, protected by a covering of boards. Aboard the sound of a man's voice could not carry from top to bottom. The archers' towers were covered with iron.' The strategy of Ch'en Yu-liang was to make sudden attacks on major lake and river cities, capturing them by assaults on their riverine walls directly from the sterns of his ships. In spite of blowing down a wide gap in the wall at the first assault, the troops of Ch'en Yu-liang were unable to take Nan-ch'ang; further ground and water-borne attacks also failing, he adopted the alternative strategy of starving out the garrison. It was a mistake. The fleet of Chu Yuan-chang sailed up the Yang-tze from Nanking and caught Ch'en Yu-liang in the bottleneck of Po'yang Lake. Outnumbered in shipping and men, the relief force had the single advantage of greater manoeuvre over the slow moving siege vessels, especially on the low summer water level of the lake. In one engagement Chu Yuan-chang's own flagship ran aground on a sand bar and stuck fast, yet his swifter craft fully exploited the predicament of the enemy. Cannon and fire ships containing gunpowder wreaked havoc amongst Ch'en Yu-liang's warships, though his determined adversary had to behead over ten commanders of squadrons which were seen to be slow in joining battle. Exhaustion of supplies and flagging morale forced Ch'en Yu-liang to attempt a break out to the Yang-tze river, and retreat to Wu-ch'ang. At the confluence of Po'yang Lake and the Yang-tze a desperate battle ended in his death and the surrender of fifty thousand of his men with their ships.

The victory, won by hard fighting against superior numbers, left Chu Yuan-chang master of the river and an augmented navy. Hunan and Hupeh were occupied and in 1367 he destroyed Chang Shih-ch'eng at Soochow. Sole pretender to the dragon throne and acknowledged leader of the

Chinese insurrection, he was ready to strike north from his now impregnable southern base at the tottering Yuan dynasty. Togan Temur did not wait for the arrival of the rebel forces in the capital; he fled to Mongolia in 1368, leaving the Empire to the care of the first Ming emperor, Hung-wu.

Though there was more than a millennium between them, Chu Yuan-chang and Liu Pang are often compared as the two commoners in Chinese history who overthrew tyrannical regimes and founded new dynasties. Both were of humble origin and gained the dragon throne through a combination of outstanding leadership and peasant cunning. Both were prepared to use the administrative skills of the scholars in order to consolidate their authority, but in the perceived relationship between emperor and official there were marked differences between them. THE EARLY MING RULERS

In 202 BC Liu Pang as Emperor Han Kao-tsu was anxious to dissociate his house from the worst excesses of Ch'in rule, identified in the minds of the people with officials who subscribed to the doctrines of the School of Law. One of the 'Hundred Schools' of philosophy in the late feudal period, Legalism held that only when custom had the sanction of dreadful punishment behind it was there any possibility of effective social organization. This was a fascist ethic of personal subordination to the state as an instrument of war, which had become dominant in Ch'in under the ministry of Shang Yang (350–338 BC), who was a leading exponent. Ch'in Shih Huang-ti, as the first ruler of the united Empire, then lacking any degree of economic integration, found strict control the most efficient way of obtaining stability. His severe decrees, imposed on the population by Ch'in garrisons, confirmed the ancient Chinese aversion to the military, already placed below the *shang* in the social order, and left Emperor Han Kao-tsu with the popular expectation that the change of dynasty meant a change in the style and form of government, even a return to some form of feudalism. This transformation occurred as *shih* of Confucian persuasion were drawn into the imperial administration, and the Former Han emperors came to model themselves on the Confucian ideal of the prince, whose virtuous rule would elicit virtue from all of his subjects.

The situation in 1368, however, was different in several ways. Emperor Ming Hung-wu had led a successful national rising against foreign invaders. Without rivals and without the political uncertainties which had faced the founder of the Former Han, Emperor Ming Hung-wu was in a very strong position, his personal authority more absolute than any previous Chinese emperor other than Ch'in Shih Huang-ti himself. The *shih* welcomed the overthrow of Togan Temur, since they had been indifferently treated under the Yuan dynasty, and they were quick to take up appointments in the Ming administration. Yet from the beginning of the Ming it was evident that the old independence of senior ministers was a past tradition. Emperor Ming Hung-wu, in 1380, reacted violently to the alleged sedition of Hu Wei-yang, an Imperial Chancellor, striking down the minister's family: he also abolished the office itself, taking personal charge of several crucial parts of the civil service such as rites, taxation, defence, foreign relations, criminal law, the examination system and supervision of the executive, and public works. This move towards despotism, which was to be the major trend in Chinese politics

The avenue to the Ming tombs, north of Peking.

until the end of the imperial era this century, had considerable dangers for the stability of the Empire, particularly at times when children or weak individuals were seated on the dragon throne. It was not until many years later, in 1449, that the disadvantages and dangers of this change were apparent. Then, Emperor Ming Cheng-t'ung, brought up in the seclusion of the inner palace, was so much under the influence of his personal attendants, the eunuchs, that he was persuaded into an unnecessary military expedition on the steppes which ended in his own capture by Mongol tribesmen. Finally, the new position in which the scholar–bureaucrats were placed can be glimpsed in the introduction of corporal punishment for maladministration or impropriety. *T'ing chang*, flogging in the court, may have been a barbaric legacy of the Mongols, but there can be little doubt that Emperor Ming Hung-wu had an intolerance of opposition that tended to manifest itself in cruelty. No longer was it the practice for condemned *shih* to commit suicide, whilst the pacifist politics common to the Two Sungs were a faded memory.

The most dynamic periods of the Ming Empire were the reigns of its founder and the third Ming emperor, Yung-lo. In breaking the time-honoured custom of taking for the dynastic title an ancient name of a locality associated with the house and choosing the epithet bright or brilliant, Emperor Ming Hung-wu was perhaps making the point that the Empire needed to be restored to its former brightness. The provinces had been racked by civil war and uprisings against the Mongols for more than twenty years. Initially, consolidation was essential. From his fortified capital of Nanking, ideally suited to govern the prosperous southern provinces, now culturally advanced by emigration from a North China which had borne the brunt of the series of devastating nomad invasions from the twelfth century onwards, Emperor Ming Hung-wu set about restoring order. The military establishment, swollen by the prolonged period of conflict, was brought within the scope of government by a system of military agricultural colonies. Soldiers and soldier-farmers were settled on state land, along the frontier and at strategic places inland; their function was to act as a structure of national defence and internal security that could be reinforced by more regular imperial forces as and when the occasion required. This partial demobilization was made easier by the wide tracts of empty land inherited by the Ming – these were the ravaged parts of the northern provinces and hunting ground previously reserved for the Mongol horsemen. Seeds, animals and tools were provided for the colonists. Although it was not until Ming Yung-lo had mounted the dragon throne that serious attention was given to foreign affairs, there were a number of significant developments before the first Ming emperor died in 1398. Along the northern frontier the possibility of a Mongol counter-attack was anticipated by campaigns extending far beyond the Gobi, and in the south-west Yunnan was annexed in 1382. This territory, formerly the kingdom of Nanchao before it was overrun by the Mongols, had always worsted Chinese armies, thus presenting a barrier to the general southward movement of economic development in the Empire. Memory of the 751 battle on the Tali plain, where an imperial army of sixty thousand men was annihilated, remained fresh enough eighty years afterwards in the T'ang court for the embassy of Nanchao to take precedence over that of Japan. Had there not been a residue of Mongol forces left there, it is not unlikely that Emperor Ming Hung-wu would have followed the Sung policy of non-intervention, and Yunnan might have preserved its independence.

Anxiety over the succession caused by the death of Emperor Ming Hung-wu's heir apparent led the ailing ruler to an unusual arrangement to secure his second choice. Three of his eldest sons were stationed in North China in command of concentrations of troops, each pledged to guarantee the accession of Emperor Ming Hui-ti, their sixteen-year-old nephew. One of these uncles defeated the others and seized Nanking. At the time, in 1402, it was believed that the young emperor had been burned alive in the destruction of the palace, but it later became known that Ming Hui-ti, disguised as a Buddhist monk, had escaped to the countryside, where he lived an obscure wandering life for forty years. Captured in 1441, after the death of the usurping uncle, he was allowed to spend his final year in quiet seclusion. The third Ming emperor, Yung-lo, was a very able ruler. In his reign there were outstanding achievements and a sense within the Empire that the glories of earlier dynasties had returned. A first decision of Emperor Ming Yung-lo was the removal of the capital from Nanking to Peking, the site of the Yuan capital and a place where he felt more at home. Though the strategic weakness of the second Ming capital, barely fifty kilometres from the Great Wall, and the immense distance that grain-tribute had to be hauled to it from South China, the two thousand kilometres' length of the Grand Canal, were to put unendurable strains on the dynasty later, the building of the magnificent city of Peking seemed to herald the beginning of a new era. Its construction in five years instead of the decade given for completion was an example of Chinese genius for manpower organization: it was a medieval 'Great Leap'.

The might and splendour of the Ming Empire, unmatched by any other state in East Asia, was dazzling to Chinese and foreigner alike. Only Tamerlane, the Central Asian conqueror, might have challenged the Ming, but he died in 1404 on the border of China. In the campaign of 1409–10 against the Mongol tribes the army of Emperor Ming Yung-lo was supplied with grain carried in thirty thousand covered wagons. Two years earlier he had reconquered Annam, the northern half of present-day Vietnam. But it is the major seaborne expeditions he dispatched into 'the southern and western oceans' sailing as far as Arabia, Africa, India, the southern islands of the Indonesian archipelago, and even Australia, that still catch the imagination. In 1405–7 the first expedition of twenty-seven thousand men sailing in sixty-two ships of special construction and very large dimensions visited Malacca, Java, Sumatra, Ceylon and Calicut. The motives behind these voyages have been variously interpreted – one not very credible suggestion is that they were a search for the refuge of the deposed Emperor Ming Hui-ti – but they did extend the bounds of Chinese knowledge of, and official contact with the world to a point never before attained. The city of Peking and maritime reconnaisance indicate the higher economic productivity of the Empire and, consequently, the reduced burden of the imperial government even at its most active periods. They were outward signs of the Chinese recovery.

Portrait of Emperor
Ming Yung-lo.

**ECONOMY AND
SOCIETY**

The Ming dynasty began with a thorough overhaul of the imperial administration, the civil code, and the conduct of public works. Its prosperous first century was due to the special interest Emperor Ming Hung-wu took in the latter; he ordered that all petitions in regard to 'water benefits', from the people as well as from officials, be brought to his attention as soon as they were received. Aware that hydraulic conservancy schemes were the unifying force in imperial history, the first Ming emperor stimulated the officials concerned with public works into frenetic activity, so that a progress report of 1395 covering all the provinces mentions the completion of 40,987 water-control projects. The Grand Canal, last dug in the Yuan Empire to connect Kanbula with the agricultural wealth of South China, was brought to perfection in 1411 by Sung Li, who solved the problem of water flow along the summit section with a mile-long dam and sluice-gates. This reservoir formed from the in-flowing rivers was divided into 'water boxes' by fourteen locks, which controlled the water through the opening and shutting of their gates. These major works were completed in two hundred days by 165,000 men. From this time onwards the sea route for transporting grain-tribute to the capital declined, a circumstance which may have inhibited maritime shipbuilding and sea power in general towards the close of the Ming. Reinforcement and repair of canals and river banks had become more sophisticated during the Two Sungs – after the devastating floods in Hopei of 1072 the Yellow River Dredging Commission had been set up and officials improved methods of collecting information on water levels by the introduction of a system of graduated poles and floating signs – but in 1595 we find an Imperial Censor, Ch'en Pang-ko, having to remind the emperor that experience had shown the need to keep the dykes low. Apart from excavation during the low-water months of summer, he recommended:

> That all official and private boats coming and going tow 'bed-harrowing ploughs', and sail with the wind, scraping the bottom as they go, so that the sand has no peace to sink and settle. Also, imitating the hydraulic mill and the hydraulic trip-hammer, let wooden machines be made which use the current to roll and vibrate, so that the sand is constantly stirred up and cannot accumulate.

Such sentiments were perfectly in accord with the ancient notion of seeking an harmonious relationship with the natural forces of the environment, 'the balancing of the Yin and the Yang'. The equipment in use has advanced without loss of the underlying philosophy.

Concentration on irrigation and transport canals in northern Hopei from the reign of Emperor Ming Yung-lo, who was anxious to improve the economy of the countryside around Peking, led to increases in population and the expansion of Chinese settlements to the north of the Great Wall as far as present-day Mukden. Yet this development in the north-east of the Empire could not obscure the reality of southern domination of both economic and social life. The migration south of cultured families had started at the fall of the T'ang dynasty in 907, when for fifty-three years the northern provinces were under the sway of short-lived houses of Turkic origin, and the exodus gathered strength after the fall of K'ai Feng to the Kin (1126). The Hakka or 'guest families' today living in Kwantung are an example of this emigration, as the closeness of their dialect to northern speech testifies. By the fifteenth century eighty-five per cent of the population lived south of the Huai River. As a result the Ming dynasty discovered that southern candidates secured a great majority of the higher places in the examinations for the civil service, while northerners were hard put to it to make any showing at all. In order to prevent North China becoming discontented it was agreed to reserve one-third of the places to northern candidates. This meant that competition at the examinations was far keener for southerners than for northerners, so that the successful southern candidates inevitably secured the senior posts in the imperial administration. The Ch'ing dynasty, the foreign one following the Ming, gave this system a final twist when it determined that one-half of government posts be reserved for its own people, the Manchus, and one-half be divided equally between Chinese from the northern and southern provinces.

Emperor Ming Hung-wu knew that he needed the *shih* to administer the Empire and in 1375 he restarted the national system of education originated by the Two Sungs. Colleges for the sons of officials were established in every prefecture; other students were only admitted to these subsidized institutions if they could show promise as a scholar and knowledge of the Confucian classics. Alongside these colleges for would-be officials was a network of village schools intended to cater for the needs of the rest of the population. Besides these state schools there were private academies supported by the high officials, wealthy landowners, or even the *shang*. Progress towards an official appointment was earned by success in a series of examinations, extending upwards from a local preliminary test through the bachelor's degree taken at the capital of the prefecture and the master's degree taken at the provincial capital, to the highest qualification only awarded in the imperial capital. Although during the Two Sungs the examination questions included technical and scientific subjects such as astronomy, engineering and medicine, the curriculum for Ming scholars was confined to orthodox literature and philosophy, a reflection of the passing of Chinese interest in technical invention and science. In 1469 there were one hundred thousand civil and eighty thousand military officials in the imperial service. Entrance for the civil service examinations was still theoretically open to all candidates, though the development of costly associated customs made advancement the privilege of the officially established. The scholar officials, however, were never as powerful in state affairs as they had been under earlier dynasties. Not only were the Ming emperors more autocratic than their predecessors but even more the growth of eunuch power in the court led to serious clashes within the administration and a diminution of Confucian influence. The Censorate (*Yu Shih Pu*) was very active, many brave *shih* perishing because of their memorials of protest, yet it was a losing battle when a number of child emperors gave unscrupulous eunuchs ample scope to repeat the worst experiences of the palace at the close of the Han Empire.

The Ming emphasis on restoration of the native heritage is conspicuous in building activity. Though space will be given to the Ming city in the later section on Peking, it is important to notice the economic significance of this public work. Defences, paved highways, bridges, temples, tombs and gardens were put in hand the length and breadth of the Empire. In the building of heavy masonry fortifications the Ming engineers excelled; the Great Wall acquired its final form in two stages of construction – one followed the reverse of 1449 at T'u-mu, the other in the sixteenth century was caused by renewed nomad attacks. The walls of some five hundred cities were also reconstructed. This enormous amount of activity was sustained by the buoyant economy, a legacy of the agricultural revolution in the Two Sungs, and not until the major epidemics of 1586–9 and 1639–44 did the increase in population slacken and level out around two hundred millions. The medical nature of the waves of epidemic disease hitting China at the end of the Ming period remains uncertain, but eye-witness accounts are agreed about how lethal they were. In some localities more than half the people survived, elsewhere no less than three-quarters of the inhabitants of a prefecture died. What these natural disasters could not do was permanently reduce the *nung*, the medieval foundation of the enormous population of modern China, but it is likely they compounded fatally the difficult circumstances of the later Ming.

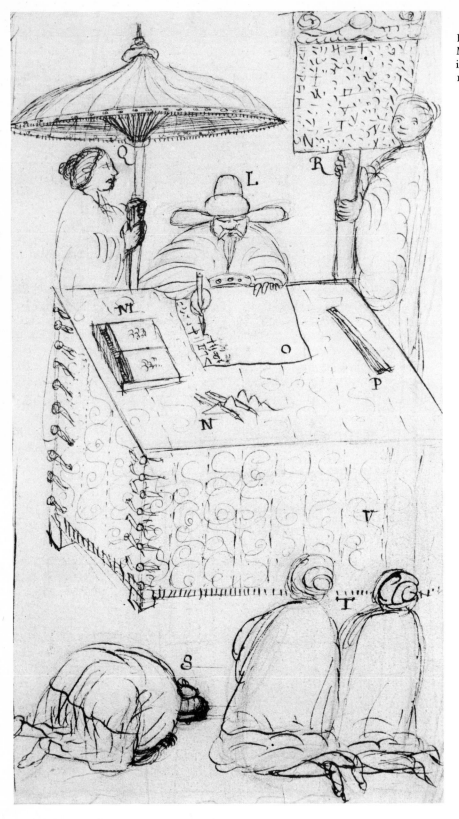

Drawing by Peter Mundy, who took part in the English attack of 1637 on Canton.

Responsibility for administration in the countryside rested with the wealthiest landowners, who had to collect the grain-tribute needed to feed the capital and imperial armies guarding the Great Wall as well as maintain the water conservancy schemes in the locality. These conscripted administrators were not usually drawn from the official class but rather well-to-do farmers 'spoken well of by the multitude', as a magistrate put it in 1435. The system worked till the end of the sixteenth century; then, as the Ming dynasty went into decline, bureaucratic corruption and incompetence made involvement onerous. Another reason for the breakdown was that suitable rural landlords became harder to find. On one hand, the concentration of ownership amongst relations of the imperial family, favoured supporters of the emperor, eunuchs, high officials, and merchants had brought into existence large estates, or plantations (*chuang-t'ien*); on the other, the fragmentation and geographical dispersal of lesser holdings reduced the number of medium-sized estates, especially in the lower Yang-tze valley. Moreover, a change in the pattern of infestment can be discerned in a transfer of wealth from the countryside to towns and cities, where trade, money-lending and real estate offered higher profits. The end of this process in the eighteenth century was the emergence of a landlord class living in cities, with agents looking after its interests in the villages, and the more active role of the scholar official in rural administration.

Around 1400 it was decreed that for commercial transactions only paper money should be used. Visiting the Yuan mint at Kanbula towards the end of the thirteenth century, Marco Polo had been struck by the novelty of paper money, which he thought 'may truly be said to possess the secret of the alchemists'. However, he was unaware of the adverse influence which this almost unrestricted practice was having on the national economy: rampant inflation and the hoarding of precious metals, which in turn worsened the currency situation, were universal. Indeed, the Ming dynasty inherited a liquidity crisis brought about by the export of coins at the end of the Mongol supremacy. China had always been short of copper, a factor behind the introduction of bills of exchange and then paper money in the ninth and tenth centuries, but the advent of a cash economy shortly afterwards added a new range of financial difficulties with which the reforms of the great Sung minister Wang An-shih had been intended to deal. Inconvertible notes, issued by Emperor Ming Yung-lo to finance his military expeditions, added to the inflationary spiral, hurting the common people most of all, whilst his conversion of overseas trade into an official tributary system through the fleets he sent into 'the southern oceans' did not encourage the import of much needed silver and gold. The later isolationism of the Ming dynasty, with its abandonment of the navy and its proscription of seaborne commerce, served merely to exacerbate matters. Internally, the development of trade and industry was encouraged by the greater homogeneity of the Empire and the opening up of new lands with their resources in the south and south-west – Yunnan, Kwangsi and Kweichou. Again, the pattern of Chinese history remained unchanged because this expansion of the economy did not improve the social standing of the merchant, nor did it cause anything akin to the rise of capitalist enterprise in Europe. Despite the changes in the countryside that can be attributed to a money economy, the status of the scholar–bureaucrat was undiminished. The

Empire remained the richest and most populous country in the world, even though at the end of the Ming dynasty the long-standing Chinese superiority in technology and science had been perceptibly lost.

The disaster at T'u-mu in 1449 was the turning point for the Ming dynasty. The inability of the resurgent Mongol tribesmen to take advantage of a battle in which the Emperor Ming Cheng-t'ung was captured reveals the extent of the Chinese recovery, the economic and military strength of the restored Empire, but the event also indicates the decline in vigour of the dynasty after the reigns of the early Ming emperors.

The author of T'u-mu was Wang Chen, the first eunuch to dominate the Ming court. Having amassed a vast personal fortune and enjoyed unchecked authority in the administration since Cheng-t'ung was made emperor in 1435 at the age of eight, Wang Chen persuaded himself that the ultimate in personal status and glory would be to lead a campaign against the Mongols, receive the congratulations of the emperor in the field after dealing the enemy a staggering blow, and then in triumph entertain the grateful ruler at his native place south-east of Ta-t'ung, a garrison town beyond the inner line of the Great Wall. Although the Oirat, or Western Mongols, under their energetic chieftain Esen, who had ambitions to unite the tribes of the steppe in imitation of Genghiz Khan, conducted a series of raids on the northern frontier, their aim was not the conquest of the Empire but rather the improvement of trade relations. The avarice of Wang Chen and his eunuch agents had subverted the tributary system: for the horses sent to China each year the Oirat should have received in return imperial gifts such as metal goods, textiles, food and luxury articles which they desired, but it was not uncommon for their envoys to go home empty-handed. Smarting under this humiliating treatment, Esen began to probe the northern defences for the impression he might make on the other Mongol leaders as much as the Ming emperor. To his surprise the Chinese overreacted and an army of half a million men marched from Peking under the command of Wang Chen, accompanied by Emperor Ming Cheng-t'ung.

Officials memorialized the throne on the dangers of an unnecessary military expedition, pointing out there were other ways of strengthening the garrison troops in the vicinity of the Great Wall. When the imperial palanquin was leaving the capital, an official threw himself in front of it and implored the emperor: 'Your Majesty may make light of your imperial person, but what of the dynasty, what of the state?' Wang Chen cursed the outspoken *shih*, Emperor Ming Cheng-t'ung was silent, and the campaign started. The last action of the emperor was to dispatch officials to the tomb of his great-grandfather, Yung-lo, in order to offer sacrifices on his birthday. Once the column had passed the Ming tombs he left all the decisions to Wang Chen, by that time so overbearing that even the highest ranking officials and generals were obliged to approach him on their knees. Inclement weather beset the army and the morale of the soldiers did not improve when, close to Ta-t'ung, the army skirted a battlefield still strewn with thousands of unburied Chinese corpses: a large force from the Ta-t'ung garrison had been overrun by Esen's cavalry. Lacking the courage and ability of Cheng Ho, the eunuch commander

A blue and white flask of the Ming dynasty, made in the early fifteenth century.

OVERLEAF Stretch of the moat surrounding the Purple Forbidden City, Peking. The notice on the embankment forbids angling, though it is unlikely that present-day offenders would suffer for intrusion the traditional penalty of decapitation.

of the maritime expeditions sent out by Emperor Ming Yung-lo, Wang Chen wavered, abandoned his plans for an advance on to the steppes, and ordered the imperial forces to retreat to Peking. After a couple of preliminary engagements the Oirat managed to trap the Chinese at T'a-mu, a post station about sixty kilometres from the inner Great Wall. Instead of sending the imperial palanquin ahead to safety or even selecting a suitable site for a camp, T'u-mu being waterless, Wang Chen insisted upon a halt, it is recorded, because he was worried that his personal baggage train, one thousand wagons loaded with valuables, had been delayed. Surrounding the imperial army and denying it access to a nearby river, Esen could wait for the best moment of attack, which came as Wang Chen tried a confused escape. The Mongols easily routed the demoralized soldiers, killing as many as half of them; Wang Chen met his death on the battlefield, possibly on the sword of an enraged Chinese officer; and Emperor Ming Cheng-t'ung was carried off as a prisoner. The twenty-one-year-old emperor displayed unusual courage, an unsuspected trait in his character and one to which he owed his life: to the wonder of the Oirat, he was found calmly seated on a carpet, in the midst of his fallen body-guard.

Raiding as far as the walls of Peking, the Oirat found they could not defeat the reinforcements coming to the aid of the capital, and their withdrawal to the steppes was an admission that the overwhelming Mongol military superiority of the thirteenth century no longer obtained. The victory of 1449 had been fortuitous. Esen sank into obscurity and the captive emperor was sent back with no conditions. When Emperor Ming Chin-ti, the prince elevated to the vacant dragon throne after T'u-mu, fell seriously ill, his elder brother, Cheng-t'ung, was restored to power by a palace *coup*, and he reigned under the new title of T'ien-shun until his death in 1465.

The lesson of T'u-mu was not learned. Under Emperor Ming Cheng-te (1505–20), who succeeded at the age of fifteen, the eunuchs reasserted their pernicious influence in state affairs. Corruption had become a widespread feature of the administration, an activity that not all the *shih* could resist. Its extent was unmasked at the fall of the Liu Chin in 1510, when it was found that this eunuch had accumulated untold riches in the abuse of his position. Ineffectual government was aggravated, too, by a number of crises in the sixteenth century: these were renewed pressure on the northern frontier, the onset of major epidemics, and recurrent famines.

The new work undertaken on the Great Wall, a symptom of Ming preoccupation with the northern threat, was sufficient to make it an effective military frontier. For the first time large-scale fortresses were added at strategic intervals and double lines of fortifications gave a stronger shield to its gates in the passes. Nevertheless, the institutional decay of the Ming Empire was paralleled by a regression in technology. When in 1592 the imperial armies were committed to the defence of Korea, whose king had appealed to Peking, as suzerain, for assistance against the invading forces of Toyotomi Hideyoshi, the Chinese discovered to their cost how lethal were the firearms used by the Japanese. These guns were based on the matchlock, introduced by the Portuguese in 1543. Though Ming soldiers were equipped with an impressive range of explosives and cannon, hard wood rather than copper or iron was the material from which personal guns were made, suggesting an underlying weakness in metallurgy. In the last decades of the Ming dynasty the services of Jesuits in casting guns were much appreciated. Though it was the work of Adam Schall von Bell in the Bureau of Astronomy that won him a high reputation and position at court, this versatile missionary was in 1636 commanded to start a foundry for the making of cannon and, in spite of his reluctance to undertake such an unpriestly occupation, he found it impolitic to disobey.

The war in Korea ended with a Japanese withdrawal on the death of Hideyoshi, and the Ming court could believe in its ability to handle external enemies. The hostilities, however, had been costly both in lives and resources, so that they fanned the flames of discontent soon to burst out in popular risings. The waning authority of the government was evident in its compromise on overseas trade. The edict of 1390 prohibiting trade with foreigners, an imperial policy renewed from time to time after the death of Emperor Ming Hung-wu, was partially lifted in 1567. Chang-chou was opened as a port from which Chinese could sail, and the depredations of Japanese pirates, long a scourge of the south-eastern coastline, were brought to an end. Their activities had been stimulated by the necessity for the clandestine conduct of international commerce.

The reign of Emperor Ming Hsi-tsung (1621–7) could not have occurred at a less auspicious time. This emperor was the tool of Wei Chung-hsien, the most infamous of the Ming eunuchs, and the fabric of government was weakened through his blatant peculation and disregard of administrative procedure. One of Wei's joys was the launching of a national programme of temple building in honour of himself. The *shih* were in disarray: some had resigned themselves to enormity of the eunuch's urge for esteem, others quit the civil service and formed themselves into opposition groups like the Tun-lin academy at Wu-hsi in Kiangsi. In 1628 when the last Ming emperor Ch'ung-chen was enthroned, the decline of the dynasty was too far advanced to give this conscientious ruler a chance of staving off ruin for his house. Famine acted as the spur for rebellion, as this memorial explains:

Your humble servant was born in Anse subprefecture, Shensi province. I have read many memorials submitted by Your Majesty's officials in connection with the present state of affairs. They say that famine has caused fathers to desert their children and husbands to sell their wives. They also say that many people are so starved that they eat grass roots and white stones. But the real situation is worse than what they have described. Yenan, the prefecture from which your humble servant comes, has not had any rain for more than a year. Trees and grasses are all dried up. During the eighth and the ninth moon months of last year people went to the mountains to collect raspberries which were called grain but actually were no better than chaff. They tasted bitter and they could only postpone death for the time being. By the tenth moon month all raspberries were gone, and people peeled off tree bark for food. Among tree bark the best was that of the elm. This was so precious that to consume as little as possible people mixed it with the bark of other trees to feed themselves. Somehow they were able to prolong their lives. Towards the end of the year the supply of tree bark was exhausted, and they had to go to the mountains to dig up stones as food. Stones were cold and tasted musty. A little taken in would fill up the

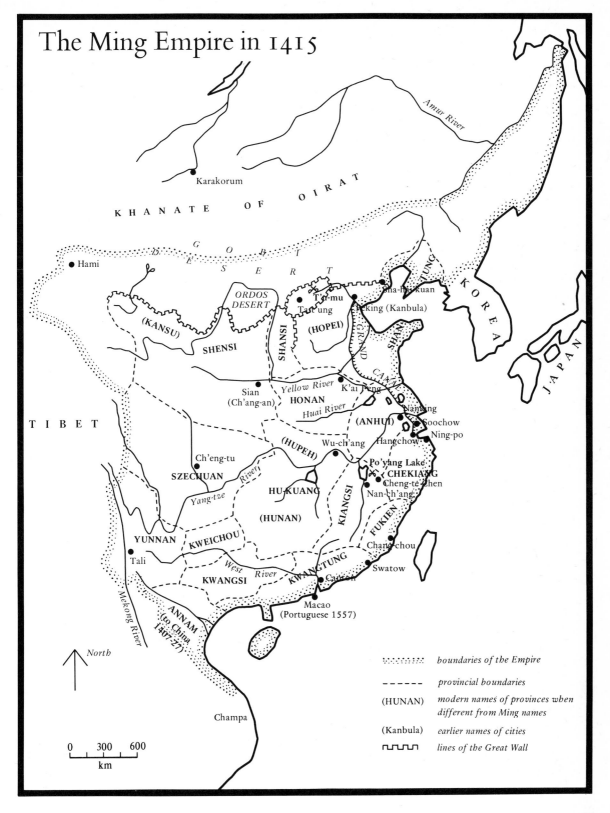

The Ming Empire in 1415

KHANATE OF OIRAT

Karakorum

Amur River

G O B I   D E S E R T

Hami

ORDOS DESERT

T'o-mu
Tatung

(KANSU)

SHANSI

(HOPEI)

SHENSI

Shan-hai-kuan

Peking (Kanbula)

GRAND CANAL

SHANTUNG

KOREA

TIBET

Sian
(Ch'ang-an)

Yellow River

HONAN

K'ai Feng

Huai River

Nanking

(ANHUI)

Soochow

Ning-po

JAPAN

Ch'eng-tu

(HUPEH)

Wu-ch'ang

Hangchow

Po'yang Lake

CHEKIANG

SZECHUAN

River

HU-KUANG

Cheng-tê-chen

Yang-tze

KIANGSI

Nan-ch'ang

(HUNAN)

FUKIEN

YUNNAN

KWEICHOU

Tali

Chang-chou

West River

Swatow

KWANGSI

KWANGTUNG

Canton

Mekong River

ANNAM
(to China
1407–27)

Macao
(Portuguese 1557)

↑ North

Champa

	boundaries of the Empire
	provincial boundaries
(HUNAN)	*modern names of provinces when different from Ming names*
(Kanbula)	*earlier names of cities*
	lines of the Great Wall

0   300   600
km

stomach. Those who took stones found their stomachs swollen and they dropped and died in a few days. Others who did not wish to eat stones gathered as bandits. They robbed the few who had some savings, and when they robbed, they took everything and left nothing behind. Their idea was that since they had to die either one way or another it was preferable to die as a bandit than to die from hunger and that to die as a bandit would enable them to enter the next world with a full stomach. . . .

The rebellious *nung* were soon joined by mutinous troops owed arrears in pay and government couriers declared redundant by the disbanding of the imperial posting system, an enforced government economy. Two rebel leaders emerged, Chang Hsien-chung and Li Tzu-ch'eng, both men of peasant stock. Chang Hsien-chung's bloodthirsty nature and hatred for the

Chart of the Indian Ocean drawn by Joan Martines in 1578, showing forts and sea routes used by the Portuguese.

shih was indulged in the Yang-tze River valley, where his commanders slaughtered and burned in grim competition with each other; slightly less brutal, Li Tzu-ch'eng gained control of North China and in 1643 declared himself first emperor of the Shun dynasty at Sian. His entrance to Peking was effected by treachery; Emperor Ming Ch'ung-chen having foolishly entrusted the defence of the city to the eunuchs, they promptly betrayed him. In the palace gardens on Coal Hill the imperial family committed suicide, bringing to a bloody close the 276 years' rule of the Ming dynasty.

THE COMING OF THE EUROPEANS

While from 1433 the Ming emperors were discouraging contact with countries overseas through a series of anti-maritime laws, the reconnaissance vessels of Portugal were wending their way down the west coast of Africa looking for a passage to the Orient. The discovery of the great southern extension of Africa beyond the Guinea coast was a discouragement for the Portuguese court, where in 1475 there was discussion of the alternative strategy of reaching the Spice Islands by sailing west across the Atlantic Ocean, an idea that inspired Columbus to set out on his famous voyage of exploration seventeen years later. The plan was not approved and further southern expeditions led to the discovery of the Cape of Good Hope by Bartholomew Diaz in 1488. Under the energetic direction of King Manuel I (1495–1521), the overseas expansion of Portugal, begun by Prince Henry 'the Navigator' with the capture of Ceuta from the Moors in 1415, reached its highest point in the establishment of a maritime dominion, which extended from the east coast of Africa to India and the islands of the Indonesian archipelago. In 1514 the first Portuguese ships put in at Canton.

The sudden progress of Portugal was brought about by the combination of two overriding motives, acquisitiveness and religious zeal. Vasco da Gama, on arrival at Calicut in 1498, told the ruler that he had come 'for Christians and spices'. The purpose of his small fleet of four vessels and less than two hundred men was primarily reconnaissance, but it was not long before outright aggression became a settled policy. Once the second and larger expedition to India under Pedro Alvares Cabral in 1500 had demonstrated the hostile attitude of Portugal to Muslims and anyone who was allied with them, there was a stiffening of local resistance to encroachment in both spheres of trade and religious belief. Yet the Portuguese declared a monopoly on all trade at Cochin in 1504 and in the following year Dom Francisco de Almeida was sent as the first viceroy of the East, with instructions to found a series of fortresses from which squadrons could harass Muslim vessels and levy heavy tolls on international trade. To this network of fortified bases were added by Alfonso de Albuquerque, viceroy from 1509 to 1515, such important strategic centres as Hormuz, Diu, Goa and Malacca, his forces having no success in an assault on Aden in 1513.

The Portuguese depredations in Africa and Asia were directed by officers responsible to the monarch, who was anxious to profit from a belated crusade against the riches of non-Christian traders. Barred from the commercial activities of the Mediterranean by the ships of Venice and Genoa, Portuguese captains had found a way into the wealth of the spice trade via the Cape of Good Hope and their response to the comparative weakness of the main eastern sea powers, the Mamluk empire of Egypt, the sultanate of Gujarat and the Javanese state of Japara, was unrestrained piracy. They had sailed into a power vacuum created by the swift run down of the Ming navy. A dim awareness of this alteration in the balance of power is found in the chronicle of Juan Gonsalez de Mendoza, an Augustinian friar, who was a member of a Spanish embassy to China in 1584. He wrote of the Chinese:

> They have found by experience that to go forth of their owne kingdome to conquer others, is the spoile and loss of much people, and expences of great treasures, besides travaile and care which continually they have to sustaine that what is got, with feare to be lost again; so that in the meantime whilest they were occupied in strange conquests, their enemies the Tartarians and other kings borderers unto them, did trouble and invade them, doing great damage and harm . . . So they found it requisit for their quietnes and profite . . . to leave all they had got and gained, out of their own kingdome, but especially the countries as were farre off.

These words should have been heeded by the Portuguese, for the burden of overseas commitment was found excessive by the end of the sixteenth century. Because of the slenderness of national resources the eastern policy had from the outset depended on the spoils of war. Without manufactures to exchange for the desired spices and luxury goods, in contrast to the finely made gifts which Chinese imperial envoys could so freely distribute, the Portuguese were obliged to seize by force a share of oriental trade. Terror was fundamental to their authority, however it was justified as righteous conflict with the heathen. No quarter was given in combat and treatment of prisoners and conquered populations was often savage. The *conquistadores* pursued scope for personal riches, a potent drive to acquire an adequate return for the enduring dangers of battle and voyage that the distant authorities in Lisbon were unable to control. Ungovernable and violent, the Portuguese colonists and adventurers in Asia were dislodged the moment local conditions ceased to favour them. Within a half a century of their arrival in 1596 the Dutch were able to take command of the seas, the Portuguese being expelled from Malacca in 1641.

Against this background of Portuguese aggression in Asia the initial relations of China and Europe have to be viewed. It has been unfortunate for international understanding that the first impressions of people from Western Europe gained by the Chinese were so uniformly bad. *Yang kuei tzu*, 'Ocean Devils', was the nickname the Ming used for Europeans. Though rumours of Portuguese truculence preceded them to China, the Ming court did not adopt a policy of exclusion until incidents confirmed the worst. In 1517, as a Portuguese ambassador was being received in the capital, a fleet under Simon d'Andrade, who had obtained a licence from King Manuel to trade with China, pillaged the southern coast near Canton. Another raiding party under the command of Alphonso de Mello had to be driven off in 1522. Yet twenty years later Portuguese trading colonies were permitted at Chang-chou and Ning-po. Arrogant behaviour troubled relations with the local population, and serious fighting broke out when the Portuguese started to construct a fortress at Ning-po. They were expelled from there in 1545, and four years afterwards from Chang-chou, whose harbour had previously been open to international shipping without incident for the previous seven centuries. At last mercantile interests in South China brought about a compromise whereby permission was given in 1557 for the Portuguese to trade from Macao, close to Canton. It was not until 1598 that Matteo Ricci, a Jesuit missionary, was welcomed in Peking, where he explained the doctrine of the Catholic faith and handed over presents from the Pope. The *shih* were opposed to his arrival, which had been largely arranged by the eunuch party; the Board of Rites respectfully reminded the throne of Han Yu's memorial of 819 on the dangers of religious excess, a renowned attempt to stem Buddhist influence in the T'ang court. Ricci did make an impression on a few officials, but Christianity made little headway after his death in 1610. Significantly the missionary noted that the imperial armies were underpowered in a letter of 1584 and Geronimo Roman, a Spanish official who read it, sent the intelligence back to Europe. 'With five thousand Spaniards, at the most', he asserted, 'the conquest of this country might be made, or at least the maritime provinces, which are the most important in the world.'

The *conquistador* mentality was covert, not dead; and the Chinese could hardly be expected to show delight at the Dutch attack of 1622 on Macao. Beaten off with heavy loss by the defenders, the Dutch turned their attention to other parts of the Chinese coastline, repeating the earlier outrages of the Portuguese. Not to be outclassed, an English squadron of three ships commanded by John Weddel bombarded Canton in 1637. Yet one of the adventurers in this party, Peter Mundy, a Cornishman, was impressed enough by what he saw to keep an illustrated diary. He noted: 'This Countrie May bee said to excell in these particulers: Antiquity, largenesse, Ritchenesse, healthynesse, Plentiffullnesse. For the Arts and manner of government I thinck no Kingdome in the world Comparable to it, Considered altogether.'

2
The Ming Revival

The city of Peking is a novel sight for a European [wrote Father Amiot in the middle of the eighteenth century]. He will not weary of admiring the manner in which the nearly three million people gathered within its vast enclosure are ruled by the authorities as schoolchildren by their masters, and dare even less than these to emancipate themselves. People coming and going fill streets wider than that which faces the Luxembourg Palace in Paris. Some are on foot, some in carts, while others ride on horseback or in sedan chairs. Some carry loads, others cry out the goods they have for sale. The crowd is beyond belief, yet peace reigns everywhere. . . .

When night falls, the barriers across the smaller streets are shut, and everyone retires to his own house. There is nothing heard but the guards sounding the hours of the night: and one meets with no one but the watchmen going on their rounds to care for public safety. They are so scrupulous in this that there are no reports of thefts or murders. At the least warning of a fire, pumps, soldiers, workmen, officials, persons of rank – and even princes – arrive from all directions.

The streets are sprinkled several times each day to lay the dust. In summer there are little booths in every piazza where people may drink iced water. On every hand one can find refreshments, fruits, tea, and eating-houses. The various kinds of foodstuffs are sold on specific days in specific places. There is entertainment everywhere for the passers-by, whether stories being read aloud, short humorous dialogues, or experts displaying tricks and curiosities. In times of natural disaster, the emperor has rice and clothing distributed to the poor. In times of celebration, all sorts of entertainments are permitted the people. . . .

The police know all that is going, even inside the palaces of the princes. They know who has arrived and who departed. They keep exact registers of the inhabitants in every house; and they make sure that all foodstuffs are in abundant supply. They see to it that all repairs required for convenience, safety and cleanliness are carried out when needed. Princes and officials, citizens and foreigners, soldiers and courtiers, bonzes and lamas, are subject to their rule; and they keep everyone on the path of order and duty without arrests, and without harsh actions, seeming hardly to interfere at all.

I will say nothing of the grandeur of the capital, of the extent of its suburbs, the beauty of its walls, the width of its ramparts, the variety of its public buildings, the alignment of its thoroughfares, the multitude of its palaces, and so forth. One has to see them to appreciate their effect. Architecture here works on a different plan to ours, its magnificence accords to

Part of the Summer
Palace, Peking.

other ideas, and its taste follows different principles; but European prejudices are powerless before the novelties that one beholds. The palace of the Emperor announces with eloquence his greatness and his power to any with eyes to see.

A hundred years after the fall of the Ming dynasty, Father Amiot, the French missionary, was as amazed by the splendour of the imperial capital as Marco Polo had been at Kanbula in the reign of Kubilai Khan. Apart from the excellence of the description of eighteenth-century Peking, which delineates the main features of Chinese cities, their spaciousness, public hygiene and strict regulation, this eye-witness account is presented as testimony of the unprecedented grandeur of Emperor Ming Yung-lo's foundation, which was inherited and embellished by the Ch'ing emperors.

In the records of the ministry of public works it is stated that 'When Yung-lo decided to establish his residence in Peking, he built a wall around the capital which was forty *li* long and pierced by nine gates'. This city wall, 23.5 kilometres in length, was the frame in which the new city was to be laid out; it followed the plan of the Mongol capital, Kanbula, the only important difference being that it was about two kilometres shorter at the northern end and about half a kilometre farther extended towards the south. The Chinese use the same word, *ch'eng*, for a city and a city wall: the external fortifications were regarded as the essential feature of a city. European cities, on the other hand, tended to expand from a nucleus such as an agora, cathedral or market-place. One of the salient aspects of Chinese architecture is the deep-rooted veneration of encircling walls. What Emperor Ming Yung-lo did in moving the capital northwards was to return to the rectangular grid plan of the classical Chinese city, which reached its perfection in seventh-century Ch'ang-an, the capital of the T'ang emperors. It was a definite reaction from the sprawling, irregular cities of South China, notably centres of commercial activity such as Hangchow, which the Southern Sung dynasty would only designate a 'temporary residence' or *hsing-tsai*, the Kin-sai of Marco Polo's *Travels*.

The chessboard pattern of Peking, the division by streets running straight in the four main directions into squares, *fang*, each one of these comprising four smaller squares, *li*, separated by narrower streets, has been partly lost through clearance and rebuilding over the last hundred years, but a glance at a map is enough to disclose its axial ground-plan. At the centre is the imperial palace, the Purple Forbidden City or Tzu Chin Ch'eng, a literary allusion to the pole-star. The imperial palace was considered the centre around which the whole terrestrial world gravitated, just as the pole-star was the centre of the celestial world. Arranged in accordance with the pole-star and the adjoining constellations, the Purple Forbidden City has a north-south orientation, all its principal façades and openings being towards the south. The middle of its three sections was the most important as it contained the great ceremonial buildings and the offices of government. Enclosed by a moat and a high wall, not quite one kilometre square, and divided internally into numerous compounds and courtyards by lesser walls and buildings, the Purple Forbidden City has its official place of entry in the Wu Men, the Meridian Gate, thought by some commentators to be the finest architectural unit in China. Erected in 1420, re-erected in 1647 and restored in 1801, this monumental gateway

The Purple Forbidden City from Coal Hill. The notice on the Spirit of Bravery Gate indicates the modern use of this section as an archaeological museum.

Ming Peking
showing city walls

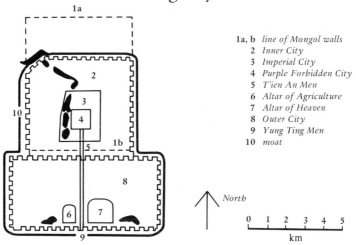

1a, b	*line of Mongol walls*
2	*Inner City*
3	*Imperial City*
4	*Purple Forbidden City*
5	*T'ien An Men*
6	*Altar of Agriculture*
7	*Altar of Heaven*
8	*Outer City*
9	*Yung Ting Men*
10	*moat*

North

0 1 2 3 4 5
km

One bastion of the Wu Men, the Meridian Gate, erected in 1420. It is the main entrance to the Purple Forbidden City.

comprises an open rectangle, the sides projecting ninety-two metres towards the south and forming at both ends a kind of bastion upon which pavilions are placed. The central building, 126 metres in length and 20 metres in height, is crowned by a double roof and pierced by five vaulted tunnels. The impression of grandeur and solidity is strengthened by the use of gorgeous colours. The walls are built of brick coated with red plaster; the wooden pillars of the pavilions are covered with thick lacquer and painted bright vermilion; the roofs are laid out with glazed yellow tiles; and the staircases and balustrades are made of white marble. 'The splendid exterior effect of the palaces', Oswald Sirén noted in his excellent study of imperial Peking, 'depends largely upon their gorgeous colouring. . . . These three colours, white, red and yellow, set against the clear sky and the green trees, or reflected in the dark water of the moats and canals, form the dominating accord in the vistas of the Palace City.'

The Meridian Gate gives access to a vast flagged court across which in a wide curve from east to west flows the Golden Water River. It is spanned by five marble bridges with carved balustrades. Straight ahead is the T'ai Ho Men, or Gate of Supreme Harmony, a pavilion with tall columns, whose middle doors, like those in all the gates, were opened only for the Son of Heaven, while his officials always passed through the side entrances. The imperial pathway can be traced in the decorative marble slabs carved with dragons and other symbolic animals that form the central sections of the gently sloping stairways leading to and from the terraced gateways, halls and temples. Standing before the Gate of Supreme Harmony are two enormous bronze lions and two marble ornaments representing the emperor's authority; on a large scale are sculptured the box in which petitions to the throne were placed and the box in which the imperial seals were kept. One hundred and eight metres beyond the T'ai Ho Men, at the northern side of an empty court, standing on an immense three-tier terrace is the Hall of the Supreme Harmony, the T'ai Ho Tien, one of the three big ceremonial buildings of the palace. Here were held the rites and formalities connected with the great occasions of the calendar, the New Year, the winter solstice, and the emperor's birthday. On a high dais, approached by three flights of steps, stood the dragon throne. The interior of the T'ai Ho Tien measures fifty-two by thirty metres, and is divided by three rows of eight columns. Several reconstructions have taken place, the most significant being the one in 1645 when the present name was adopted. Immediately behind the Hall of Supreme Harmony on the high terrace are the Chung Ho Tien, the Middle Harmony Hall, and the Pao Ho Tien, Protecting Harmony Hall. A small building

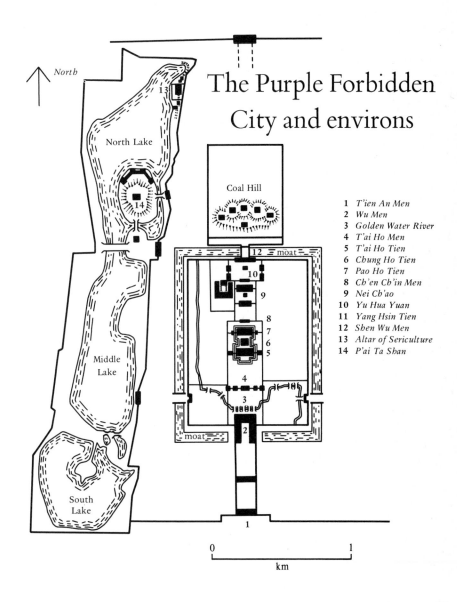

The Purple Forbidden City and environs

1 *T'ien An Men*
2 *Wu Men*
3 *Golden Water River*
4 *T'ai Ho Men*
5 *T'ai Ho Tien*
6 *Chung Ho Tien*
7 *Pao Ho Tien*
8 *Ch'en Ch'in Men*
9 *Nei Ch'ao*
10 *Yu Hua Yuan*
11 *Yang Hsin Tien*
12 *Shen Wu Men*
13 *Altar of Sericulture*
14 *P'ai Ta Shan*

sixteen metres square, the Middle Harmony Hall served as a tiring room for the emperor prior to the ceremonies held in the T'ai Ho Tien. The Protecting Harmony Hall is much larger, the outside measurements being forty-nine by twenty-three metres, and it was in this building that the successful candidates in the palace examinations were received by the emperor. The courtyard to the rear of the Pao Ho Tien terminates in the Ch'en Ch'in Men, a one-storied hall and entrance to the Inner Court, or Nei Ch'ao. Northwards the axial avenue continues with three small halls that balance the ceremonial edifices of the outer courtyards, and ends in a beautiful garden, the Yu Hua Yuan, where the emperor could rest from the cares of government. The northern wall of the Purple Forbidden City is penetrated at the Shen Wu Men, or the Spirit of Bravery Gate, near the foot of Coal Hill. The private rooms of the emperor were situated in the Yang Hsin Tien, the Hall where the Heart is Nourished, a large building on the western side of the Nei Ch'ao.

A glimpse of the dazzling brightness of the court as it survived under the Empress Dowager T'zu Hsi, who dominated the Purple Forbidden City through her eunuchs from the 1860s till her death in 1908, is available in this report of an American visitor:

> Her Majesty's Throne room at the Winter Palace fronted on a court which was surrounded by well built walls with curiously shaped doors and windows and ornamental yellow and green tiled designs at intervals. In the centre of the wall in front was the immense gateway, with wooden folding

Plan of T'ai Ho Tien
in the Purple Forbidden City, Peking
(after Sirén)

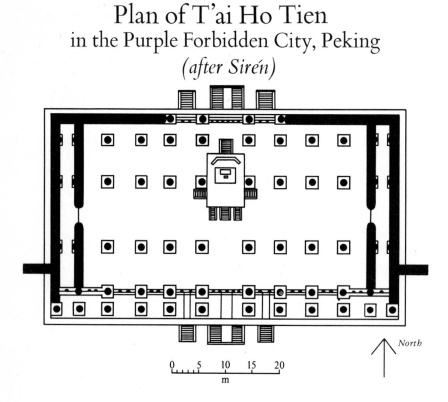

0   5   10   15   20
m

North

Chung Ho Tien, the
Middle Harmony Hall,
in the Purple Forbidden
City, Peking.

doors, which had just opened for her passage. . . . Entering, I was struck by
the beauty of the great central hall, the harmony of its proportions, the
sombre splendour of its colour. It seemed to me as the most satisfying, the
most picturesque of all the restful, harmonious Chinese interiors I had seen.
Its dull red walls, splendid coffered ceiling, glowing in colour and glinting
in gold, its central dome, with elaborately carved pendatives, was painted
in brilliant primary colours, subdued into a rich harmony by the demi-
obscurity, for it had no 'latern' and received its light from the windows
below. . . .

The hall was paved with great blocks of highly polished black marble,
which dimly reflected the glowing splendour of the walls and the ceiling.
In the centre of one side was a low dais, richly carpeted, on which stood a
great antique throne and foot stool of red lacquer, framed in ebony and
inlaid with cloisonné – the three-leaved screen behind was of bronze with
landscapes in low relief. On each leaf a poem in golden characters gave the
needed touch of brilliancy to the sombre massiveness of the dull bronze.

Close to the Purple Forbidden City were other areas reserved for imperial
use. While Coal Hill, so named according to tradition because an emergency
supply of coal was stored there by one of the Yuan emperors, served as a

55

Overlooking a portion
of the three western lakes
in the Imperial City,
Peking.

recreation and pleasure ground for the inhabitants of the palace, temples and smaller residences were dotted on the islands and shores of the three western lakes, whose origins probably date from the Kin Empire (1125–1212). Most of the buildings were erected by the Ch'ing dynasty, though P'ai Ta Shan, or White Pagoda Mountain, on the large island in North Lake has been identified as the Green Mount of Kubilai Khan, who according to Marco Polo had a live forest of 'handsome' trees moved to cover this artificial eminence. The lakes offer rare and unusual perspectives to the observer; indeed, one is liable to forget that they are situated near the centre of a great city encircled by several massive walls. At the north-eastern tip of the Pei Hai or North Lake is an enclosure containing the Altar of Sericulture, where the empress performed certain rites to ensure the safe breeding of the silkworms. Legend has it that the Chinese were introduced to sericulture by the wife of the Yellow Emperor, the cultural founder-hero.

Two sacrificial altars attended by the Son of Heaven are south of the Purple Forbidden City on either side of the Yung Ting Men or South Gate. Emperor Ming Yung-lo performed the sacred rites as the One Man on a single site in the vicinity, but about 1530 it was decided, after a thorough historical investigation by a commission of scholars, that separate altars should be built not only for Heaven and Earth but also to the Sun and Moon as well as other spiritual powers. Within a three-hundred-hectare enclosure is the T'ien Tan or Altar of Heaven, a three-tier terrace nearly five metres in height, and the well-

The 'Dragon Pavement' in the Purple Forbidden City. Besides the dragon, a symbol of imperial authority from earliest times, other fantastic animals decorate the path reserved for the emperor. They include the dragon horse (*lung-ma*), the phoenix (*fung-huang*), and the composite tiger, horse and dragon (*cha-ya*).

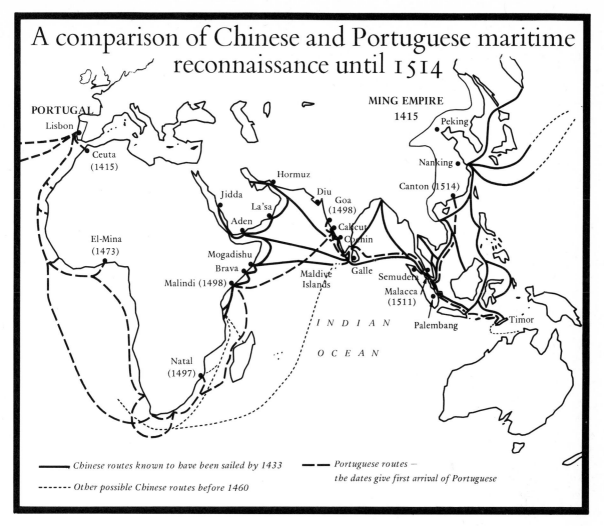

A comparison of Chinese and Portuguese maritime reconnaissance until 1514

PORTUGAL
Lisbon
Ceuta (1415)
El-Mina (1473)
Natal (1497)

MING EMPIRE 1415
Peking
Nanking
Canton (1514)

Hormuz
Jidda
La'sa
Diu
Aden
Goa (1498)
Calicut
Cochin
Mogadishu
Brava
Malindi (1498)
Maldive Islands
Galle
Semudera
Malacca (1511)
Palembang
Timor

INDIAN OCEAN

——— Chinese routes known to have been sailed by 1433   – – – Portuguese routes –
                                                             the dates give first arrival of Portuguese
------- Other possible Chinese routes before 1460

known Ch'i-nien Tien, a circular edifice with a triple roof of blue tiles, usually called the Temple of Heaven. In this beautiful hall the emperor offered prayers for a prosperous year. Nearby is the Hsien Nung T'an, the Altar of Agriculture, whose sacrifices were connected with the spring ploughing and were directed at the securing of good harvests. Beneath the architectural use of monumental terraces in the composition of the Purple Forbidden City lay an ancient religious tradition, stretching back to the primitive mounds or altars dedicated to the god of the soil in the earliest settlements. The loess soil of North China was eminently suited to the formation of stone-lined terraces, whether sown for crops or prepared as foundations for religious or secular buildings.

MARITIME
EXPEDITIONS

In nautical technology the Empire of the Two Sungs had been supreme. For the first time the imperial navy was established on a permanent basis and in defensive actions against the invading Kin, and later the Mongols, it won numerous victories. Inland its man-powered paddle-wheel warships were able to seal off rivers and artificial waterways that stood in the way of the

59

樓
船
圖

Armoured war junk, a type which may have been involved at the battle of Po'yang Lake (1363).

nomad advance; along the shore its squadrons of sailing ships kept a close watch on enemy movements besides acting as ferries for reinforcements of troops sent to relieve invested coastal cities. The sea and the Yang-tze River had become the new Great Wall, as warships were substituted for watch-towers. Only the acquisition of a naval arm by the Mongol invaders through the services of captured provinces brought about the complete conquest of China, the last Southern Sung prince losing his life in a sea battle in 1279 off what is now Hong Kong. Inheriting Chinese maritime skills, Kubilai Khan was able to put together a fleet of 4,400 ships to attack Japan in 1281 and, twelve years later, an expeditionary force was carried to Java in 1,000 ships. Both ventures were unsuccessful, but they testify to an impressive naval capacity. Its successor, the navy of the Ming, extended the supremacy of Chinese fleets into the Indian Ocean itself.

From 1405 to 1433 the Ming dynasty mounted seven major seaborne expeditions which caused the authority and power of the Son of Heaven to be acknowledged by more foreign rulers than ever before, even distant Egypt sending an ambassador. The renown of the Chinese Empire was increased by these voyages in which the foremost navy in the world paid friendly visits to foreign ports; and states which accepted the suzerainty of Peking were guaranteed protection and gifts were bestowed on their kings. 'Those who refused submission', the histories tell us of the first expedition, 'they over-awed by the show of armed might. Every country became obedient to the imperial commands, and when admiral Cheng Ho turned homewards, sent envoys in his train to offer tribute. The emperor was highly gladdened, and before very long commanded Cheng Ho to go overseas once more and scatter largess among the different states. On this, the number who presented themselves before the throne grew ever greater.' The expeditions, it would seem, were neither commercial in design, nor privately sponsored, but sailed under the personal direction of a eunuch solely responsible to Emperor Ming Yung-lo, whose desire to display power and acquire prestige for the Empire was a corollary of the Chinese recovery. These were the heroic years of the Ming dynasty, before reverses in Annam forced the occupying Chinese forces to withdraw in 1427, and the disastrous conduct of Wang Chen at T'u-mu resulted in the contraction of the northern frontier to the line of the Great Wall.

The maritime expeditions had, in fact, a dual function – the reassertion of Chinese authority in the southern ocean after the expulsion of the Mongols, and a return to the state-controlled overseas trading system of the Two Sungs. The import of luxury items such as drugs, ivory, rhinoceros horn and pearls had been a severe drain on the limited supply of metal coinage in the Sung Empire; hence a regulation issued in 1219 specified the commodities to be used in place of cash to pay for foreign imports – silk, brocades, and porcelain. The latter became the chief item of exchange during the Ming dynasty, and porcelain vessels were used in places as far apart as East Africa and North Borneo. They were welcome gifts from the Son of Heaven, who received in return luxury goods and precious commodities sought after by the court. The Sultan of Malindi, the ruler of the Zinj Empire, sent an embassy to China in 1415 with various gifts, among them a magnificent specimen of a giraffe for the imperial zoo. At the palace gate Emperor Ming Yung-lo personally received the animal, together with a 'celestial horse' and a 'celestial stag', perhaps a zebra and an oryx. To mark his appreciation the ambassadors were conducted all the way home to East Africa on the fifth voyage of 1417–19.

How different the Ming expeditions were from those of the Portuguese. Instead of pillaging the coastline, slaving, seeking to establish colonies and monopolize international trade, the Chinese fleets were engaged on an elaborate series of diplomatic missions, exchanging gifts with distant kings from whom they were content to accept formal recognition of the overlordship of the Son of Heaven. There was neither intolerance of other religious beliefs nor the search for one's personal fortune in the discovery of Eldorado:

the two dominant traits of *conquistador* mentality. The voyages of the early Ming were unique in nature and intention, good reasons for us to look at them in some detail and consider the historical significance of the later Chinese neglect of sea power.

Most of the finance for the building of the expeditionary fleet was raised by Emperor Ming Yung-lo outside the usual methods of taxation. Continuing the resettlement policies of his father, the first Ming emperor, he sold off to farmers and landlords the remainder of the imperial hunting domain inherited from the Yuan dynasty. With the vast sums that accrued, a scheme for overseas ventures could be devised by the court, beyond civil service control, and as the emperor's own agent the eunuch Cheng Ho was put in command of the fleet. A strong ruler and an able soldier, Emperor Ming Yung-lo had no need to fear eunuch influence, though his successors whose experience of life was confined to the palace did repeat the worst errors of the Later Han emperors; his choice of Cheng Ho was probably conditioned by the memory of how important naval power had been in founding the Ming dynasty and his fear that a well-equipped fleet in the hands of any one other than a eunuch could pose a threat to his own usurpation. In Cheng Ho he found an extraordinary man, a first-rate ambassador and admiral. Born in Yunnan about 1371, Cheng Ho's original name was Ma Ho and his forbears were Mongols of Muslim belief. He came to the notice of the emperor in the suppression of a rebellion in Yunnan, after which he was promoted a 'grand eunuch' and received the surname of Cheng. Such were his abilities and demeanour at court he was appointed admiral-in-chief of the six expeditions which sailed progressively westwards between 1405 and 1421 during the reign of Ming Yung-lo as well as the seventh and last one of 1431–3, sent to the western ocean at the behest of Emperor Ming Hsuan-te. Two years later Cheng Ho died, at the age of sixty-five, in Nanking, but his fame has persisted as legend in several of the lands he visited, including Thailand where for centuries a temple has made sacrifices to him.

The 'treasure ships', the Ming name for vessels piloted by Cheng Ho, were built in yards on the Yang-tze River near Nanking. The first order was for two hundred and fifty ships, many of them larger than ever previously launched. The best *kung*, selected by examinations, were transferred from other work, such as the building and repair of palaces and temples. Sixty-two very large junks which formed the nucleus of the expeditionary fleet had dimensions of one hundred and thirty-four metres in length and fifty-five metres in beam. They possessed four decks, a hull divided into watertight bulkheads and buoyancy chambers, and no less than nine masts. A special kind of sail, made out of bamboo, permitted sailing against the wind, so that reliance on oars only occurred in a calm. With a crew of five hundred men, each junk had a displacement in excess of 1,500 tonnes. Traditional accounts of the magnitude of these vessels were disbelieved, or regarded as overstatements, until the discovery in 1962 of a rudder-post of one of Cheng Ho's 'treasure ships'. It is twelve metres long and sufficient for a rudder capable of steering a vessel up to one hundred and sixty metres. The contrast between Portuguese and Chinese ships is striking and would have been even more obvious had any of Vasco da Gama's craft of 300 tonnes encountered off the African coast a 'treasure ship' of 1,500 tonnes.

赤龍舟圖

Small war junk armed with missiles.

The distant shores that the Chinese navy reached in the early Ming period included the countries of South-east Asia, Ceylon, India, Persia, the eastern coast of Africa as far south as Zanzibar, and Arabia. Yet even in the third voyage of 1409–11, when Cheng Ho sailed with a force of thirty thousand troops in forty-eight 'treasure ships' to Champa, Java, Malacca, Sumatra and Ceylon, the fleet had not entered waters previously unvisited by Chinese junks. Ibn Batutah, the great Arab traveller, noticed thirteen ships of the Mongol navy anchored at Calicut in 1330. The admiral in command behaved like a 'great Emir' and had with him one thousand men. It was the last four Ming expeditions which converted this presence into an undisputed naval supremacy, making the Indian Ocean into a Chinese lake.

On the third voyage, however, the most serious opposition to Chinese claims for hegemony in the southern and western oceans took place. Sailing homeward in 1410 or 1411 Cheng Ho made a stop at the port of Galle in Ceylon, where he had enjoyed a peaceful visit to the Buddhist shrines and temples on his first expedition. The Sinhalese monarch, Alagakkonara, enticed the expeditionary force inland and then demanded huge quantities of gold and silk as presents, meanwhile sending troops to sink the Chinese junks. Resolute and resourceful, Cheng Ho marched on the capital, overcame its defenders, and captured the royal family. Fighting several battles on his way back to the coast, he routed the Sinhalese army, and set sail for China. Emperor Ming Yung-lo treated the prisoners kindly; he had them returned to Ceylon after a relative of the deposed king had been installed on the throne, apparently satisfied that 'those who refused submission [were sufficiently] over-awed by the show of armed might'. The contrast with the imperialism of Portugal is inescapable: neither had Cheng Ho taken his revenge for the treachery by firing the limbs of his prisoners at the Sinhalese army, as Portuguese commanders were to do with Muslim captives over Indian cities, nor had the Chinese emperor for one moment entertained the idea that cruelty should be used as an aspect of imperial policy. The tenor of Cheng Ho's approach to relations with southern countries can be gauged from the text of a stele he had set up at Galle. The stele, inscribed in three languages, Chinese, Tamil and Persian, is dated 15 February 1409, the day on which the following was composed in China:

> His Imperial Majesty, Emperor of the Great Ming, has despatched the Grand Eunuchs Cheng Ho, Wang Ch'ing-lien, and others, to set forth his utterances before the Lord Buddha, the World-Honoured One, thus.
>
> Deeply do we reverence Thee, Merciful and Honoured One, of bright perfection wide-embracing, whose Way and virtue passes all understanding, whose Law pervades all human relations, and the years of whose great *kalpa* rival the river-sands in number; Thou whose controlling influence ennobles and converts, inspiring acts of love and giving intelligent insight into the nature of things; Thou whose mysterious response is limitless! The temples and monastries of Ceylon's mountainous isle, lying in the southern ocean far, are imbued and enlightened by Thy miraculously responsive power.
>
> Of late we have despatched missions to announce our Mandate to foreign nations, and during their journeys over the oceans they have been favoured with the blessing of Thy beneficent protection. They have escaped disaster or misfortune, journeying in safety to and fro, ever guided by Thy great virtue.
>
> Wherefore according to the Rites we bestow recompense, and do now reverently present before the Lord Buddha, the World-Honoured One, oblations of gold and silver, gold-embroidered jewelled banners of varie-gated silk, incense-burners and flower-vases, silks of many colours in lining and exterior, lamps and candles, with other gifts, in order to manifest the high honour of the Lord Buddha. May His light shine on the donors.

The inscription ends with a list of the presents: one thousand pieces of gold, five thousand pieces of silver, one hundred rolls of silk, and so on. Here we have a Moslem ambassador from China dedicating gifts to a Buddhist monastery in Ceylon from the Son of Heaven, the One Man of Confucian ethic. More fascinating still is the circumstance that the other inscriptions do not translate the Chinese one. From the Tamil we learn that the One Man, having heard of the fame of Tenavarai-nayanar, an incarnation of Vishnu, caused the stone to be set up; whilst in the Persian version praise is accorded to Allah and the great saints of the Islamic faith. Again there is a painful juxtaposition with the Portuguese, who were soon to bring into the Indian Ocean the ancient enmity of Christianity and Islam which had bedevilled the Mediterranean with the Crusades, while in the sixteenth century they transplanted to their colony of Goa the most tyrannical feature of the Counter-Reformation, the Holy Inquisition. The Chinese urbanity was, of course, nothing more than an extension of their own historical involvement with religion, typified as it was by a rejection of exclusive creeds and an absence of 'holy wars'. The members of the Ming expeditions were able to discourse about the religious beliefs of the people of the southern countries without forsaking the basic teachings of the Chinese sages.

There were only two other occasions when Cheng Ho had to resort to force. In 1406 he crossed swords with a pirate chief who had pillaged merchants and attempted to surprise the Chinese camp at Palembang: subsequently, the leading Chinese resident in the town, 'Shih Chin-ch'ing who was a man from Kwantung', Ma Huan relates in *Ying-Yai Sheng-Lan* or *The Overall Survey of the Ocean's Shores*, had bestowed on him by Emperor Ming Yung-lo 'a hat and girdle . . . to rule over the territory'. This has the appearance of imperialist expansion into Sumatran affairs until it is realized that the pirate king who was sent back to China for sentence hailed from Kwantung and the authority of Shih Chin-ch'ing probably ran for the Chinese community only. The second conflict also happened in Sumatra, seven or eight years afterwards, when Cheng Ho was ordered by the emperor to restore Sultan Zain Al' Abidin to the throne of Semudera. He did so, the usurper being executed in China. Representative of Ming overseas policy would be the treatment of the ruler of Malacca, which Cheng Ho used as a base for reassembling the various squadrons of the fleet at the end of a voyage. The Chinese were welcomed at Malacca, a city which had only recently gained its independence, the ruler travelling to the Ming court three times to offer tribute.

On the death of Emperor Ming Yung-lo in 1425 voyages were suspended, and, despite the seventh expedition of 1431–3, the era of maritime reconnaissance and diplomacy was over. Not all the reasons are apparent for this momentous alteration in policy, which left a vacuum in the Indian Ocean and the China Sea to be filled unwittingly by the European powers. A combination of circumstances seems to be responsible. The *shih*, strongly against the ventures from the beginning, were even more strongly opposed to the prestige Cheng Ho and the eunuchs derived from their success. They were also becoming less profitable and no alternative sources of finance remained to be tapped. But not to be overlooked are the improvements of Sung Li to the Grand Canal, henceforth the focus of Chinese nautics. Inland craft replaced ocean-going junks in the sixteenth century as the anti-maritime party reached its height. In 1525 coastal officials were ordered to destroy all junks with two or more masts. Although there was a later recovery of mercantile shipbuilding, the run down of the imperial fleet was dramatic and irreversible, so that naval architecture ossified during the Ch'ing dynasty, when a deliberate policy of indifference to sea power exposed China to the aggressive ambitions of nineteenth-century European imperialist nations.

Copious scholarship was the hallmark of the Ming revival. The gigantic *Yung-lo Encyclopedia (Yung-lo ta-tien)* was prepared in four years by more than two thousand *shih*; on completion in 1407, its 11,095 volumes and 22,000 chapters were judged to be too numerous for a printed edition, a misfortune today because the main collection of hand-copied rolls perished when the British sacked the Summer Palace in 1860. The encyclopedia, in which books from all over the Empire were copied, was a reflection of intellectual attitudes amongst the *shih* returned to public office under the Ming emperors. They were preoccupied with the past. Though this antiquarian emphasis in learning led directly onto the establishment of the new disciplines of philology and phonetics, with a consequent reassessment of the authenticity of ancient texts, the intellectual revival in China contrasts with the scientific aspects of the European Renaissance, and appears strangely anti-scientific in the context of the previous millennium of technological advance pioneered by the Chinese. In the Two Sungs, Joseph Needham has written, 'one finds a major

ARTISTIC AND
INTELLECTUAL
ACTIVITIES

The Idle Fisherman. An anonymous Ming painting (1368–1644).

focal point . . . for the applied as well as the pure sciences'. Whatever the inhibiting factors on the development of scientific method in Ming China – at the moment no consensus of opinion can be said to exist – the historical fact is that the initial progress of Chinese science was discontinued and the scientific revolution of sixteenth and seventeenth centuries in Europe gave to the western nations a temporary advantage in technology.

Despite the prevailing atmosphere at court and in educational institutions there were a number of individuals who did make contributions to scientific knowledge. Notables were the botanists, Chu Ting-wang and Chu Hsien-wang, respectively the fifth son and grandson of Emperor Ming Hung-wu; they maintained a large botanical garden near K'ai Feng and published in 1406 the *Chiu-huang pen-ts'ao* or *Herbal for the Prevention of Famine*, which contained the first woodcuts of plants anywhere in the world. The culmination of such codifications came in the *Pen-ts'ao kung-mu*, or *Outline of Herbal Medicine*, the basic text on herbs for the Chinese doctor from its completion by Li Shih-chen in 1578. The pharmaceutical values of two thousand plants and animals, exhaustively described and illustrated, preceded more than eight thousand prescriptions. Noted yet more by his contemporaries was the philosopher Wang Yang-ming, whose idealist mode of thought chimed with the inwardness and isolation of the later Ming. Wang Yang-ming (1472–1529), an official of high rank, was profoundly influenced by the idealist doctrines of Buddhism. As the last and chief teacher of the *Hsin-Hsueh*, or Mind Doctrine School of Neo-Confucianism, he stressed that all knowledge existed within one's inner self and that it could not be acquired by interrogating outward things. Intuitive knowledge, *liang-chih*, was an expression of the essential goodness of mankind and the absolute unity which existed throughout the universe. 'The mind in man', Wang Yang-ming said, 'is a heavenly pool to which nothing is not vouchsafed. Speaking fundamentally, there is only one Heaven, and it is only through the obstruction of selfish lusts that this original unity with Heaven is lost. Thus, if every thought is used in extending intuitive knowledge, then the barriers and obstructions will be entirely cleared away. Then the substance of Heaven will be recovered and there will be again the heavenly pool.' Sublime though this conception of the alert and concentrated mind was, the tendency towards abstraction necessarily downgraded the value of empirical observation, much to the detriment of the natural sciences. Henceforth the sage acted from inner knowledge, the correct response to attunement with the nature of all things.

In painting the rift between the court and the scholar-painters, voluntarily living away from the capital which had arisen during the Yuan dynasty, was widened into a gulf under the stimulus of private patronage, the owners of the *chuang-t'ien*, the great estates, gathering together collections of Sung and Yuan masterpieces along with the works of contemporary artists. At the Ming Court painting lost its vitality, conforming more and more to academic stereotype, while the *wen-jen*, the literary painters who traced their origins back to Wang Wei in the T'ang period, cherished their independence in the provinces and sought to extend the recent achievements of Yuan landscape painters like Huang Kung-wang (1269–1354) and Ni Tsan (1301–74). Both these voluntary exiles from the Mongol capital had had strong connections with Taoist quietism: Huang Kung-wang wandered the mountains and valleys of southern provinces, while Ni Tsan spent most of his life in a houseboat on the lakes of Kiangsi. The austerity and power of the latter's landscapes partly explain his influence on Ming artists. By the economical use of ink and the eschewing of colour he managed to convert landscape into an expression, a bodying forth of an inner mood, something that can be seen to have appealed to Lu Chih (1496–1576) in his own *Taoist Retreat in Mountain and Stream after Ni Tsan*. As Sherman Lee commented:

> Ink painting during the three-hundred-year period of the Sung dynasty developed a wide vocabulary of brush strokes and a broad grammar of pictorial structure. The virtuoso usage of these basic elements for a new purpose was achieved in the succeeding Yuan dynasty, [when] ... a smaller number of literati, members of the scholarly elite, experimented with the structure provided by the great Northern Sung masters as a means, not of pictorial creation, but of written confession – using landscape, almost alone, as the means of personal expression through brush work.

The Wu school, a name taken from Wu-hsien near Soochow, where were born its leading painters Shen Chou (1427–1509) and Wen Cheng-ming (1470–1559), consolidated the *wen-jen* tradition and ensured its future pre-eminence. Deservedly renowned for the series of paintings of gnarled pine trees that Wen Cheng-ming executed in his last years, this pupil of Shen Chou found little scope for his abilities in the capital. The famous *Old Pine Tree*, now in the collection of the Cleveland Museum of Art, could stand as the symbol of his own experience, the inner strength and hardy age of the retired artist. A scholar-painter who did achieve official distinction was Tung Ch'i-chang (1555–1636). He also worked in ink and wrote about the aesthetics of the literary tradition of painting. Referring to old masters of wet and dry ink, he wrote, 'Li Ch'eng spared the ink as if it had been gold; Wang Hsia splashed the ink abundantly with water. Students of painting should always keep in mind these four words: *Hsi mo, p'o mo* (spare ink, splash ink); if they do it, they will understand more than half of the Six Principles and the Three Classes of painting.' Thus, seeing the origins of *wen-jen* tradition in the Ch'an Buddhism of the T'ang period, Tung Ch'i-chang favoured those painters who delighted in the sudden and the spontaneous, cursive lines of accomplished calligraphers.

In literature, as in painting, it was the exclusion of the *shih* from the civil service after the founding of the Yuan dynasty that stimulated the development of new forms – the play and the novel. Attention was no longer focused on the classics studied for the imperial examinations, so that scholars were at liberty to venture into new fields of composition. Outside the pale of respectable literature, drama before the fourteenth century was either associated with popular performances derived from folk legend or entertainments put on by actors from 'the Western Regions' for the court. Whether or not another influence entered China during the Mongol invasion is uncertain because Yuan plays do not reveal features which suggest outside additions to the native dramatic material. A favourite subject of the theatre was the pilgrimage to India of Tripitaka, the historical Hsuan Tsang (seventh century) who brought back to the T'ang Empire copies of the Buddhist scriptures:

Ming jade carving of
a Mongolian pony.

his fantastic adventures, richly elaborated by folk stories and plays, were also
the inspiration of Wu Cheng-en (1505–80) in *Pilgrimage to the West*, possibly
the most widely read book in Chinese literature. The knockabout humour
and frank speech of this novel may surprise Western readers, though the
wisdom of honest laughter was appreciated long before the reign of Ch'in Shih
Huang-ti and the sceptical tradition of Confucian thought soon discovered
in ridicule a potent weapon against religious fanaticism. The Ming novels
were, in fact, the first major works to be composed in colloquial language.
Indeed, it was only in the twentieth century that the novel was admitted to the
select ranks of Chinese literature.

The supreme novel of manners *Chin Ping Mei*, or *Golden Lotus*, was pub-
lished anonymously at Soochow in 1610. Much impressed by its candour was
Lu Hsun (1881–1936), the earliest practitioner of the modern novel in China.
In his study of Chinese fiction, Lu Hsun wrote that *Chin Ping Mei* 'holds such
a variety of human interest that no novel of that period could surpass it', the
author having achieved a subtle 'condemnation of the whole ruling class'.
Here, the central character Hsi-men Ching is being abused by his mistress
Golden Lotus, whose husband he had poisoned.

'You scoundrel!' said Golden Lotus. 'You've reminded me of something
I'd forgotten. Spring Plum, show him those slippers!' She turned back to
Hsi-men, 'Do you recognize these slippers?'
'Indeed I don't,' said Hsi-men.
'What a picture of innocence!' jeered Golden Lotus. 'A fine way you
carried on with Lai-wang's wife behind my back, treasuring her stinking

slippers like some jewel in your card-box with writing paper and incense in the cave in the garden. Are they such treasures? What use are they? No wonder that cursed bitch went to Hell when she died!' And pointing to Autumn Aster, she scolded: 'This stupid creature produced them, thinking they were mine. I gave her a good beating!' She ordered Spring Plum: 'Throw these objects away at once.'

Spring Plum passed the slippers on the floor and said with a glance at Autumn Aster: 'You can have them.'

Autumn Aster picked them up, remarking: 'Madam's slippers are so small, I can hardly get my toes in.'

'You cursed slave!' exploded Golden Lotus. 'Why say "madam"? She must have been your master's mother in his last existence: otherwise why should he keep these as a treasure? No doubt they're a family heirloom. How disgusting!'

As Autumn Aster was walking out, Golden Lotus called her back. 'Bring me a knife! Let me chop the bitch's slippers up and throw the bits in the piss-pot, so that she'll have to stay in Hell and never come to life again.' She rounded on Hsi-men: 'The sadder you look, the smaller I'll cut them up.'

Hsi-men laughed. 'You bitch! Just throw them away. I don't care a damn . . .'

Other famous Ming novels were the two historical romances by Lo Kuan-chung, namely *The Romance of the Three Kingdoms (San Kuo Chih Yen I)* and *All Men are Brothers (Shui Hu Chuan)*. These tales looked back at periods of decline or disruption in Chinese history; they have enjoyed immense popularity ever since their appearance at the beginning of the fifteenth century.

To many people outside China the Ming dynasty is identified with ceramics. Sir Harry Garner noted:

Fine piece of fifteenth-century blue and white. A stem cup.

In the long history of the development of decorated pottery and porcelain no single type has had more widespread influence than that which is known as 'blue and white'. It reached its heyday in China during the Ming dynasty and its manufacture spread to the countries of the Near East, to other oriental countries, Japan and Korea, and finally to Europe. Although from the early eighteenth century onwards the more brightly coloured porcelains came into favour everywhere, blue and white still retained much of its popularity. In England, for example, the printed wares of Staffordshire were largely blue and white and in many instances, such as the well-known Willow Pattern, were based on Chinese designs.

Painting in underglaze blue was introduced during the Yuan dynasty. This Persian invention of the twelfth century – the technique and the imported cobalt which produced the 'Mohammedan blue' colour – was transformed by Chinese potters into the dominant mode of decoration for porcelain, not least by the discovery of a way of preventing the cobalt from running. The *kung* found that the addition of native cobalt, which contained manganese, avoided the problems encountered by Persian potters. Manufacture centred on Ch'ing-te Chen, Kiangsi, where there were plentiful supplies of high-grade china-clay and china-stone, the two materials that combine to make the body of the porcelain. The Chinese method had only one firing. Pigment was applied to the unglazed body, the whole was covered with glaze, and the piece was then fired, so that the complete fusion of all the materials resulted in an unequalled brilliance and luminosity.

Pieces of first-rate quality were not produced for the court alone. Certain designs and forms were restricted for the use of the imperial household; at one time the dragon when depicted with five claws may have referred exclusively to the emperor's person. Demand for blue and white, however, grew both within the borders of the Empire and without from countries wishing to enter into relations with Peking or initiate trade agreements. Cheng Ho distributed the largesse of Emperor Ming Yung-lo partly in the form of porcelain, and the Victoria and Albert Museum in London houses a fine bottle inscribed 'Jorge Anrz, 1557', a personal commission from this Portuguese traveller. As a result more centres of manufacture specializing in wares for export came into existence, such as Swatow in Kwangtung, and others in Annam, Korea and Japan. According to legend the first porcelain made in Japan was by Gorodayu go Shonzui, who had gone to Ching-te Chen in 1510 and spent five years learning the art. Nevertheless, the prime function of the Chinese porcelain industry was the supply of wares for the court. The size of the imperial orders undertaken can be appreciated from the surviving documentary evidence. In 1534, for instance, a small request was made for 6,000 bowls, cups and dishes, while in 1544 an order was placed for 1,340 table services, comprising 35,000 pieces, and in 1554 another 100,000 were required for the court.

3

The Founding of the Ch'ing Dynasty

On his capture of Peking in 1644 Li Tzu-ch'eng seemed about to found a lasting dynasty, the Shun. Though Li Tzu-ch'eng was a man of little education, his abilities as a commander were manifest and the domination of the Ming court by the eunuchs encouraged the feeling that a change of imperial house might not be disadvantageous, providing it was a native one. People recalled how the founder of the Ming had been of humble origins and how the vigorous action of the early Ming emperors against nomadic tribes had contained the problem of encroachment from the steppe. Under a vigorous dynasty the Empire would be able to cope with the rising power of the Manchus, now dominant beyond the Great Wall.

A factor not taken into full account by Li Tzu-ch'eng was the susceptibilities of the general responsible for defending the line of the Great Wall immediately north of the capital. This man, Wu San-kuei, who was neither a fanatical adherent of the Ming nor a contender for the dragon throne, found himself drawn into a personal quarrel with the Shun pretender. After the fall of Peking, Li Tzu-ch'eng had taken into his harem Ch'en Yuan, the favourite concubine of Wu San-kuei, and he was not prepared to restore her. Unwilling to tolerate this situation and eager for vengeance, Wu San-kuei turned to the Manchus for support, opening the gates in the Great Wall at Shanhaikuan. This strategic position – a translation of the name is 'the Pass between Mountain and Sea' – controlled the road between China and Manchuria: upon it the Ming system of northern defence had hinged. Whatever Wu San-kuei expected to be the result of alliance with the Manchus, the admission of these warlike tribesmen to the northern provinces was a fatal move. Once they were embroiled in civil strife they proved impossible to expel or control. Driven from Peking by the combined army, Li retreated westwards until he was finally overcome and destroyed by Wu San-kuei, whilst the Manchus, temporarily withdrawing from the conflict, installed their seven-year-old king as Emperor Ch'ing Shun-chih (1644–61).

The Manchus were related to the Kin tribesmen who had conquered North China between 1125 and 1212. Their home was the woodlands between the Liao River and the Korean border, country suited to a mixture of pastoralism and rudimentary agriculture. Settlement by Chinese farmers north of the Great Wall was a source of friction between the Ming Empire and the Manchus, who raided the farmlands in the lower Liao valley once the military strength of the Ming declined. Nurhachu (1559–1626) was the first leader of all the Manchus and a man possessed with the vision of conquest. He devised the politico-military system of the 'banners', administrative units

Abahai, Manchu chieftain, known by the posthumous title of Ch'ing T'ai-tsung.

charged with the maintenance of a certain number of fighting men. The
'banners' were headed by officials loyal to Nurhachu, who was concerned to
weaken the influence of hereditary chieftains, and by 1644 there were some
170,000 fighting men enlisted under twenty-four 'banners'. In border raids
they worsted Ming forces sent against them, forcing the latter to fall back to
the security of the Great Wall. Under Abahai (1626–43), known also by the
posthumous title Ch'ing T'ai-tsung, the Manchus overran Korea and Inner
Mongolia, thus gaining ascendancy over all of the lands adjoining the
northern frontier. Dorgon, Abahai's brother, was regent when Wu San-kuei
surrendered the gates at Shanhaikuan and gave the bannermen access to
North China.

For thirty years the authority of the Ch'ing dynasty, as the Manchus
styled their house, was restricted to the North. Wu San-kuei was left to deal
with the remaining pretenders in the South, which was then divided between
himself and two lesser generals. Emperor Ch'ing Shun-chih proved a feeble
ruler, easily misled by the eunuchs whom he inherited with the imperial palace,
and the future of his house was by no means certain in 1661 when the young
K'ang-hsi succeeded. Had Wu San-kuei chosen this moment to revolt it is
quite possible that the Ch'ing dynasty would have been toppled. Not until
1673 did the people of the southern provinces rise in rebellion. By then Emperor
Ch'ing K'ang-hsi had dispensed with his regents and his own energetic handling of the crisis was decisive, though the alliance Wu San-kuei established
with dissident Mongol tribes came close to breaking Manchu power. Age
and the rigours of campaigning as much as anything else undermined Wu
San-kuei, who died undefeated in 1678. Disagreement among his sons
opened the way to final victory for the Manchus four years later.

The last centre of rebellion to be subdued was Taiwan, the base of Cheng
Ch'eng-kung, or Koxinga as he was known to Westerners. This rebel leader,
the descendant of a pirate, was the staunchest supporter of the deposed Ming
dynasty. Finding a permanent foothold in the Yang-tze valley hard to
maintain, he shipped his forces to Taiwan, an island not previously under

Warriors and horsemen
at the time of K'and-hsi.

Chinese jurisdiction. The Dutch had occupied the coastal areas in 1624 and their garrisons had to be ejected before he could convert the island into a rallying point for Ming loyalists. A constant source of anxiety for the Ch'ing dynasty, whose naval strength was no match for Cheng's squadrons, the independence of Taiwan was only ended in 1683. Then the Manchus, aided by strife among the grandsons of Cheng, invaded and annexed the island with the assistance of Dutch vessels. The foundation of the Ch'ing dynasty was secured.

K'ANG-HSI, THE MODEL RULER (1661–1722)

Though the Council of Princes and High Officials had not agreed with me in 1673 [Emperor Ch'ing K'ang-hsi reflected later on the rebellion of Wu San-kuei] I had pushed ahead. It seemed possible that, if we were thorough enough and showed that we were in earnest about the transfers of the three southern princes, then they would have no choice but to follow through. So I briefed two commissioners and sent them to Yunnan to discuss details of the move with Wu; I sent other commissioners to Shang and Keng; I told the Boards of War and Civil Office to start selecting potential appointees for the new vacancies opening up in the South; and I set the Board of Revenue to estimating the land and building needs for the princes and their retinues in Manchuria. I have said that even then I did not anticipate a war, but it would have been folly not to take certain precautions: I started standardizing each Banner company at around one hundred and thirty men, to make rapid mobilization of our troops simpler; and with a few close advisers I made certain contingency plans on defensive zones and staging areas.

The sense of personal responsibility for the suffering endured by the *nung* caught up in the civil war never left Emperor Ch'ing K'ang-hsi. It remained in his mind as a terrible example of the difficulty of making correct decisions. After endless debates over policy towards the southern holdings, he had decided to retire the three generals to Manchuria and the eight years of conflict that ensued wrought havoc throughout populous Kiangnan.

In the campaigns he was furious at the dilatoriness of Manchu leaders, especially on learning that attacks on rebel concentrations were most often spearheaded by Chinese generals. That Emperor Ch'ing K'ang-hsi remained upon the dragon throne and removed the last rivals to his house depended as much on the support of the *shih* as on the military prowess of the bannermen. Under Dorgon and Emperor Ch'ing Shun-chih a series of measures had been adopted which were aimed at binding the Confucian scholars to the Ch'ing dynasty. All officials of the Ming were encouraged to serve alongside Manchus and throughout North China local notables were asked to recommend suitable candidates for public service. The Imperial University received substantial gifts and several colleges were founded in Peking for the education of Manchus. Not least the conduct of the bannermen was kept under strict observation so that they did not act like conquerors and claim any spoils at the expense of the native population. Yet to Emperor Ch'ing K'ang-hsi must go credit for winning over the majority of the *shih* who had served the fallen dynasty. Apart from purging the palace of four thousand eunuchs and bringing into policy formation the senior scholars of the day, his own studious disposition and love of learning impressed the *shih* enough for them to disregard the fact that he was a foreign emperor. His humane approach to government and his reverence for Confucian tradition were recognized as the attributes of a model ruler. Noted in the entry for the year 1670 in the annals of the Han-lin Academy, the stronghold of the Confucian party, was this remark of Emperor Ch'ing K'ang-hsi to the officials of the Board of Rites: 'To learn the art of government, one must explore the classic learning of the ancients. Whenever we can find a day of leisure from the affairs of state, we spend it in the study of the Classics.'

In 1684 Emperor Ch'ing K'ang-hsi visited the shrine of Confucius at Ch'u-fu, a pilgrimage first undertaken by a Chinese ruler in 72, when Emperor Han Ming-ti offered sacrifices to the Sage of Lu as one 'who had given good laws to the people'. There the young Manchu emperor heard the ritual music and listened to lectures on the classics; he was shown the famous collection of precious objects, including the ritual vessels donated by

Portrait of Emperor Ch'ing Ch'ien-lung by William Alexander, who painted a number of watercolours while accompanying Lord Macartney's mission to China (1793–4).

Emperor Han Chang-ti in the first century and a renowned example of the calligraphy by Emperor Sung Hui-tsung dating from the twelfth century; and he talked at length with K'ung Shang-jen, the sixty-fourth generation descendant of Confucius. Carefully pointed out to him also was the place in a wall where the ninth-generation descendant of the philosopher hid the classics when Emperor Ch'in Shih Huang-ti burned the books. But the *shih* knew that they need have no anxiety about the intentions of Emperor Ch'ing K'ang-hsi.

Lacking a distinct culture of their own, the Manchus were unable to resist the strength of Chinese traditions once their leaders adopted the policy of alliance with the *shih*, the officials, scholars and gentry. Numerically small – the Manchu minority was never larger than two per cent of the total population of the Empire – they were obliged to identify with the official élite and the Confucian orthodoxy which underpinned the authority of the One Man. However, the genuineness of Emperor Ch'ing K'ang-hsi's admiration for Chinese civilization was never in doubt. He was learned and his calligraphy, the hallmark of the scholar, drew praise from even partisan supporters of the Ming in the dissident South. In the nineteenth century the danger for China was to lie in the ultra-conservative tendency within such respect for tradition. Then, an alien ruling class clung adamantly to the customs of the past when the only hope of survival for the country as a sovereign state was in adaptation to the conditions of the modern world. Under the later Ch'ing, Chinese culture ossified.

Thoroughly Confucian though Emperor Ch'ing K'ang-hsi was, his mind remained open to new ideas from the Jesuits at court and his attitude towards matters of administration was refreshingly practical. His provincial governors were expected to be efficient not ceremonial, as this comment indicates:

> On appointing Ch'en in 1711, I told him: 'When you get to Kwangsi you must ensure harmony between civil and military, and keep troops and commoners at peace. The governor is responsible for the troops, and must drill them constantly. You've been to the Han-lin Academy for many years, so I am going to make a special experiment of appointing you to a senior post, and see how you are able to manage things.' At first his memorials were too long and in the wrong format, and he passed on a report that a magical *chih* fungus had been found on a mountain top under a fragrant cloud, sure proof of the Emperor's virtue and promise of long life to come; and even though he knew I did not value such auspicious omens, he was duty-bound to send it in to the palace, so I could examine it or use it for medicine. I replied that the *Histories* are full of these strange omens, but they are no help in governing the country, and that the best omens were good harvests and contented people. Later his memorials were shorter, there was no more *chih* fungus, and he became a sensible governor.

ABOVE The blue robe. The summer garment of Emperor Ch'ing Ch'ien-lung.

Dragon dance and fire-crackers at the New Year Festival. Design on a dish made during the reign of Emperor Ch'ing Ch'ien-lung (1735–95).

Such practicality was of inestimable value to the Ch'ing dynasty in dealing with restive Kiangnan. Between the provinces of the North and the South there was a marked difference of attitude amongst the Chinese towards the Manchu invasion. The entrance afforded by the gates at Shanhaikuan meant that the experience of the population in the North was a more or less peaceful takeover of power, whilst the rebellion of Wu San-kuei turned the

South into a battlefield. The benefits of the new regime too were felt in the northern provinces because the Manchus preferred to retain Peking as the capital for the reason that it was near their homeland.

> When one is beyond the Great Wall [Emperor Ch'ing K'ang-hsi remarked], the air and soil refresh the spirit; one leaves the beaten road and strikes out into untamed country; the mountains are densely packed with woods, 'green and thick as standing corn'. As one moves further north the views open up, one's eyes travel hundreds of miles; instead of feeling hemmed in, there is a sense of freedom. It may be the height of summer, but there is dew on the trees, and some of the leaves are turning yellow already, as if it were late autumn; you have to wear a fur jacket in the mornings, even though in Peking it is so hot that you hesitate about having the eunuchs lead the consorts out of the palace to greet you on your return.

It seemed to many living in Kiangnan that their wealth was being drained for the sake of a foreign house, despite the rapid cultural assimilation of Manchus through the acquiescence of the North. There is, indeed, truth in the view that sees the establishment of the Republic in 1912 as the culmination of southern agitation against the Ch'ing. Nevertheless, the sagacity of Emperor Ch'ing K'ang-hsi did ensure that the government of Kiangnan contributed to its rising prosperity. He avoided oppression, the symptom of fear and mistrust exhibited by later emperors.

Instead, his scholarly instincts and knowledge of the classics led him to espouse the rational thought of Neo-Confucianism. In 1712, by the emperor's order, the Sung philosopher Chu Hsi was elevated to the rank of 'most distinguished follower' and took his place alongside the Sage of Lu's other great disciples in Confucian temples. The commentaries of Emperor Ch'ing K'ang-hsi on the Confucian canon, as conceived by Neo-Confucianism, became standard works which all students, who wished to become candidates in the civil service examinations, had to master. His concern for ethics is evident in the sixteen maxims of the *Sacred Edict*, which was issued in 1669. Exalted were the twin virtues of filial piety and brotherly love as the basis of harmonious relations in society. Teachers and students were ordered to assemble twice a month to recite aloud the edict, a copy of which had to be on display in every classroom.

The attitude of Emperor Ch'ing K'ang-hsi to theological differences among the Christian missionaries illustrates his maxim on the importance of traditional belief. Jesuit tolerance of non-Christian practices, when of a moral purpose like ancestor worship, had been denounced by other religious orders and in 1705 Maillard de Tournon, a papal legate, arrived to settle the controversy. Though the legate was supposed to arbitrate impartially, he was already in possession of a secret document that ruled against any accommodation of Confucian rites and his stay of five years in China comprised a bitter struggle against the Jesuits resident at Peking. Emperor Ch'ing K'ang-hsi received Tournon with kindness, gifts were exchanged and imperial anxiety expressed for the poor health of the legate, but the Jesuits retained their favoured position at court. Having commissioned the *K'ang-hsi Tzu Tien*, the standard dictionary of the Chinese language, the emperor found it difficult to accept that he was in error over the usage of certain words. Yet it

Ch'ing jade ear-ring, dating from the seventeenth century.

Scene of life at the Ch'ing
court. Anonymous
seventeenth-century
painting.

P. MATTHÆVS RICCIVS MACERAT. of the Society of Iesus, the first propagator of the Christian Religion in the Kingdo of China.

LY PAVLVS GREAT the Chinese propagator of y

LEFT Father Matteo Ricci with a prominent Chinese convert. From Athanasius Kircher's *China monumentis qua sacris qua profanis, illustrata*, published in Amsterdam in 1667.

In 1629 an imperial decree gave to Hsu Kuang-ch'i, a Christian official, and Adam Schall von Bell (BELOW), his Jesuit teacher, the task of reforming the calendar.

was insisted that *T'ien Chu*, not *T'ien* or *Shang Ti*, was the correct term for God. Moreover, the legate's injunction against participation in Confucian ceremonies by Chinese Christians was an open act of defiance to the will of the throne, which accepted the interpretations of Matteo Ricci. Neither was Emperor Ch'ing K'ang-hsi prepared to countenance the claim of the Pope to international authority nor was he willing to import religious dogmatism into the Empire. He commented thus:

> Every country must have some spirits that it reveres. This is true of our dynasty, as for Mongols and Mohammedans, Miao or Lolo, or other foreigners. Just as everyone fears something, some snakes but not toads, some toads but not snakes; and as all countries have different pronunciations

and different alphabets. But in this Catholic faith, the Society of Peter quarrels with the Jesuits, Bouvet quarrels with Mariani, and among the Jesuits the Portuguese want only their own nationals in their church while the French want only French in theirs. This violates the principles of religion. Such dissension cannot be inspired by the Lord of Heaven but by the Devil, who, I have heard Westerners say, leads men to do evil since he can't do otherwise.

Therefore, edicts were issued to regulate the activities of the missionaries and discourage would-be converts. 'Hereafter', Emperor Ch'ing K'ang-hsi told Tournon, 'we will permit residence in China to all those who come from the West and will not return there.' The number of Catholics in the Empire gradually declined: by 1798, the year of Lord Macartney's embassy, there were only five thousand living in Peking and about one hundred and fifty thousand altogether. On his death in 1722, after sixty years on the dragon throne, Emperor Ch'ing K'ang-hsi bequeathed to his successors a tolerant court and a humane administration, the two requisites for dynastic continuity.

IMPERIAL CLIMAX   After the fall of the last Ming stronghold on Taiwan in 1683, Emperor Ch'ing K'ang-hsi was free to turn his attention to external security, particularly along the troublesome northern frontier. Since earliest times the threat of mounted raiders from the north had a permanent place in the anxieties of the Chinese mind and the maintenance of the Great Wall was a gigantic attempt to divide the two mutually antagonistic environments of the steppe and the sown. During militarily powerful Chinese dynasties such as the Han and the T'ang, the authority of the Son of Heaven had reached out westwards into Central Asia and the early Ming rulers had also adopted a forward policy against the Mongols. Yet the Great Wall remained the basic northern frontier, beyond whose defences the nomadic peoples were encouraged to bicker and fight amongst themselves. To the Manchus this lack of direct control of the northern grasslands seemed a dangerous weakness, not least because of the ease with which they had penetrated the northern defences at a time of civil strife. In consequence, pacification of the steppe became a fundamental of Ch'ing foreign policy.

Before their entry to China in 1644, the Manchus had succeeded in subjugating Korea and Inner Mongolia. An advance into Outer Mongolia was therefore a strategic possibility and in 1697 Emperor Ch'ing K'ang-hsi personally led an expedition which ended with a decisive victory near Urga. All of Mongolia was now a vassal, and the Ch'ing armies drove north-westwards against the Dzungars, a Mongolian tribe whose influence covered Chinese Turkestan, the valley of the Ili River, and the Altai Mountains. The expeditionary force met with little success and again in 1732 the Dzungars drove off the invaders. Not until the reign of Ch'ing Ch'ien-lung did the kingdom of Dzungaria fall to the imperial forces after a fierce campaign lasting three years (1755–7). Manchu expansion on the steppe proved of lasting strategic benefit to China because it ended the ancient menace of nomad raiders, despite the new conflicts of the nineteenth and twentieth centuries with the Russians who were simultaneously occupying other parts of Central Asia and Siberia.

The Founding of the Ch'ing Dynasty

Another outcome of rivalry with the Dzungars was the conquest of Tibet. Lamaism, the Tibetan form of Buddhism, had been made the official religion of the Yuan dynasty sometime before the end of the thirteenth century, yet the expulsion of the Mongols from China did not in any measure reduce its influence on the Mongolian tribes. When advantage of a schism in the Lamaist church was taken by the Dzungars to invade Tibet in 1717, Emperor Ch'ing K'ang-hsi dispatched two armies against them. By 1720 he had driven out the Dzungar forces and installed the Dalai Lama as the spiritual and temporal head of state at Lhasa, where a Ch'ing garrison was permanently stationed. Further interventions in 1728 and 1750 led to the strengthening of the occupation force, the acceptance of Ch'ing direction of Tibetan affairs through resident officials who advised the Dalai Lama, and the annexation of the area adjoining Szechuan. The greatest extension of Manchu authority in the Himalayas occurred in 1792 when a defeat was inflicted on the Ghurkas, their sole reverse on the battlefield, and Nepal acknowledged the suzerainty of the Son of Heaven.

To stabilize the southern frontier, the Ch'ing dynasty adopted two lines of approach. First, the system of indirect rule for minorities living within the Empire was abolished. Indigenous peoples such as the Miao, who inhabited the less accessible parts of Yunnan, Kweichou and Kwangsi, had a separate administration under their own hereditary chieftains. Disputes between Miao and Chinese settlers were not easy to resolve because of this duality, nor was it a simple matter to curb the behaviour of an intractable chieftain, especially when his people were likely to revolt. The change in administration whereby all inhabitants came under the direct jurisdiction of the provincial government was introduced between 1726 and 1731. Secondly, external relations were put on to the footing of tributaries of the One Man. Vietnam – Annam to the Ch'ing – accepted this status, though in 1789 Emperor Ch'ing Ch'ien-lung

People at work. A lady with bound feet (LEFT) is making socks; a *kung* (BELOW) busily cuts and shapes; and a *shih* (OPPOSITE) copies a painting. Notice the pigtails worn by the men, the required way of dressing the head for Chinese under the Ch'ing dynasty.

sought to increase his authority by sending in troops to quell the popular Tay Son rebellion. As all recognized authorities had collapsed before this movement there was an opportunity for intervention; the Manchus entered the country, only to sustain a serious reverse. Henceforth, the Ch'ing were content to exercise indirect control. At the same time the kingdom of Burma acknowledged itself as a vassal, whilst in Siam the power of the Ch'ing Empire received a tacit recognition that saved the bother of a demonstration of arms.

China in the eighteenth century was a great imperial power. The Ch'ing dynasty ruled over a vast land empire, the greatest area ever to have acknowledged the authority of the Son of Heaven. Along the land borders there was no challenge to its armies and from the sea the only annoyance came from missionaries, traders and pirates – objects unworthy of imperial notice. Neglect of naval forces, a policy inherited from the later Ming, continued, the idea being 'coastal defence, but no battles at sea'. European trade was restricted to the port of Canton from 1757, a restriction intended to minimize contact between the Empire and non-tributary nations. Always uneasy about the loyalty of Kiangnan and suspicious of European aims, the Ch'ing court preferred to regard the coastline as a second Great Wall, making it a punishable offence for a Chinese to voyage overseas or build seagoing vessels. The dreadful consequences for China of such an exclusion policy were all too clear in the nineteenth century, when European navies had complete command of the coastal waters.

But no seaborne threat existed on the accession of Emperor Ch'ing Yung-cheng in 1722–3. Having reigned for sixty years and having no fewer than thirty-five sons, Emperor Ch'ing K'ang-hsi was vexed over the choice of a successor. When Prince Yung-jeng, the heir apparent, had to be put aside through the onset of a mental illness, the rumours and intrigues in the palace almost threatened the dynasty itself. It is likely that only on his death bed did Emperor Ch'ing K'ang-hsi designate his fourth son. Possibly the fraternal strife in the final years of his father's reign left its mark on him, for Emperor Ch'ing Yung-cheng was severe and strict, not hesitating to execute those members of his family whom he suspected of treason. Conscious of the succession issue he decided that his own choice would not be known while he was living. Concealed in two envelopes the name of Ch'ien-lung, also his fourth son, remained a secret till 1735, when the Emperor died.

The administration of the Empire was ably conducted under Emperor Ch'ing Yung-cheng, who took a close interest in finance and supervised the selection of officials for senior appointments. He laid emphasis on moral example and moral persuasion, fundamentals of Confucian orthodoxy which he expounded in his commentary on the *Sacred Edict* of his father. Yet his laudable desire for sound government and his own close involvement with the daily matters of state encouraged the process of concentrating power on the occupant of the dragon throne, an incipient despotism that can be traced back to Emperor Ming Hung-wu's attitude towards the *shih*. By the establishment of an inner cabinet, or privy council of ministers and princes, Emperor Ch'ing Yung-cheng put the officials of the civil service at one remove from policy formation and decision-making. The benefits to the provinces of such imperial concern far outweighed any resentment harboured by the less influential scholar-bureaucrats, for Emperor Ch'ing Yung-cheng's suspicious disposition rarely got the better of his conscience, but in the long term the diminution of bureaucratic responsibility was to weaken seriously the apparatus of government, not least when a faction of the imperial family dominated the Purple Forbidden City. In parallel with this concentration of power went a stiffening of the philosophical arteries of Confucianism. Emperor Ch'ing K'ang-hsi's fascination with European mathematics almost seemed a lapse in a court that prized adherence to the traditions celebrated in classical texts, now the sole basis of examinations for entry to the civil service. An ultra-conservative outlook began to typify the scholar-bureaucrat, Chinese and Manchu alike. Trained to conform strictly to a narrowed view of the world,

A mandarin's lady and her attendant, painted by William Alexander.

these officials accepted the existence of a rigorous censorship, even though the reduction in the number of places available to Chinese candidates for office led to a growing disenchantment among the *shih* of Kiangnan. It seemed to many educated southerners that the North lived off the wealth and toil of the South, whilst the bannermen, the politico–military system retained by the Ch'ing emperors as an internal security force and the core element of the imperial armies, lost their justification once the conquests of Emperor Ch'ing Ch'ien-lung had rid China of its enemies on land.

The long reign of Emperor Ch'ing Ch'ien-lung (1735–95) was the most glorious period of Manchu power: it was the climax of the late Empire. The authority of the Son of Heaven was recognized by countries and peoples never previously within the Chinese sphere of influence, and the order and prosperity of late eighteenth-century China became a legend in the West. There was peace until the 1790s when the 'White Lotus' secret society fermented widespread disorder in the Huai River valley. The origins of this sect – which believed that the coming of the future Buddha Maitreya was at hand and that a descendant of the Ming dynasty was about to drive out the Manchus – can be found in the twelfth century, but significantly its fame had been established in the popular movements of the 1340s against the Mongols. The rebellion of the 'White Lotus' was a harbinger of the disorders of the nineteenth century as well as an indicator of impending dynastic decline.

Emperor Ch'ing Ch'ien-lung, the only occupant of the dragon throne whose name has become widely known in the West, was an enthusiastic patron of the arts and he gave a status to painters which they had not enjoyed since the reign of Emperor Sung Hui-tsung (1101–26). The enlargement of the imperial collection of art treasures was one of his chief concerns. Old masters or copies of paintings from earlier dynasties were sought throughout the Empire, an antiquarian zeal that exactly matched the complacency of Emperor Ch'ing Ch'ien-lung in his relations with European nations at the end of his reign. The conservative taste of the Ch'ing court was also reflected in architecture. The rebuilding of the Purple Forbidden City, largely carried out on the orders of Emperor Ch'ing Ch'ien-lung, closely followed the style of the Ming and was imitation on the grand scale: there was no fresh development in style. Such uncritical admiration for Chinese tradition continued as the main feature of the Ch'ing dynasty throughout the troubles of the nineteenth century, when reform of the social and economic order was a desperate need. Though the Manchu tongue was an official language and all documents were issued in both Manchu and Chinese, Manchu remained mostly a formality, and long before 1912 it had changed into a 'dead language' which the Manchus themselves were forced to study in schools.

Typical of this process of cultural absorption was Emperor Ch'ing Ch'ien-lung himself. A prolific writer of Chinese verse, a connoisseur of painting and calligraphy, he was seen as the 'scholar emperor', an ideal of the enlightened despot, by the *philosophes* of the Enlightenment, those observers from the safe distance of another continent. Yet China was blessed with peace and prosperity under Emperor Ch'ing Ch'ien-lung. The population of the Empire had doubled to reach the incredible figure of three hundred millions, compared with well under two hundred millions for the whole of Europe and

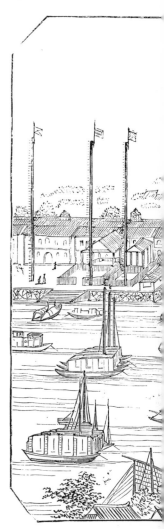

Canton. A nineteenth-century engraving of the waterfront, showing a few of the foreign warehouses on the left as well as the city walls. This area suffered considerably in the various naval bombardments of the Opium Wars.

Russia; whilst the flow of revenue to the imperial coffers was so great that on several occasions it was considered unnecessary to levy taxes. The pomp and circumstance of the Ch'ing dynasty impressed the outside world, though Lord Macartney discerned beneath the splendid surface the first signs of decay. It was not insignificant that the minister with whom the British Ambassador had most contact during his negotiations, Ho-shen, the favourite courtier of Ch'ing Ch'ien-lung, should be impeached for corruption and the abuse of office after the emperor's death. Reminiscent of the cupidity of the eunuchs under the later Ming emperors was this Manchu official's colossal greed, for it was revealed in 1799 that he had used his ascendancy to amass a fortune equivalent to ten years' revenue of the Empire.

THE EMBASSY OF LORD MACARTNEY (1793-4) In 1757 Emperor Ch'ing Ch'ien-lung decreed that all foreign trade must be transacted at Canton. It was part of Manchu policy towards Kiangnan and the 'Ocean Devils' that international commerce should be kept in semi-official

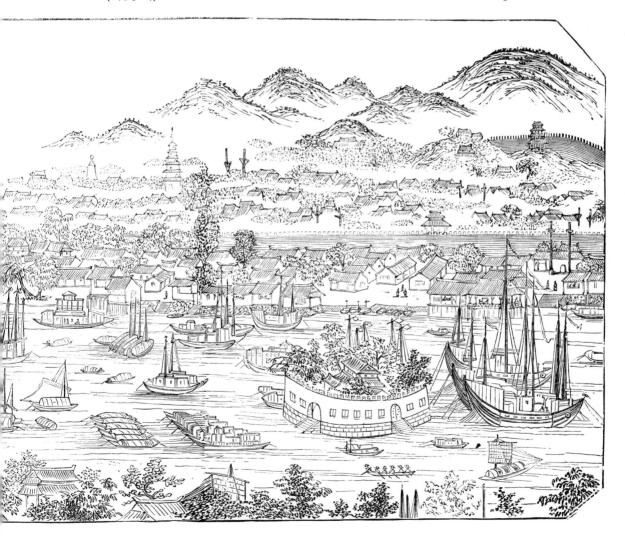

limbo at a port remote from the capital. At such a vast distance, trade was out of sight and out of mind, but problems of regulation could not solve themselves. The Hoppo, a Manchu official appointed for a term of three years by the court, was in charge of foreign trade and it was accepted practice for him to extort the maximum financial benefits from barbarian merchants, since he had to buy his office and maintain it by giving 'presents' to the powerful. Corruption and extortion were thus added to the taxes taken by the Imperial Treasury.

The 'squeeze' on trading vessels putting into Canton was not the only problem. The rapacity of the Hoppo and the difficulties faced by the *shang* in arranging the long overland haul of goods from the Yang-tze River valley, the main centre of production, were serious hindrances, but a more profound financial crisis enveloped the China trade at the end of the eighteenth century. The East India Company, the largest trader in Canton, found itself unable to obtain enough silver to pay for the tea and silk it needed. Because the Ch'ing court regarded the economic self-sufficiency of the Empire as a prime virtue and the British were not possessed of products desired by the Chinese in any great quantities, the balance of trade was heavily in favour of China. As the export of tea continued to expand yet the import of English manufacturers remained constant, pressures built up for a freer approach to Chinese markets. Manchu exclusiveness – foreign merchants resident in the small factory area at Canton were forbidden to learn the Chinese language – was blamed for the situation and in 1792 the British government sent Lord Macartney to China in order to establish diplomatic relations and negotiate a trade treaty. The East India Company was less concerned with diplomatic relations than with an easing of restrictions in

The Emperor Ch'ing Ch'ien-lung being carried in procession to the imperial audience tent at Jehol on 14 September 1793, when Lord Macartney was first presented. Painting by William Alexander.

Emperor Ch'ing Ch'ien-lung receiving homage from allied tribesmen at Jehol.

trade, especially in North China where British woollens might be sold. Though the company hoped that Lord Macartney would create a favourable impression of the British character at the Ch'ing court, it urged him to be cautious and not press for things likely to upset the existing position in Canton.

After a voyage of ten months aboard HMS *Lion*, a warship of sixty-four guns, and the *Hindostan*, an East Indiaman of 1,200 tonnes, the embassy found itself off Macao in June 1793. There it was learned, Lord Macartney records in his *Journal*, 'that the news of an Embassy from England had been received at Court with great satisfaction, that the Emperor considered it no small addition to the glory of his reign that its close should be distinguished by such an event, and that orders had been dispatched to all the seaports of China to give the most hospitable and honourable reception to His Majesty's ships whenever they should appear on the coasts.' Five weeks later HMS *Lion* and the *Hindostan* dropped anchor outside the bar on the estuary of the Pei River where the gifts brought for the emperor and the luggage of the suite were transferred to smaller craft, so that the embassy might proceed inland by water. The senior officials who met Lord Macartney made the arrangements for the rest of his journey to Jehol, the summer residence of the court. North of the city of Tientsin, whose 'crowds of people . . . on shore and in the boats on the river were quite astonishing', the embassy quit the river and reached Peking by road.

In the *Journal* are already noted the beginnings of the differences between the imperial officials and the British embassy which later undermined his purpose. Lord Macartney wrote:

We have indeed been very narrowly watched, and all our customs, habits and proceedings, even of the most trivial nature, observed with an inquisitiveness and jealousy which surpassed all that we had read of in the history of China. But we endeavoured always to put the best face upon everything, and to preserve a perfect serenity of countenance upon all occasions. I therefore shut my eyes upon the flags of our yachts, which were inscribed 'The English Ambassador bringing tribute to the Emperor of China', and have made no complaint of it, reserving myself to notice it if a proper opportunity occurs.

This difference in attitude towards the relationship of the Empire and Britain was no less apparent in the question of court ceremonies, which had been tactfully broached by the Chinese officials. On being informed that respect was paid to the emperor by kneeling upon both knees and making nine inclinations of the head to the ground – the *kowtow* – Lord Macartney said in England it was somewhat different, and that though he desired to behave in the most agreeable manner, his first duty was to do what would be agreeable to his own sovereign. In the event Emperor Ch'ing Ch'ien-lung accepted the English ceremony, and the British ambassador bent a knee but was not permitted to kiss the emperor's hand at his presentation on 14 September. Reflecting on this gracious reception, he felt 'the commanding feature of the ceremony was that calm dignity, that sober pomp of Asiatic greatness, which European refinements have not yet attained'.

Hearing of the curiosity of the embassy about China, Emperor Ch'ing Ch'ien-lung ordered that Lord Macartney be conducted around the great park of the Summer Residence at Jehol. A 'charming place', we read in the *Journal*, that would have provided 'Capability' Brown with his 'happiest ideas'. One feature above all struck the ambassador: it was 'the happy choice of situation for ornamental buildings. From attention to this circumstance they have not the air of being crowded or disproportioned; they never intrude upon the eye but wherever they appear always show themselves to advantage, and aid, improve and enliven the prospect'. Although the Grand Secretary Ho-shen and other chief officials were in attendance and every courtesy was paid, Lord Macartney remained aware that 'the same jealousy prevails towards us which the Chinese Government has always shown to other foreigners, although we have taken such pains to disarm it, and to conciliate their friendship and confidence'. There was a reluctance on the part of the court to discuss the purpose of the embassy. Both the emperor and his ministers were polite to the British suite and solicitous for the health of Lord Macartney, who suffered a great deal from rheumatism, yet there was no meeting of minds. Ho-shen, the effective chief minister, could not understand the desire of the British for an exchange of permanent envoys: these were customs of Europe, not the kind of ceremonies acceptable to the Son of Heaven. Nor were the British requests for trading facilities at Ning-po, Chusan, an island nearby, and Tientsin, for the use of a small, unfortified island in the neighbourhood of Chusan as an *entrepôt* and place of residence for merchants, and for the ending of surcharges and local taxation on commerce at Canton likely to receive a welcome in a court that preferred to ignore the increasing activities of the Western nations in East Asia.

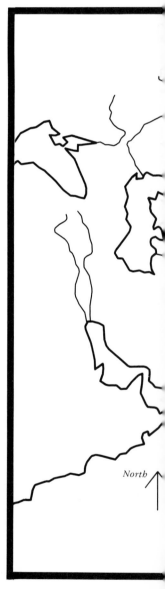

North

92

Once it became obvious to Lord Macartney that he would not be allowed to reside in China as the British ambassador, he determined to return home with the edict written by Emperor Ch'ing Ch'ien-lung to King George III. The tenor of this communication left him in no doubt concerning the failure of the mission. Not only was the residence of an ambassador stated as inconsistent with 'the Celestial Empire's ceremonial system' but, even more, the need for developing trade between the two countries was rejected outright. The continuation of the seclusion policy was unmistakable, notwithstanding the ceremonial language. The edict said:

> The Celestial Empire, ruling all within the four seas, simply concentrates on carrying out the affairs of Government properly, and does not value rare and

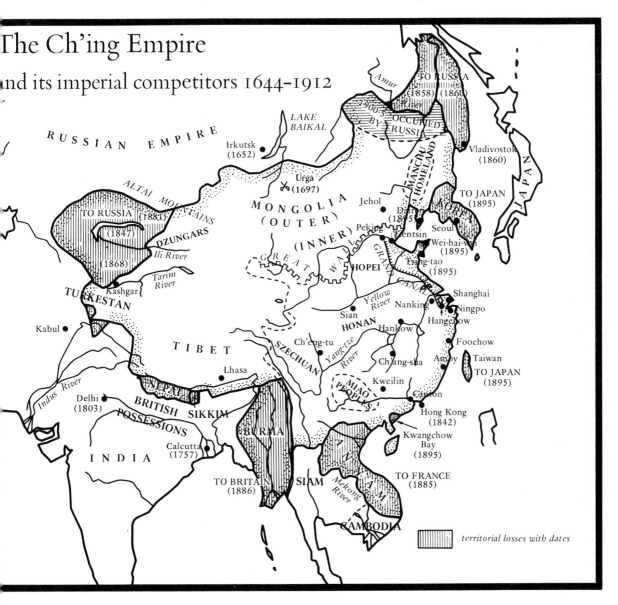

The Ch'ing Empire and its imperial competitors 1644–1912

territorial losses with dates

precious things. Now you, O King, have presented various objects to the throne, and mindful of your loyalty in presenting offerings from afar, we have specially received them. In fact, the virtue and power of the Celestial Dynasty has penetrated afar to the myriad kingdoms, which have come to render homage, and so all kinds of precious things from 'over mountain and sea' have been collected here, things which your chief envoy and others have seen for themselves. Nevertheless we have never valued ingenious articles, nor do we have the slightest need of your country's manufactures.

A classical exposition of the relationship between China and the West, as viewed by the ultra-conservative Ch'ing court, this edict served notice that diplomatic relations with China on the European pattern were impossible. The export of tea, silks and porcelain were merely a sign of the benevolence of the One Man, who was prepared to furnish the outer barbarians with commodities which made their lives bearable: at no time should the commercial transactions in Canton be construed as an encouragement to international trade. It was a concession, nothing more.

On the first stage of his homeward voyage, the journey down the Grand Canal and along other waterways to Canton, Lord Macartney had time to reflect on his baffling reverse.

How are we to reconcile the contradictions that appear in the conduct of the Chinese Government towards us? They receive us with the highest distinction, show us every external mark of favour and regard, send their first Minister to attend us as cicerone for two days together through their palaces and gardens; entertain us with their choicest amusements, and express themselves greatly pleased with so splendid an embassy, commend our conduct and cajole us with compliments. Yet, in less than a couple of months, they plainly discover that they wish us to be gone, refuse our requests without reserve or complaisance, precipitate our departure, and dismiss us dissatisfied; yet, no sooner have we taken leave of them than we find ourselves treated with more studied attentions, more marked distinction, and less constraint than before. I must endeavour to unravel this mystery if I can.

A satisfactory answer he was unable to find, though the *Journal* records the views of two close observers. First, Father Amiot, a Jesuit long resident in Peking, thought that the embassy 'would have met with fewer difficulties at its outset if it had arrived before the Government had been alarmed by the news of great troubles in Europe, the inhabitants of which are indiscriminately considered by them as of a turbulent character'. Despite the unsettling tidings of the French Revolution, the priest was convinced that the favourable impression made by Lord Macartney could be strengthened by an exchange of letters between monarchs. As yet the Chinese considered embassies as 'mere temporary ceremonies, sent on a particular occasion only' and had 'no favourable ideas of treaties with distant powers, but they might be rendered sensible of them if applied to and solicited without precipitation, and managed with caution and adroitness, for nothing was to be expected as attainable on the sudden'. Another point of view was expressed by Sung-yin, a Mongol Grand Councillor, who told Lord Macartney to lay aside the uneasiness he seemed to feel about the edict because it was not meant 'to convey anything unfavourable or unpleasant'. He simply reminded him 'that the laws and usages of China were invariable, and that the Emperor was so strictly observant of them that no consideration could ever induce him to infringe them'.

The final entries in the *Journal*, written as the British ambassador awaited ship in Canton, dismiss the notion of dominion in China as an extravagance of Lord Clive, the conqueror of India. The development of commerce in China would not be aided by its dissolution, nor could any immediate advantage be gained by drawing in other European imperial rivals. Yet, if such a situation should occur, Lord Macartney was certain that Britain, as 'the first political, marine and commercial power on the globe', would 'prove the greatest gainer . . . and rise superior over every competitor'. Wrong in anticipating dismemberment in his own lifetime – the first serious clash, the First Opium War, only occurred in 1839–42 – his description of the Empire, on the other hand, was prophetic in that the modern reconstruction of China could not commence until a new basis for society was established. Lord Macartney concluded:

> The Empire of China is an old, crazy, first-rate man-of-war, which a fortunate succession of able and vigilant officers has contrived to keep afloat for these one hundred and fifty years past, and to overawe their neighbours merely by her bulk and appearance, but whenever an insufficient man happens to have the command upon deck, adieu to discipline and the safety of the ship. She may perhaps not sink outright; she may drift some time as a wreck, and will then be dashed to pieces on the shore; but she can never be rebuilt on the old bottom.

4

The Celestial Empire

One April evening in 1778, the conversation of a leading literary figure in London turned to foreign travel. Boswell records that Dr Johnson, who professed an inordinate partiality for tea, also

> talked with an uncommon animation of travelling into distant countries; that the mind was enlarged by it, and that an acquisition of dignity of character was derived from it. He expressed a particular enthusiasm with respect to visiting the Wall of China. I catched it for the moment, and said I really believed I should go and see the Wall of China had I not children, of whom it was my duty to take care. 'Sir,' he said, 'by so doing, you would do what would be of importance in raising your children to eminence. There would be a lustre reflected upon them from your spirit and curiosity. They would be at all times regarded as the children of a man who had gone to view the Wall of China. I am serious, Sir.'

Though Boswell never saw the masonry of the Great Wall, his mentor's excitement over this formidable line of defence was part of the general admiration of China in Europe during the eighteenth century. In the Celestial Empire the *philosophes* of the Enlightenment considered that they had discovered a model form of government because of the lack of hereditary privilege and a powerful clergy, unlike Europe of their own day.

It was from Jesuit descriptions of China that influential thinkers and writers, such as Leibniz and Voltaire, obtained a tantalizing glimpse of an alternative tradition to the West. One early source was the diary kept by Matteo Ricci, who succeeded in converting several eminent members of the Ming court once he exchanged the clothes of a Buddhist monk for those of a scholar in 1594. Attempting to gain entry into the highest levels of Chinese society so as to secure official acceptance of the Jesuit mission, Ricci was prepared to tolerate local religious practices like ancestor worship and to identify himself with the *shih* when he realized that in China priests did not enjoy the degree of respect bestowed on them in Europe. He wrote that a

> remarkable fact and quite worthy of note as marking a difference from the West, is that the entire kingdom is administered by the Order of the Learned, commonly known as the Philosophers. The responsibility for orderly management of the entire realm is wholly and completely committed to their charge and care. The army, both officers and soldiers, hold them in high respect and show them the promptest obedience and deference, and not infrequently the military are disciplined by them as a schoolboy might be punished by his master. Policies of war are formulated and

An anonymous Ch'ing painting of characters from *The Dream of the Red Chamber*, a Yuan novel.

Pl. 54.

The Elevation of a Temple partly in the Chinese Taste.

10 9 8 7 6 5 4 3 2 1   10 fe.

An illustration from W. and J. Halfpenny's *New Designs for Chinese Temples*, published in 1752.

military questions decided by the Philosophers only, and their advice and counsel has more weight with the King than that of the military leaders. In fact very few of these, and only on rare occasions, are admitted to war consultations. Hence it follows that those who aspire to be cultured frown upon war and would prefer the lowest rank in the philosophical order to the highest in the military, realizing that the Philosophers far excel military leaders in the good will and respect of the people and in opportunities of acquiring wealth.

A View of the Wilderness, with the Alhambra, the Pagoda & the Mosque, in the Royal Gardens at KEW

The pagoda in the Royal Gardens at Kew. An eighteenth-century engraving.

Although the custom of castrating young boys for service in the imperial palace was deplored by Ricci, along with the great influence of the eunuchs in the affairs of state, the general impression of his narrative is of a brilliant civilization in which education and administrative order coincided. Of Confucius he proclaimed that 'his self-mastery and abstemious ways of life led his countrymen to assert that he surpassed in holiness all those who in times past, in the various parts of the world, were considered to have excelled in virtue. Indeed, if we critically examine his actions and sayings as they are recorded in history, we shall be forced to admit that he was the equal of pagan philosophers and superior to most of them.'

The impact of China on the European *philosophes* was profound, though the Chinese 'Philosophers' were not so powerful as the Jesuits believed or claimed. Gottfried Wilhelm Leibniz (1646–1716) was in constant touch with the mission and he edited and published in 1697 a collection of material on China entitled *Novissima Sinica, Historiam Nostri Temporis*. Three years later he was reading a Jesuit commentary on the *I Ching*. Aware that the Chinese were lacking in the art of scientific demonstration – 'they have remained content with a sort of empirical geometry' – he was nevertheless adamant in his defence of their conception of the natural order of the world against those who attacked the Jesuit appreciation of Neo-Confucianism cosmology. In his *Letter on Chinese Philosophy*, written in 1715, he pointed out the underlying harmony and unity of this idea: 'space, not as a substance with parts, but as the order of things'. For, Leibniz realized, 'the Chinese, far from being blameworthy in the matter, merit praise for believing that things come into existence because of natural predispositions, and by a pre-established order. Chance has

A literary gathering in a garden. The 'ink boy' is making sure that the scholar about to compose verse will not have to pause once he dips his brush. A late seventeenth-century silk hand scroll of uncertain authorship.

nothing to do with it, and to speak of chance seems to be introducing something which is not in the Chinese texts.' The *li*, the pre-established harmony of Neo-Confucian philosophy, may have provided crucial confirmation of Leibniz's organic theory. Seeking an explanation of the world that was realist but not mechanical, he rejected the current Western view of the universe as a vast machine and proposed the alternative concept of it as a living organism, every part of which was an organism, or 'monad'. These 'monads' fitted into a pre-established harmony, whose arrangement and workings could be partly fathomed by mathematics.

The rational emphasis in Neo-Confucian philosophy had particular appeal to the Enlightenment. Most of its leaders were deists: their belief in 'natural religion' was strengthened by the discovery of a system of morality that did without supernatural sanction. The Chinese, wrote Voltaire (1694–1778), 'have perfected moral science, and that is the first of the sciences'. In his *Essai sur les moeurs* he portrayed China as the land of tolerance, a utopian state in comparison with which the shortcomings and prejudices of eighteenth-century Europe were legion. Emperor Ch'ing Ch'ien-lung has become the supreme example of the philosopher–king. Strangely, the ceremony of the spring ploughing, the *keng chi*, when the emperor with his own hands turned the first furrow for the spring cultivation, fascinated the *philosophes*, to whom it appeared a perfect token of the solicitude of the ruler for his people; a benevolent paternalism. In 1756, Louis xv, at the suggestion of the encyclopaedist Quesnay made through La Pompadour, followed the example of the Chinese emperors. This annual rite of Confucian orthodoxy was described in Du Halde's *Description de la Chine*, which was published in 1735 and immediately acclaimed for its detail of Chinese customs. An earlier work of Sinophile literature which was appreciated in England, Kircher's *China Illustrata*, may have found its way into the library of Pepys. He recorded in his diary on 14 January, 1667, 'to my bookseller Martin and there did receive my book I expected of China, a most excellent book with rare cuts.' At the beginning of the upsurge of interest in things Chinese this volume is noteworthy as being the first major work by a Jesuit scholar who had never set foot in China.

A less intellectual import was the habit of tea-drinking. Pepys mentions in his diary on 25 September, 1666: 'I did send for a cup of tee, a China drink of which I never had drunk before.' The fashion for tea was quickly established and within a century the tea trade became a considerable factor in the world's economy. In the early 1770s the annual shipments from Canton ran to ten million kilograms. Cargoes of porcelain, silks and lacquered objects were not in lesser demand, though the vogue brought into existence centres of manufacture in the West itself. The development of the rococo style, swift and eclectic though it was, bears witness to the influence of the Celestial Empire on the taste of eighteenth-century Europe.

> Of late, 'tis true, quite sick of Rome and Greece
> We fetch our models from the wise Chinese;
> European artists are too cool and chaste
> For Mand'rin is the only man of taste.
> James Cawthorn: *Of Taste* (1756)

A Manchu general, from an early nineteenth-century engraving.

Artists and designers were encouraged by the beauty and delicacy of its products to visualize the landscape and architecture of China as a kind of fairyland. Pavilions started to pimple the European garden, just as Greek temples were to do from the 1760s. In painting there was nothing like rococo furniture – Chippendale designed a lacquered bedstead for a room with Chinese wallpapers, mirrors and chairs at Badminton, the seat of the Duke of Beaufort – but it has been suggested that in the landscapes of Jean Antoine Watteau (1648–1721) can be found echoes of Sung masters. Whilst by 1761 Oliver Goldsmith could jibe at the contemporary enthusiasm for *chinoiserie* in *The Citizen of the World,* mocking rooms where 'sprawling dragons, squatting pagodas, and clumsy mandarines were stuck upon every shelf', yet he has one of his characters say that the history of the Celestial Empire shows a civilization 'established by laws which Nature and reason seem to have dictated'.

'A PEOPLE OF ETERNAL STANDSTILL'

The eighteenth-century admiration of the Chinese model in Europe rested on the belief that it was still possible to find a philosopher–king. China was seen as an ideal for the reason that it remained in accord with the ideals of a great past. Such an attitude, the perfect expression of those thinkers devoted to the *ancien régime,* declined before the social and political upheavals in Europe at the end of the eighteenth century as well as the more far-reaching economic changes wrought by the Industrial Revolution. A belief in progress became typical of the nineteenth century. In this new atmosphere the apparent changelessness of China – summed up by Ranke's phrase, 'eternal standstill' – was soon converted into a justification for European superiority and impatience. Yet it remains a matter of historical fact that the contemporary experience of the Chinese people was of change, albeit the uncertain beginning of the massive transformation only reaching completion today.

Population increase was dramatic. Under the Ch'ing dynasty the Chinese population rose from over 200 millions in the seventeenth century to 417 millions in 1851, after which date census figures were disrupted by the T'ai P'ing Rebellion. Although New World crops like maize, peanuts and potatoes were introduced and there was an expansion of the acreage under cultivation, the agricultural economy barely kept pace with population growth. No agricultural boom occurred like the one experienced in Kiangnan during the period of the Two Sungs and farming tended more and more towards food grain production at the expense of commercially valuable crops like cotton. The largest single handicraft industry in China in the Ch'ing dynasty, cotton manufacture, suffered shortages of raw materials as demand for food accelerated. The demographic impact on the cotton industry can be best appreciated when it is recalled that mechanization of the British textile manufacture was integral to the Industrial Revolution. Whereas the British were able to import cotton from the New World, tripling consumption between 1741 and 1775, the self-imposed isolation of the Chinese from international trade left them with little scope for adjustment. Commerce and industry had to manage within an economic system proving itself to be less and less satisfactory. The sheer extent of the Empire had made the exclusion policy possible. Originally, there were sufficient resources in the different provinces

Bedstead of wood, lacquered black and gilt. Designed 1755–60 by Chippendale for the Duke of Beaufort, who was one of the original subscribers to *The Gentleman and Cabinet-Maker's Directory.*

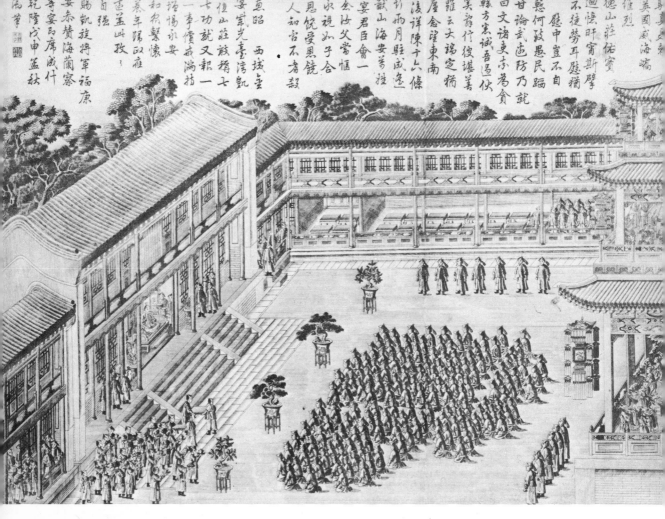

to meet the needs of an elaborate state and a large population, but this balance
was lost in the nineteenth century in spite of the confidence in imperial self-
sufficiency expressed by Emperor Ch'ing Ch'ien-lung. A part of the price
that China had to pay for isolationism was temporary economic deterioration,
with the resulting danger of military weakness. To Lord Macartney, the
apostle of free trade, lack of interest in economic developments outside China
was foolhardy. He appreciated that distrust of Europeans was 'encouraged by
the government, whose political system seems to be to persuade the people
that they themselves are already perfect and can therefore learn nothing from
others; but it is to little purpose. A nation that does not advance must
retrograde, and finally fall back to barbarism and misery'. Such economic
shortsightedness was ascribed by Lord Macartney to the peculiar political
conditions of the Empire. 'The government as it now stands', he wrote in the
1790s, 'is properly the tyranny of a handful of Tartars over more than three
hundred millions of Chinese.' The edict of 1757 which prohibited international
trade in all seaports except Canton could be cited as an example of tyrannical
interference with Western notions of a free market, but for the Chinese state
control over large sectors of the economy was a long-standing tradition and
the authors of trade restriction were the Ming, not the Manchu, emperors.
Control over foreign trade characterized Chinese policy during most of the

late Empire, the system only breaking down after 1842 when China was compelled by Great Britain to sign the Treaty of Nanking and open other ports to unrestricted international commerce. Perhaps the significance of governmental limitation of foreign trade and contacts was that it coincided with a period of internal economic decline.

The accompaniment of sustained population increase was a loosening of social bonds, particularly in the rural areas where the overwhelming mass of the people lived. Profound unrest among the *nung* had been evident in the rebellions led by Chang Hsien-chung and Li Tzu-ch'eng at the end of the Ming dynasty. Most disturbing for the *shih* at this time was the pent-up hatred and fury of the landlords released in the *nung* by these disturbances. It was the anger of the abject tillers of the soil which convinced the powerful families that any revival of serfdom was perilous. In 1681 Emperor Ch'ing K'ang-hsi approved a memorial from the governor of Anhui to the effect that: 'Henceforth, when landlords are buying and selling land they must allow their tenants to do as they please. They may not sell them along with their fields or compel them to perform services.' By the beginning of the nineteenth century there were no traces of this practice left and the countryside had become predominantly a world of smallholders – independent *nung* with small holdings and petty landlords. No longer was investment in land seen as profitable. On the contrary, the wealthy people of Kiangnan, the *shih* and the *shang*, found that they obtained better returns from money lending, commerce and urban real estate. Though land remained the chief form of security, the way in which one generation could transmit status to the next, the difficulties of collecting rents and the heavy burden of tax disinclined the well-off from acquiring large estates. There was a steady tendency towards fragmentation as holdings were divided equally between male heirs, without any successful member of the family seeking to restore the ancestral estate. Absentee landlordism became the pattern where ownership was retained to any extent, since the amenities of the towns and cities were a powerful magnet. The relationship, therefore, between tenant and landlord was reduced to the cash nexus. Pawnbrokers and moneylenders from market towns and cities, the local suppliers of capital, took over as the dominant social group in the rural community.

Great social mobility was not without its problems. The Chinese *nung* were less constrained than the peasantry of contemporary India or Japan, but the closeness of the 'rich' smallholder and the 'poor' labourer combined with the fluctuations of fortune caused by the vagaries of the climate and growing civil disturbances to produce an atmosphere of hostility. The anxieties of many *nung* found solace in the activities of secret societies, which flourished throughout the Empire, whilst the inclusion of land distribution in the programme of the T'ai P'ing rebels shows that they clearly sought to end social grievances of a fundamental kind. The catalyst was Western imperial pressure after the 1840s but conditions requisite for radical social change were being prepared by a people far from 'eternal standstill'.

Numerous secret societies grew up in response to the general decay of society during the nineteenth and early twentieth centuries. These associations provided protection in disturbed times, such as the rapid decline of the Ch'ing dynasty after the Treaty of Nanking, and in the decades prior to the revolution

An audience given in 1788 by Emperor Ch'ing Ch'ien-lung to senior military officials who had put down a rebellion on Taiwan. The calligraphy is the emperor's own.

of 1911 they were often republican in temper. 'The Triad' was a secret society with considerable support in Kiangnan and Nanyang, that is from the people of the southern provinces and those living in overseas settlements: its main thrust, like that of the northern 'White Lotus', was against the Manchus. 'Restore the Hung [Ming] and exterminate the Ch'ing' was its slogan. Actively opposed to the Ch'ing dynasty for a couple of centuries, 'The Triad' had strong connections with the T'ai P'ing revolutionary movement and 'T'ung-meng-hui', the 'Sworn League' of republican agitators formed in 1905 and led by Dr Sun Yat-sen. Influential among the poor of both town and countryside, 'The Triad' fermented the Hong Kong dock strike of 1885, a patriotic protest over the presence of a French warship, *La Galissonière*, which had taken part in the Tonking campaign against Annamese and Chinese forces; and it co-operated with the 'T'ung-meng-hui' in organizing the 1906 insurrection of the P'ingsiang coal-miners of Hupei against the Ch'ing dynasty.

Although the various secret societies were castigated by the *shih* as perverse and vicious sects of dissidents or bandits, there was agreement that their membership was partly united by religious sentiment. Perhaps because of this implicit challenge to Confucian orthodoxy as represented by the state, clan and family, the attitudes as well as activities of members belonging to most secret societies were looked upon as corrupt. Mutual antagonism was typical, as Father Leboucq noted in 1875:

> The recruitment chiefs in general mistrust scholars, especially those with inherited wealth and a reputation for honesty. Moreover, since their aim is to overthrow authority, honorary titles bestowed by the emperor, whether in literary examinations or military contests, are not of a kind to inspire them with confidence in those that bear them. They do not openly refuse them admission but they despise and mistrust them. I know a bachelor full of talent and ambition who, having succeeded in gaining the certificate of membership, could not attain even the lowest official rank – not even that of decurion.
>
> I do not know whether European secret societies admit women to their midst, but in China it is the harpies of the Water-Lily who hold sway in that society. It is they who inspire and encourage the faint-hearted. Should the Water-Lily Society ever come to set up a Committee of Public Safety or a Commune . . . it is certain that it would not lack women fire-raisers.

The freedom of action given to female members is noteworthy. It seems to have caused the French Jesuit most anxiety. Possibly in a traditional society like that of late imperial China the revelation of a liberal attitude to women took him by surprise. Yet this progressive outlook – on one hand, a coolness towards the male dominance explicit in Confucian tradition and, on the other, the placing of men and women on an equal footing in the society – was part of a wider movement towards more democratic forms to be found in other associations. The custom of binding women's feet was strictly forbidden in the provinces captured by the T'ai P'ings, whilst even in the Boxer Rising of 1900, when members of the 'Righteous Harmony Fists' captured Peking and be-sieged the 'Ocean Devils' in the diplomatic quarter, women were very active.

The removal of landowners from the countryside weakened the control which they could exercise over their tenants. Instead of direct contact, the daily relations of the important family in its country residence with the immediate neighbourhood, they were obliged to rely on salaried agents as well as understandings with local officials. Tenancy changed in character as did the role of the landlord, now a permanent town-dweller. Choice of residence for the well-off widened as the number of market towns began to multiply and there occurred the start of the process of suburban growth which was to make Chinese cities some of the largest in the twentieth-century world. The walled-city-in-the-country had been the effective seat of government and administration from the Han Empire (202 BC–AD 220) onwards. It dominated the rural landscape: within its walls were the state granaries that held the grain-tribute or tax upon which organized government depended, the food surplus that maintained the official class, the standing army and the conscripted labour force involved in water-conservancy schemes. But during the eighteenth and nineteenth centuries new settlements came into existence as market centres, the result of population growth and the rise of local pawn-brokers and money-lenders. The origins of these towns were very diverse. Some grew up at bridges, confluences of waterways and customs stations; others appeared near temples, the residences of powerful families, the warehouses of rich merchants and industrial centres like potteries; others coexisted with military establishments or depots of government monopoly products such as salt. 'Anyone who is tempted to think of the late Chinese rural economy as "cellular", "self-sufficient", or "uncommercialized" has only to look at this network and its density', Mark Elvin has well remarked, 'to realize how inapplicable these terms are.'

The influence of the *shang* on the countryside can be noticed in the following report about Anhui made by a Censor in 1814.

> In the region of the two market towns of Shuang-lo and San-lo, in the neighbourhood of Liu-an in Lu-chou in this province, there is a rice merchant called Lu. He has built granaries along the river for over thirty kilometres, and has dominated this area for many a year. At harvest time he gathers in a million piculs, buying cheap and selling dear.

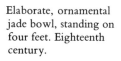

Elaborate, ornamental jade bowl, standing on four feet. Eighteenth century.

Possibly this merchant, an important local figure, also contracted for the collection of taxes. Yet his economic power remained at odds with his social position: trade and finance were no substitute for education and official rank. Merchants might gather vast fortunes but prestige could only be gained through association with those honoured by society, the highly born and the officials. Hence, the descendants of hard-working and frugal Lu, in the second and third generation after the original fortune had been made, would acquire very different habits. They then sought status, spending enormous sums in the endless quest for social esteem. Schemes for the benefit of the general public, sponsorship of scholars as well as institutions of learning, besides ostentatious displays of personal interest in gardens, books, paintings and music, diverted the family wealth from investment aimed at further accumulation. Not until the 1905 abolition of the *k'o-chu*, the imperial examination system, did the stigma attached to commercial activities cease to hinder the social progress of the *shang*, though capitalism enjoyed only a brief respite before state interference reappeared under the People's Republic. Even so the strength of traditional discrimination against trade is evident in its survival among overseas communities, where leading businessmen are still expected to take the lead in supporting not only Chinese education but also cultural activities.

In a survey of eighteenth-century towns throughout the world Fernand Braudel wrote:

> No independent authority represented a Chinese town as a whole in its dealings with the state or the enormously powerful countryside. The countryside was the very living centre of living, active, thinking China, 'the vegetable mould which continues to feed Chinese thought'. The town, residence of officials and nobles, was not the property of either craftsmen and merchants. There was no comfortably expanding middle class there. No sooner did this middle class evolve than it thought about desertion, being fascinated by the splendours of the mandarins' life. . . . Only the West swung completely over in favour of its towns. The towns caused the West to advance. . . . What would the Chinese towns have become if junks had discovered the Cape of Good Hope at the beginning of the fifteenth century, and had made full use of a chance of world conquest?

Marco Polo's wonderment at the enormous size and activities of Chinese cities serves to remind us that in the West urban concentration was a late event. At Zaiton, or Chuang-chou, he found the pepper trade alone 'so considerable, that what is carried to Alexandria, to supply the western parts of the world, is trifling in comparison, perhaps not more than the hundredth part'. Of greater note, then, is the extent of urban development generated within the late Empire by internal trade. Added to the ancient foundations of cities like Nanking and Peking were a host of newer settlements, one of which market centres was soon to become the internationally renowned Shanghai. When the foreign inhabitants of the latter petitioned the Ch'ing court for a 'charter' in order to conduct their civic affairs on the European model of a free city they were met with blank bewilderment. Their request was simply not understood: it had no place in a tradition where towns were under the control of the official class and undifferentiated from the countryside. Whilst Braudel is correct in his contrast of towns in the West and China, the implication of missed opportunities for overseas development connected with Ming maritime exploration reveals a somewhat Western prejudice. China has never been expansionist in this sense, its people from Shang times (1500–1027 BC) moving outwards from the Yellow River valley only through a gradual extension of the area under cultivation. Relations with neighbouring states, Korea, Vietnam and Japan, were conducted on a tributary basis in recognition of Chinese cultural and economic superiority. The Chinese had planted no forts, founded no colonies and attempted no conversions in the Indian Ocean. Although the Manchus certainly enlarged the land area under the authority of the One Man, their exclusion policy after 1757 was more in accord with Chinese sentiment, except in its extreme forms of xenophobia.

Finally, a word needs to be said about the impact of money on the civil service. The purchase of studentships, offices and official titles started during the eunuch ascendancy at the close of the Ming dynasty. After 1850 the possession of money began to overshadow higher academic qualifications as a determinant of social status. The examination system had ceased to be the main channel of social mobility as well as a politically and socially stabilizing factor. Periodic sales of qualifications in the late Ming had opened the way to social advancement for some wealthy merchants – licensed salt-boilers being among these recruits to officialdom – but the examination system remained the primary route to status up to the outbreak of the T'ai P'ing Rebellion. Thereafter a harassed dynasty and a divided country had little time for formal education. Furthermore, the decline of the examination system in the eyes of the Chinese was not unconnected with its use to maintain Manchu supremacy. As Lord Macartney observed earlier, 'whatever might be concluded from outward appearances, the real distinction is never forgotten by the sovereign who, though he pretends to be perfectly impartial, conducts himself at bottom by a systematic nationality, and never for a moment loses sight of the cradle of his power'.

Buddhist saint with a tiger, a favourite subject. Blanc de chine porcelain, eighteenth century.

CH'ING ART AND LETTERS

The antiquarian tendency of the M'ing period gathered strength after the Manchu conquest of the southern provinces, the scholarly interests of Emperor Ch'ing K'ang-hsi acting as a spur to both painters and men of letters. The eighteenth-century encyclopedic movement far outstripped anything done by Ming scholars: the hallmark of their Ch'ing successors was perspiration rather than inspiration. It was the age of great collections and the greatest collector of all was Emperor Ch'ing Ch'ien-lung, to whose diligence we owe the survival of so many paintings today.

Court painters were noted for elaborate, detailed scenes taken from literature or events of ceremonial interest. Elegance of expression combined with meticulous brushwork to produce a style of painting that was amazingly intricate and profoundly conservative. The tradition of figure painting started by Ku K'ai-chih (c.334–406) thus ended in punctiliousness. The slightest detail in a composition was carefully depicted, whether it were the texture of lacquer furniture, a jade brooch or a bronze ornament. Nor did the incorporation of perspective in some of these works cause any fundamental change in this tradition, though the synthetic style of Joseph Castiglione, a

Lapis lazuli mountain, carved towards the close of the eighteenth century. A Taoist immortal gathers the fungus of longevity near a subterranean river and a rock inscribed with a poem composed by Emperor Ch'ing Ch'ien-lung.

mixture of Chinese medium and technique with Western naturalism, was much admired. Having arrived in Peking in 1715, the Italian Jesuit not only executed paintings as interior decoration but also designed for Emperor Ch'ing Ch'ien-lung a variety of pleasure pavilions for the Summer Residence, the Yuan-ming-yuan, at Jehol.

Untouched by either the restriction of taste in the Ch'ing court or the Western technique of perspective were the *wen-jen*, the literary painters. Most notable were the 'Four Wangs' – Wang Shih-min (1592–1680), Wang Chien (1598–1677), Wang Hui (1632–1720) and Wang Yuan-ch'i (1642–1715). From their dates it can be observed that they belonged as much to the Ming period as the Ch'ing. When they are bracketed by Chinese art historians with Wu Li (1632–1718) and Yun Shou-p'ing (1633–90) as the 'Six Great Masters of the Ch'ing Dynasty', this overlap takes on a greater significance. For the foremost Ch'ing painters were spiritual survivors from the preceding Chinese dynasty, and they owed little debt to the inspiration of the Manchu occupation. Although Wang Yuan-ch'i, the grandson of Wang Shih-min, rose to high office under Emperor Ch'ing K'ang-hsi, becoming head of the Han-lin Academy, and wrote at the imperial behest on painting and calligraphy in 1708, his work remained separate from the court tradition of painting. Wang Yuan-ch'i drew upon the landscapes of the Yuan masters and Tun Ch'i-ch'ang. The most gifted *wen-jen* was undoubtedly Wang Hui, who was discovered by Wang Chien in 1651. So impressed was the elder painter with the young man's abilities in calligraphy and painting that he introduced him to the leading scholar-painter of the day, Wang Shih-min. This meeting was of the utmost importance for Wang Hui. He was invited to live at Wang Shih-min's studio near Soochow, where he had access to many famous paintings of the past. Assiduous copying taught Wang Hui a range of techniques that he was able to put to excellent use in his own landscapes.

Eclectic though his works were, their recreation of aspects belonging to previous masterpieces was original and satisfying. Wang Hui 'pursued the ancients' in order to recapture the essence of landscape and his originality in large scale compositions is apparent in paintings like *The Colours of Mount T'ai-hang*, executed in 1669. The genesis of composition is given by the artist in an inscription placed at the top right-hand corner. It reads:

> Once at Kuang-ling, in the home of a powerful family, I saw a small scroll by Kuan T'ung, *Cloudy Peaks Racing Together*. In spirit it was luxuriant and dense, truly, it might 'pierce the heart and startle the eye'. Even today, I remember one or two tenths of it: accordingly I have imitated its method and made this *Colours of Mount T'ai-hang*. It should have the deep and heroic atmosphere of the North, and not become attractive with pretty details. . . .

This was not slavish copying, the obsession with correctness of later court painters, nor was it conformity to the dogma of the *wen-jen-hua*, the school of the scholar-painters; rather it was an expression of the extent to which the most talented artist of the Ch'ing dynasty had turned to the past. It was the pursuit of antiquity. The insoluble problem for literary painters after the death of Wang Hui, which comprises the majority of the Ch'ing period, was the difficulty of going beyond previous models, the avoidance of mere imitation by artists unendowed with exceptional ability.

The seventeenth century also boasted a few worthy outsiders, artists for whom the political conditions in the conquered Empire made contact with polite society impossible. Thus Kung Hsien (*c.* 1620–1700), like the Yuan masters, chose seclusion in Kiangnan, where he painted strikingly unusual landscapes of desolate, craggy mountains wreathed with sombre mists and cloud. He said that he followed no one and no one could follow him, an apt comment on his haunting *A Thousand Peaks and a Myriad Ravines*. Another isolate was Chu Ta (1626–1705), a distant relation of the deposed Ming emperor who became a monk, a gesture of despair at the world of politics and art. Again, his paintings are unlike anything executed by his contemporaries. From Ch'an Buddhism perhaps he acquired his daring brush-strokes as well as his intense fascination with animal life, which is evident in the famous *Fish and Rocks*.

After the death of Emperor Ch'ing Ch'ien-lung the status of court painters declined steeply, till at the end of the nineteenth century they were hardly superior to palace servants. Nearly as steep was the lowering of standards among the scholar-painters, who progressively substituted exact imitation for the syncretic masterpieces of the original Wang Hui. As Wang Shih-min is reputed to have remarked, 'Anyone who thinks Wang Hui copies the works of the ancients does not understand painting.' The revival of originality within traditional Chinese painting had to wait until the twentieth century when two great artists reinterpreted the role of the painter: namely, Ch'i Pai-shih (1863–1957) and Huang Pin-huang (1864–1955).

A similar decline took place in the quality of porcelain, lacquer and carved jade. The clear, smooth, slightly greenish glaze of eighteenth-century 'blue and white' was replaced by a glaze of poor colour, sometimes even greyish, with a slightly uneven surface. The imperial kilns at Ch'ing-te Chen had produced outstanding porcelain during the reign of Emperor Ch'ing K'ang-hsi, but in the nineteenth century the popularity of 'blue and white' gave way to brightly coloured wares. In Europe, too, these more ornate products, along with Japanese porcelain, were preferred. Other handicraft factories existed than those concerned with the supply of the Ch'ing court and the official class, and they concentrated upon the desires of the *shang*, the well-off living in the expanding urban centres, and the export market. Lacquer furniture and carved stone ornaments were favourites. One of the immediate consequences of territorial expansion under the early Ch'ing emperors was the wider range of hardstones made available to the *kung*. The Ch'ing dynasty was able to command new sources of supply so that there was scope for more virtuosity in carving. Stones of striking colours came into use – bright green and yellow jade, violet-pink quartz, red chalcedony and blue lapis lazuli. Archaic themes were common, as well as the naturalistic treatment of such things as flowers and small animals. Over-production in the nineteenth century led to a loss of delicacy in technique, though the finest examples of jade carving remain superb. In taste the Ch'ing court was content to follow the tradition it inherited from the Ming dynasty, hence its contribution to architecture was a thorough restoration of existing monuments, notably in Peking.

Looking back on the cultural achievement of the Ch'ing dynasty from the vantage point of 1920, Liang Ch'i-ch'ao, the ardent supporter of reformer

Grey jade duck, with feathers finely carved in low relief. Eighteenth century.

K'ang Yu-wei, concluded that its fundamental shortcoming was a lack of progress. 'Although Ch'ing art, especially painting, cannot be called greatly inferior to that of the previous dynasty', he wrote, 'it certainly never developed in any new direction.' As for 'Ch'ing literature, its poetry, for instance, certainly was in a state of extreme deterioration.' The harshness of this judgment may have partly derived from the critic's wish to free the twentieth-century Chinese intellect from aspects of culture under the Manchus that had tended so dangerously towards narrowness or affectation.

Notwithstanding the charge of corruption levelled at him by Liang Ch'i-ch'ao, the best-known poet of the Ch'ing dynasty was Yuan Mei (1716–79), whose collected works may have been purchased by Lord Macartney. The life of Yuan Mei as much as his work provides us with an insight into the lot of the poet during the Manchu occupation. Born of poor parents in Hangchow at the end of Emperor Ch'ing K'ang-hsi's reign, Yuan Mei was helped to acquire a sound education through the interest of an aunt and in 1736 he was advanced enough to be a candidate in a special examination held at Peking. Although Yuan Mei was not selected as one of the fifteen 'talented' scholars and recruited to the civil service, his candidature at the tender age of twenty caused a sensation. Yet beneath the young man's scholarship lurked a discontent with the formalities of the examination system and the exclusive study of the Confucian classics. In 1739 he passed the highest civil service

Jade buffalo and boy, a favourite subject. Eighteenth century.

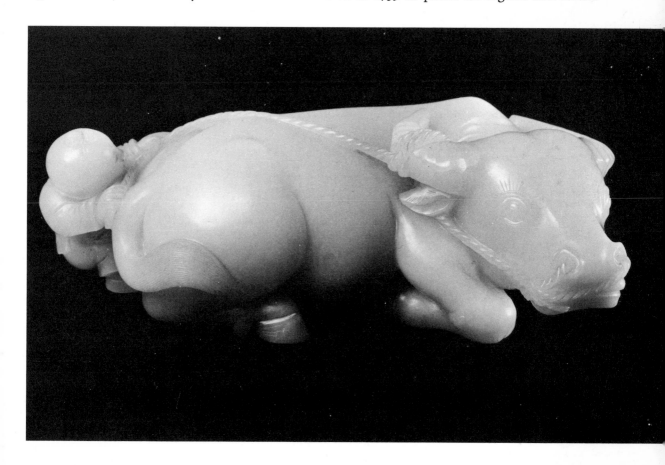

examinations and became a scholar of the Han-lin Academy, but his personal preference was for reading and composing poetry. At this time he acquired as patrons two eminent Manchu statesmen, Yin-chi-shan (1696–1771) and Ortai (1680–1745). Yin-chi-shan, the minister responsible for law and order, was impressed with the poem Yuan Mei had written in one of his examination papers, though the poet disappointed both patrons by his singular failure to master the Manchu language.

In 1743 Yuan Mei was appointed to Kiangnan, where he was in charge of a district near Nanking. Two years later, through the influence of Yin-chi-shan, he was transferred to the city itself and his responsibilities were for a number of wards. Though he enjoyed a reputation for good administration – a book was later published on his decisions as a magistrate – there can be no doubt from the following lines that he tired of office.

> Morning after morning at the fifth watch I climb into my carriage;
> I must pay my respects to those above me, meet, them, see them off,
> Answer the questions of their clients and guests while time flies away.
> The inner wall of Nanking is sixty leagues round,
> To do the whole circuit of the town is about a day's job.
> When at last I manage to get home the lamps are beginning to be lit;
> Through the dusk I trundle to the fold, as do the cows and sheep.
> Womenfolk holding their brats block the entry to my house,
> And while the children tug at my skirts their elders make excuses:
> 'We all said what a pity it was that you were kept so late;
> It never occurred to anyone that you had not had your supper.'
> Gasping with hunger, yet holding out, I put my papers in order;
> Just on the verge of reaching a decision I go back again to the start.
> I am haunted by the fear that further delay may do harm to my people;
> Yet I know well that when I hurry I make a lot of mistakes.
> The tangled threads are straightened out; at last I am leaving my office
> When a young Bachelor turns up, and wants to show me an essay:
> 'Knowing that your Worship was previously employed in the Han-lin Academy
> I felt I should not be doing my duty if I did not pay my respects.'

So at thirty-two years of age he decided to retire as an official. Except for a brief spell from 1752, Yuan Mei kept to his resolve and lived in a garden residence at Nanking, where he could take pleasure in writing as well as in the company of his concubines and young men. Perhaps he found distasteful the increasing vigilance of the Manchu censorship, whose search for literature subversive to the dynasty had brought about in 1753 the banning of *All Men are Brothers*, a Ming novel based on the ancient and hallowed notion of the right of an oppressed people to rebel. The absurd lengths to which officials of Emperor Ch'ing Ch'ien-lung were prepared to go in order to stifle intellectual dissent became apparent fifteen years later, when Ch'i Shao-nan, an acquaintance of Yuan Mei, was dispossessed for the crime of having composed a preface to a book written by his cousin in which there were passages disrespectful to the Manchus. Ch'i Shao-nan's preface was forty-three years old at the time of his conviction.

Yuan Mei derived his income from the composition of tomb inscriptions

Sui Yuan in Nanking, an old garden acquired in 1757 by the poet Yuan Mei, who remodelled it. Particularly admired were the bamboos and plum blossoms.

and the sales of his literary works, whose printing he personally supervised. At least two patrons were rich merchants, men anxious to display their support for literature. Besides writing poetry, Yuan Mei issued collections of strange stories; these were wonder-tales, relating irrational events, encounters with the unknown and accounts of curiosities. He also wrote a history of poetry and a cookery book, entitled *Shih-tan* (*The Menu*). Right to the end of his life Yuan Mei remained unmoved by either the forms of Confucian orthodoxy or the practices of Buddhist religion. He was a hedonist, a poet who cultivated his own secluded garden of sensual delights. Typical of his contempt for the religious rituals associated with ancestor worship was the following injunction in his will:

> As for the recitation of Scriptures, chanting of liturgies and entertainment of monks on the seventh days – these things that I have always detested – you may tell your sisters to come and make an offering to me, in which case I

shall certainly accept it; or to come once and wail; at which I shall be deeply moved. But if monks come to the door, at the sound of their wooden clappers my divine soul will stop up its ears and run away, which I am sure you would not like.

About 1765 was published *The Dream of the Red Chamber* (*Hung-lou meng*). It is the novel of sentiment. For some people this tale of star-crossed love represents the finest achievement of Chinese fiction, and even Liang Ch'i-ch'ao had to admit that it 'stood unique for all times'. The tragic love of the two cousins Precious Jade, or Pao-yu, and Black Jade, or Tai-yu, arises from the social customs of late traditional China, when arranged marriages were common practice among the well-to-do. Delicate and cultivated, Tai-yu composes poems lamenting her position, a poor orphan secretly admired by her artistic cousin Pao-yu, whose wife must be chosen for him from a family of status and wealth. The cousins exchange letters and poems but consumptive Tai-yu dies broken-hearted on the wedding night of Pao-yu, a most reluctant groom. Insanity then engulfs Pao-yu, refuge from which affliction is only found in joining a monastic community. The artistic pair had wilted under the implacable indifference of convention. Alike in its rejection of social norms was *The Scholars*, a satirical novel published in 1803. Wu Ching-tzu (died 1754) probably wrote this assault upon social abuses at the end of the reign of Emperor Ch'ing Yung-cheng. His main target, as the title itself suggests, was the official class, which may partly explain the popularity of the novel in present-day China.

No discussion of Ch'ing letters can afford to omit the influence of K'ang Yu-wei (1858–1927). Famous as a scholar and a man of action, this Cantonese reformer had an immense impact on the thought of the final years of the Ch'ing dynasty. After the humiliation of the Second Opium War, Liang Ch'i-ch'ao tells us,

> resolute men of purpose [literally, 'those clenching their fists and grinding their teeth'] sought ways to redeem themselves. The revival of the conception of practical studies for the service of the state burst forth like an unextinguishable, raging fire. With the lifting of the ban on oceanic communication, so-called 'Western learning' gradually came in: first the study of industrial arts and then political institutions. Scholars hitherto had lived as if in a dark room, unaware of what was beyond it; now a window was suddenly opened, through which they peered out and discovered all sorts of radiant objects which they had never seen before. Looking back into their own room, they saw only depressing darkness and piled-up dust.

K'ang Yu-wei was the leader of those who raised 'the rebel's flag against the Orthodox School'. He had already rejected the artificialities of essay style demanded in the examination system and his attention was held by 'Western learning', which a visit to the British Crown Colony of Hong Kong in 1879 had helped to bring into clearer focus. Worried by the rising tide of confusion and its exploitation by ambitious European powers as well as Japan, K'ang Yu-wei tried to provide an intellectual basis for the changes in Chinese society that were necessary to save the Empire. Teaching and writing in Kwantung, he attempted to transform Confucianism and Buddhism into a viable system of thought that could hold its own in the modern world. In

1891 his first book, *Forged Classics of the Hsin Dynasty* (*Hsin-hsueh wei-ching k'ao*) created in scholarly circles an uproar which was not diminished the following year by the publication of *Confucius as a Reformer* (*K'ung-tzu K'ai-chih k'ao*). Enraged officials in Peking attacked *Forged Classics of the Hsin Dynasty* as sacrilegious and unscholarly, so that at their request it was banned, and the printing blocks were burned. Nothing, however, would deter K'ang Yu-wei and his followers in bringing to the notice of the throne the cause of reform. Local setbacks in Kwantung failed to discourage them and Liang Ch'i-ch'ao became editor of a newspaper, *Current Affairs* (*Shih-wu pao*), founded to propagate nationally K'ang Yu-wei's ideas for change.

The disaster of the Sino-Japanese War (1894–5) vindicated the position of K'ang Yu-wei, who had perceived how unprepared the Empire was for its entry into the hostile world of the twentieth century. Defeat in Korea would have been the catalyst, but for the Empress Dowager Tz'u Hsi and the habitual cautiousness of the *shih* themselves. The Hundred Days of Reform in 1898, when K'ang Yu-wei had the ear of the young Ch'ing Emperor Kuang-hsu, were followed by swift reaction and exile. On the run in Japan, America, England, India – to name a few of the places where he lived in fear of assassination by government agents – K'ang Yu-wei continued to write and plot for the reformation of the Empire. Although the sudden death of Emperor Ch'ing Kuang-hsu in 1908 undermined his confidence in affecting institutional improvement under the Manchus, he deplored the revolution of 1911–12, and considered it the wrong solution for China's problems. He stuck by his belief in a constitutional monarchy along with a programme of social and economic reform. The best of the *shih*, K'ang Yu-wei was sacrificed along with the Empire on the altar of ultra-conservatism. Yet the influence of 'Western learning' on the development of his thought pointed the way to the contemporary intellectual renewal that has come through Communist theory.

His final point of view can be found in *The One-World Book* (*Ta T'ung Shu*), a work he completed at Darjeeling, India, in 1902. K'ang Yu-wei outlined the practical steps by which mankind could reach utopia, a world society of small democratically self-governing communities, each equally represented in a world parliament. The 'compassionate natures' of people have to be developed and conducted along this path by the example of their leaders. At last 'the men and women of One World are entirely equal. Through the abolition of the family, women are no longer burdened with the age-old duties of caring for children, nor are they merely playthings for men. There being no essential differences between men and women as human beings, women are not regarded any differently than men when it comes to work or to holding office.'

大清國慈禧皇太后

5

Western Imperialism and the Collapse of the Chinese Empire

In the 1840s an exhibition at Madame Tussaud's which was popular with Londoners represented 'Commissioner Lin and his Favourite Consort, Modelled from life, by the Celebrated Lamb-Qua, of Canton, with Magnificent Dresses actually worn by them'. Publicity for this singular wax-work display went on to declare that Lin was 'the author of the Chinese War!' and 'the Destroyer of £2,500,000 of British Property'.

Blame for the outbreak of the First Opium War (1839–42) was attributed to China not only by the general public. At Westminster it was the view of the government that the concern of the Chinese emperor about the bad effects of opium on the health of his people was not genuine, and it was assumed to conceal his real motives for the suppression of the traffic. Lord Palmerston claimed that the Ch'ing court was primarily concerned to reduce the outflow of silver and to protect the cultivation of the poppy at home. The 1840 debate on the opium problem and the war revealed some of the worst attitudes of nineteenth-century European imperialism. Profitability carried the day. The authority of the British gunboat was reckoned to be superior to that of the Chinese emperor, whose right to determine the morality of drug traffic within his dominions was found quite unacceptable. However, the opium question, because of the efforts of missionaries and humanitarian agitators, was guaranteed to raise the political temperature in both Houses of Parliament. Gladstone made a fine speech against governmental acquiescence in the traffic of opium, pointing to the fact that smuggling could be ended without any blockade on the Chinese coast. It could be brought under control by a prohibition on the cultivation of the poppy in India. Of the hostilities between China and Great Britain he declared 'a war more unjust in its origin, a war more calculated in its progress to cover this country with permanent disgrace, I do not know, and have not read of'. Yet Gladstone was able to manage his own conscience in such a way that in a debate of 1870 he contended that opium had become a commercial commodity through the imposition of an import duty. What he chose to overlook was that this concession had been wrung from an unwilling China in the Treaty of Tientsin (1858) after the further intervention of gunboats. Like most nine-teenth-century politicians, Gladstone was impressed by the powerful impact of a modest naval force on the tottering Manchu Empire. European domi-nance, as temporarily expressed in industrial technology and expanding capitalist activity, seemed a natural progression in world history. A similar opinion was held by the British electorate, who returned Lord Palmerston with a thumping majority for his gunboat diplomacy at the height of the *Arrow* incident (1856–7).

Portrait of the Dowager Empress T'zu Hsi, the uncompromising opponent of reform.

The moral issues of the opium trade were forgotten in the revenue accounts of the British Empire. To our lasting shame, India was used to grow the drug in such vast quantities that the *shih* became alarmed at the rapid spread of the habit, with its appalling destruction of hundreds of thousands of people. It was an import that also did little to alleviate the general bad impression of Europeans gained by the Chinese population since the Ming period. As Manchu propaganda asserted, they were really 'Ocean Devils'.

The Anglo–Chinese War of 1839–42, known as the First Opium War, was more than a skirmish over trade. It was the inevitable collision of two governments whose views were totally different: two diametrically opposed social and economic systems had met head-on. Brushing aside the failure of Lord Macartney's embassy, London sent other ambassadors to establish diplomatic relations with Peking. In 1816 Lord Amherst was unable to achieve anything at the Ch'ing court, whilst in 1834 Lord Napier was prevented from travelling beyond Canton, though the recommendation in his report that the island of Hong Kong be acquired as a naval and commercial base did influence later British strategy. The expiration of the East India Company's charter in the year of Lord Napier's embassy soon led to a situation where conflict arose. Trade, now in the hands of private merchants, grew apace, and the steep annual increase in opium imports compelled Emperor Ch'ing Tao-kuang to intervene directly. Because the British authorities informed the Chinese that they were unable to prevent traffic as private vessels carried the opium – to the Ch'ing court, the centre of all authority in the Empire, this seemed a very hypocritical attitude – a Special Commissioner, Lin Tse-hsu, was sent to Canton in 1839 with instructions to stamp out the whole business. The action which he took was to destroy the opium stocks without compensation, and to insist that European merchants promise to end the traffic in the drug. The British merchants were uneasy about this suppression and the murder of a Chinese by a group of drunken British and American sailors added the wider question of extra-territoriality to the dispute. When the British were unable to ascertain which man had delivered the fatal blow and refused to surrender the entire group, Lin Tse-hsu ordered that supplies be withheld from foreign shipping. At Kowloon a clash occurred, casualties were sustained by both sides, and the British were formally excluded from Canton.

An expeditionary force, consisting of about twenty warships, including steamers – according to Lin Tse-hsu 'cart-wheel ships that put the axles in motion by means of fire, and can move rather fast' – arrived off Macao with 4,000 British and Indian troops. After attacks on Canton, the British fleet, further reinforced from India, sailed northwards in 1841 to intimidate Peking. Coastal towns and cities were sacked, the Manchus having little defence against the superior fire-power of the invaders, and in the face of general panic the Ch'ing court was obliged to sign the Treaty of Nanking in 1841; immediately afterwards the English put up notices in occupied areas announcing where 'opium is on sale very cheap – an opportunity not to be missed'. The opium ships had accompanied the Royal Navy in its glorious sweep up the Yang-tze River, a fact usually unmentioned by British historians. The shock of Chinese capitulation to such a small seaborne expedition was enormous, for the fragility of the Manchu Empire was demonstrated to the world. It signalized that China was besieged.

Explicit imperialism in this cartoon from *Punch*, 22 December 1860. Opium is of course unmentioned.

WHAT WE OUGHT TO DO IN CHINA.

Early nineteenth-century Chinese view of a British man-of-war.

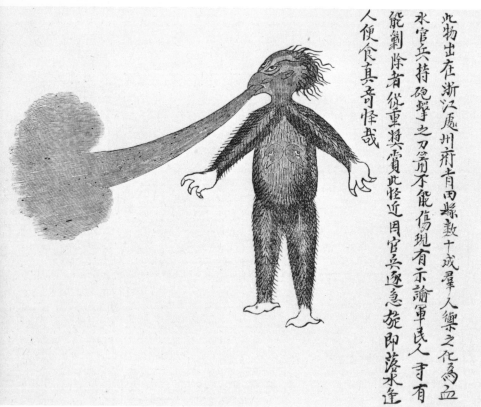

此物出在浙江處州府青田縣數十成羣人樂之化為血水官兵持砲擊之刀箭不能傷現有示諭軍民人等有能剿除者從重獎賞此怪近因官兵逐急旋即落水逢人便食真奇怪哉

An Ocean Devil. A caricature of a fire-breathing English sailor, which appeared in 1839 as part of Ch'ing propaganda designed to increase Chinese xenophobia. Yet there was little in the behaviour of the Briton to suggest that he was other than 'truly a wonderful monster'.

By the Treaty of Nanking the five ports of Canton, Amoy, Foochow, Ning-po and Shanghai were opened to the residence and trade of British subjects, who were exempt from Chinese jurisdiction. The island of Hong Kong was ceded to Britain for the development of a naval and commercial base. Agreements were reached on a uniform and moderate tariff on exports and imports which could only be varied by mutual consent, the establishment of equal relationships between British and Chinese officials in Treaty Ports, and the payment of an indemnity for the opium destroyed by Commissioner Lin. China also agreed that whatever privileges it might grant to any other nation, it would also grant to Britain, as the 'most-favoured-nation'. The Treaty of Nanking became a model for later agreements which Western powers imposed on the Empire. To the Chinese it was the first of the 'unequal treaties', because the benefits provided in the agreement went exclusively to the European nation at the expense of China. The principle of extra-territoriality was to become particularly obnoxious once sizable enclaves of foreign residents came into existence. Chinese alive today can recall the sign which once hung on the entrance of a park in Shanghai: it read, 'Dogs and Chinese Not Allowed'.

The Treaty of Nanking, hopefully looked upon by many Westerners as the beginning of a new era of international relations for China, took into account neither the historical sentiments of the official class nor the aspirations of the mass of the southern Chinese. To the *shih* and their Manchu masters the concessions were made to gain a respite from external pressure: to the Chinese people this accommodation of the 'Ocean Devils' was an encouragement to rebellious activities against the Ch'ing dynasty, a major focus of sedition being 'The Triad' secret society. Actual insurrection on a national scale occurred through the T'ai P'ings, whose capital was Nanking from 1853 to 1864. It is noteworthy that the Ch'ing dynasty was aided by Western nations in the struggle with the T'ai P'ing rebels. Not only was the brand of Christianity propagated by the rebellion considered to be heretical, but even more the T'ai P'ing campaign against the opium habit had depressed sales of the drug dramatically and there were at stake many valuable treaty concessions recently agreed with the Manchus. When it came to the point, the 'Ocean Devils' preferred propping up the Ch'ing dynasty to its overthrow, which would have produced either a national resurgence or, more likely, a prolonged period of disunity and conflict, conditions unsuited to the development of trade.

Lord Palmerston, bent on gaining the greatest advantages for British commercial interests, welcomed the *Arrow* incident as a new opportunity for dressing down the Chinese. In October 1856, the lorcha *Arrow* and its crew of twelve men were seized by the Chinese authorities near Canton. The vessel, owned by a Chinese, had previously been registered at Hong Kong and until September, the month before seizure, was entitled to fly the British flag. Angered by the *virtual* insult to the flag, the British consul at Canton demanded the sailors and an apology. Though opium smuggling was probably involved, the Chinese authorities released the men, but with no apology. In the heady days of the Great Exhibition, that ritual celebration of industrial progress at the Crystal Palace, this near-affront was enough to start the Second Opium War (1858–60). In concert with Britain over the Crimean

War, France decided that the execution of a Catholic missionary in Kwangsi, where he had been stirring up rebellious feelings among the inhabitants, also entitled it to any benefits derived from renewed hostilities.

Lord Elgin was chosen to conduct the 'gunboat diplomacy' on behalf of the Allies. Making no impression on the Ch'ing court by the capture of Canton, he directed his expedition northwards and seized Tientsin, a city less than one hundred and thirty kilometres from the capital. This action obliged the Manchus to agree to the terms of the Treaty of Tientsin (1858), whereby the *kowtow* was abolished for Western ambassadors in audience with the emperor, and new Treaty Ports were declared along with other trading privileges, including the legal importation of opium. Again, with the *shih* dallying over the implementation of the terms, an incident at Tientsin allowed Elgin in 1860 to march on Peking itself. 'I thought bitterly', Lord Elgin wrote at the time, 'of those who for the most selfish object are trampling underfoot this ancient civilization.' But his orders were to resort 'to the most violent measures of coercion and repression on the slenderest provocation', and he more than succeeded in overcoming his finer feelings by ordering the burning of the Summer Palace as a reprisal for the deaths of several British envoys. In this sound thrashing of the devious natives posterity was deprived of a universally esteemed building as well as many of the paintings and other works of art belonging to the Imperial Collection.

The Conventions of Peking (1860) converted the Empire into an adjunct of the European economic system. An Englishman, Robert Hart, was even appointed as Inspector General of Chinese Customs, a post he held from 1863 until 1909. Ten new Treaty Ports were designated, several of them in the middle course of the Yang-tze River. Ambassadors were to have the right of residence in Peking, while there were to be no restrictions on the activities of Christian missionaries and their converts. England received Kowloon, a useful addition for growing Hong Kong, and the inevitable indemnity was imposed on China to meet the Allied expenses in the recent hostilities – but this time, of course, there was Robert Hart to ensure that a regular revenue would be available to pay it. The Russians too had not missed an opportunity to advance their boundaries in Central Asia and in Siberia. With the British and French invading China from the sea and the T'ai P'ing rebels ascendant in Kiangnan, the Ch'ing court was hardly in a position to refuse the pressing Russian offer of mediation in return for territorial concessions. In 1858 China ceded the region north of the Amur River to Russia, and two years later was hustled into giving up sovereignty over the land between the Ussuri River and the Pacific. By adroitly exploiting the difficulties of the Manchus Russia gained a territory larger than Texas without ever firing a shot. Other nations were to follow this example, though the steady reluctance of England to seek dominion in China as it had in India and the attitude of the United States of America did much to hinder the process of disintegration. The French, who had first exhibited an interest in Annam during the Second Opium War, wrested the former tributary from the Chinese sphere of influence in 1885, after setbacks on land at the hands of Annamese and Chinese forces. Naval power and the bombardment of important coastal cities, such as Foochow, proved decisive once more. The same year the British completed the annexation of Burma to their Indian empire, and, in 1890, had the Ch'ing

The entry of Lord Elgin into Peking in 1860 to sign a new peace treaty with China. The natives had been soundly thrashed again.

court recognize Sikkim as a British protectorate. Equally energetic, however, in pressing territorial claims against China was to be Japan, an oriental country which after some hesitation had adopted a policy of modernization on Western lines.

Whilst with hindsight the Conventions of Peking may be discerned as the moment at which the besiegers of China literally and metaphorically took the citadel, the full extent of the defeat was not apparent to all. The court, under the sway of Empress Dowager Tz'u Hsi, from 1862 until her death in 1908, saw to it that the new Foreign Office, the *Tsungli Yamen*, was unable to exercise any initiative in relations with 'barbarians'. From the point of view of the Ch'ing dynasty, the presence of foreigners in the capital, not submissively bearing tribute but making endless demands for concessions, was a token that the Mandate of Heaven had been forfeited. Manchus like Tz'u

Hsi were anxious about the condition of the Empire, but the future of the Ch'ing dynasty touched them in a more personal way and monopolized their interest. Yet there were very many Chinese scholars who also regarded European ways as inimical to the Confucian state. Their fears were expressed by Liu Hsi-hung, a member of the first permanent mission sent to the West. In a diary recording the establishment of a Chinese embassy in London, he wrote:

> But everything in this world has advantages and disadvantages. The West considers the building of steamships and trains as progress. But I dare not say whether this is real progress or retrogression. . . . If this comes from the Will of Heaven however, a man can do nothing about it. For example, with steamboats we Chinese did not at first want to imitate the foreigners, but now we have about twenty or thirty boats. Now we have steamboats, we must use more coal. To make more iron cannons we must have more iron. Having to use more iron and coal, and not being able to ask for them from Western countries, the question of opening mines arises. But then, what will be needed for the transport of coal and iron? What about the cost of labour and the difficulty of the roads? We must naturally then discuss the construction of railways. This shows how things are mutually related. One thing will lead to another, and we will not be able to refuse them.

Liu Hsi-hung had realized how fundamental was the process involved in modernization. It was impossible for China to accept only what it wanted from Europe and reject the rest. One adopted everything or nothing, and once embarked on a course of adoption, there would be no end to the undermining capacities of Western technology and finance.

'Let me give examinations to the scholars instead of the Manchus,' Hung Hsiu-ch'uan declared in 1843, after his fourth failure as a provincial candidate at Canton. When the enraged village schoolmaster threw his books to the ground, his mind seething with rebellious thoughts, it is doubtful whether any neighbour or relation realized that this gesture of exasperation was also the beginning of the T'ai P'ing revolutionary movement. Nor could anyone know that exactly ten years later in Nanking the Heavenly King, as Hung Hsiu-chuan was then to be styled, would hold the first T'ai P'ing government examination, open to all scholars regardless of qualifications. The potential of this national rebellion, the greatest of the nineteenth-century social revolutions in the world, was not lost on Karl Marx, who noted as early as 1853: 'Perhaps the next uprising of the people of Europe may depend more on what is now taking place in the Celestial Empire than on any other existing political cause.'

THE T'AI P'ING REVOLUTIONARY MOVEMENT (1851–66)

One of the direct causes of the popular revolutionary upsurge behind the T'ai P'ing movement was the Western impact on China. After the fiasco of the First Opium War there grew up a general impression among the southern Chinese that the future of the Ch'ing dynasty was uncertain. Although Hung Hsiu-ch'uan provided the single spark which lit the prairie fire, the size of the conflagration, once the flames had caught hold, was unprecedented and overwhelming. Most of the southern and central provinces remained under T'ai P'ing control for over a decade in spite of the ebb and flow of battle fronts. These were the populous areas of the Empire, accounting for over 200 million of the 430 million inhabitants. Given the scale and ferocity of the civil conflict, it is hardly surprising that estimates of casualties range from 20 millions to as high as 100 millions. There are no accurate statistics on the number of deaths but the extent of depopulation in areas affected by fighting can be gauged by the fact that in 1911 the census revealed a population between 375 and 400 millions. Added to the human toll was an irretrievable loss of historical buildings, art treasures, books, and outstanding works of craftsmanship. Besides the iconoclasm of the T'ai P'ing Christians, whose hatred of idolatry brought wholesale destruction to shrines and temples, whether Confucian, Buddhist and Taoist, over six hundred cities were stormed, for many of which ruthless pillage followed recapture by imperial forces or their Western allies. The costly defeat of the T'ai P'ings gave a respite to the weakened Ch'ing dynasty but the throne's reliance on the military, coupled with the embarrassing terms of the 'unequal treaties', paved the way for a more radical revolution that overthrew the Empire itself. On one hand the T'ai P'ing rebellion produced Yuan Shih-k'ai and a generation of warlords; on the other, tales of its heroic exploits moulded the character of Dr Sun Yat-sen, who as a boy cherished the nickname 'Hung Hsiu-ch'uan the Second'. Though the rebel defeat destroyed forever the chance that China might be converted to Christianity, the ideology of the T'ai P'ing revolutionary movement was significant in that for the first time it looked outside Chinese civilization for its inspiration. In this sense the T'ai P'ings indicated the direction of future national renewal, through democratic ideals to the Communist theory of today.

Starting in forested Kwangsi province, in the far south, the T'ai P'ings laid careful plans for their rebellion: recruits were hand picked and trained, understandings reached with clan groups and secret societies, effective military groupings arranged under able commanders, and adequate quantities of weapons and foodstuffs stockpiled. The leader of this determined movement was Hung Hsiu-ch'uan (1814–64). A Hakka whose ancestors had migrated from North China to Kwantung at some period after the T'ang dynasty and held various government offices under the Southern Sung (1127–1279), he was nurtured in an atmosphere of sturdy independence, acquiring an unswerving belief in nationalism as well as a pronounced dislike of the Manchus. After his third failure at the provincial examination in 1837, Hung Hsiu-ch'uan evidently had a nervous breakdown, which turned into a conversion to Christianity, a religion he encountered through the agency of Protestant missionaries and tracts in Canton. Seriously ill, he was visited by strange visions over a number of days, the import of which only became obvious to him in 1843 when he found a key in the half-forgotten Christian pamphlets. Thereafter, Hung Hsiu-ch'uan perceived himself as a man directly enlightened by God: he was to be the Heavenly King, God's own instrument in bringing about peace on earth and goodwill among men, Chinese and *wai hsiung ti*, 'foreign brothers'. A tragedy for the T'ai P'ing rebels was the coldness of the majority of Europeans living in China, especially those with commercial interests at stake or missionaries anxious over differences concerning doctrine. The T'ai P'ings initially regarded the Europeans as co-

Title page of the Old Testament in Chinese. The two dragons flying through the clouds and the calligraphy style of the Sung Empire were favoured by the T'ai P'ing Christians, whose authorized edition this was.

A popular drawing of battles in the T'ai P'ing revolutionary movement. The sketch records the intervention of 'terrible barbarians who have disturbed the peace of the people and the land': these were of course the European allies of the ailing Ch'ing dynasty.

religionists and allies against the Manchus: on both accounts they were to be cruelly disappointed.

The theology of Hung Hsiu-ch'uan was defective on some points, not least because his limited sources – the Protestant tracts he had been given in Canton – concentrated on the evils of the prevailing superstitions and of all forms of idolatry. God was presented not as the loving Father of the New Testament but as the angry and jealous God of the Old Testament, the Jehovah who destroyed cities and punished transgressors of the law by death. However, the astonishing early success of the T'ai P'ing rebellion and his own sincere belief in the divine origin of his visions left Hung Hsiu-ch'uan immune to charges of unorthodoxy, despite numerous attempts of Protestant missionaries to elucidate obscurities in his interpretation. He remained firmly convinced that he had been given 'a sword, and commanded to exterminate the demons, but spare his brothers and sisters'. His followers implicitly believed in the divine mission of the cause – the establishment of a Christian kingdom in China and the expulsion of the Manchu invaders – and were willing to accept a strict moral code of behaviour, in startling contrast to the imperial forces. The T'ai P'ings had to accept orders without question, tolerate a strict segregation of men and women, avoid causing any trouble to the people, relinquish personal property and disputes, and dedicate both mind and body to the struggle.

By 1850 the 'Society of God-Worshippers', the name of Hung Hsiu-ch'uan's followers since about 1847, was ready to defy the corrupt local administration in Kwangsi. The strength of his following had increased to twenty thousand, trained and organized for insurrection. First blood was drawn from 'the demons' in December 1850, when a force of government

Painting of Miao tribesmen by Joseph Castiglione, a Jesuit who arrived in Peking in 1715.

soldiers and local militiamen was overrun, a Manchu general falling in the engagement. A month later, in January 1851, Hung Hsiu-ch'uan assumed the title Heavenly King, the T'ai P'ing T'ien Kuo, or 'Heavenly Kingdom of Eternal Peace and Prosperity' being formally declared. The seriousness of the uprising was appreciated by the Manchus, but the dispatch of Lin Tse-hsu, the scourge of the opium traders, to handle the critical situation in Kwangsi was frustrated by the official's death on his journey south. Therefore efforts to contain rebel activities were unco-ordinated, with the result that Kweilin, the provincial capital, had to endure a siege lasting over thirty days. Although the T'ai P'ings did not capture the city, the action welded the rebels into an army, in which women had a place in the ranks alongside men. Undeterred, they marched northwards through Hunan, where proclamations attacking the Ch'ing dynasty and extolling the Christian religion attacted humble recruits but alienated the local gentry and scholars. Imperial units sent against the T'ai P'ings could not stem the triumphant tide of revolution: towns and cities found difficulty in resisting a rebel army swollen to 100,000, until in 1853 the Heavenly King entered Nanking. The capital of the first Ming emperor, Hung-wu, became 'Little Heaven', the capital of the T'ai P'ing T'ien Kuo.

The decision to move eastwards into the lower Yang-tze River valley instead of striking northwards through Honan in order to reach Peking proved a strategic mistake. At this juncture, a northern thrust by the T'ai P'ings would not have been opposed by either the militia armies soon to be raised by loyal *shih* or the Mongolian and Manchurian cavalry forces being hurriedly mustered from the steppe. Moreover, the robust southerners who formed the core of the T'ai P'ing army might have fared better in an all-or-nothing campaign in North China, where even the lukewarmness of the local population towards the rebel cause could have served to strengthen their own dedication; rather than, as was the case, the choice of Nanking for a permanent base took these unsophisticates into the richest part of Kiangnan, presenting them with the insidious problems of luxury and urban organization. The T'ai P'ings did make use of what was the 'key economic area' of the Empire, by conscription and voluntary recruitment increasing their military strength to over one million, but the retention of Shanghai for the Manchus by the Europeans, who eventually launched an army from it to turn the T'ai P'ing flank, meant that after the northern expedition had turned back at Tientsin in 1854, the insurgents were on the defensive. The defence of Hopei, and therefore the imperial capital, against the T'ai P'ings was due to the raising of militia forces by diligent local officials and gentry, in response to an order sent out to all provinces on the fall of Nanking. Most formidable of the militia armies opposed to the T'ai P'ings was the 'Hsiang Army', created at Ch'ang-sha by the famous Hunanese scholar Tseng Kuo-fan (1811–72). The civil service examinations for the humble Tseng Kuo-fan, unlike Hung Hsiu-ch'uan, had opened the door to high office and fortune. His devotion to Confucian philosophy also led him to a belief in unqualified loyalty to the throne, a duty he was willing to undertake even if he was looked upon as cruel and stern. At Ch'ang-sha in 1853, Tseng Kuo-fan deemed local conditions to be so out of hand that he imposed martial law, executing one hundred people in two hundred days, for which he was branded 'the head-shaver'. By this name the inhabitants meant that he was fierce enough to go beyond the partly shaved head demanded of the Chinese by the Manchu authorities.

Needing warships to carry on a campaign against the T'ai P'ings along the Yang-tze and among the inland lakes, Tseng Kuo-fan built them. Foreign cannon were purchased to equip these vessels, and also for the use of the 'Hsiang Army'. After the rebellion was over, Tseng Kuo-fan pursued his interest in the manufacture of guns and ammunition and the building of ships: he became the chief advocate of modernization. There were dangers for the Manchus in such competence, as Emperor Ch'ing Hsien-feng was reminded by a Chinese official on hearing the news of the victory at Wu-chang in October 1853. He was told: 'Tseng Kuo-fan with the status of a Vice-President on home leave is no more than a mere commoner. A mere commoner staying in his native place rose up and by shouting a slogan could rally over one hundred thousand followers under his command. It is not a blessing to the Empire.' Thus, the emperor dropped his idea of a special promotion, leaving his ablest field commander with nothing more than an honorary title and no authority over officials in the provinces where he campaigned so

Nineteenth-century photograph showing two European missionaries in Chinese attire.

successfully against the T'ai P'ings. Of Tseng Kuo-fan, however, the court had nothing to fear, but the organization of the 'Hsiang Army' did create new problems. Based on close personal loyalties to its commander and officers, this excellent fighting unit, though unrecognized at the time, was the prototype of the personally recruited armies of the later warlords. Like the T'ai P'ings, the 'Hsiang Army' soldiers were expected to conduct themselves in a civilized manner, Tseng Kuo-fan's stern emphasis on Confucian morality finding reinforcement in the daily observation that the habitual tendency of imperial troops to pillage or pilfer was a reason for the support given to the rebels by the *nung*.

The furious massacres of opponents, rebel sympathizers, and innocent bystanders perpetrated by imperial troops found little or no counterpart in the actions of the T'ai P'ings. The religious idealism of the movement expressed itself in a revolutionary social programme which precluded wanton violence. Moral exhortation was aimed at all classes, none being excluded from the joyous life of the T'ai P'ing T'ien Kuo. An official publication declared:

> Scholars, peasants, workmen, and merchants should engage in their own occupations peacefully,
> Paying taxes and performing governmental duties obediently as ordered in regulations.
> Every kind of trade are they free to conduct,
> Excepting the prohibited articles – tobacco, opium, and wine – which must not be dealt with clandestinely.

In addition, the status of women was greatly improved, with opportunities for service on the battlefield or in administration. Foot binding was specifically forbidden, though the original T'ai P'ing countrywomen seemed not quite to understand how painful it was to have one's feet suddenly unbound. Throughout the rebellion we encounter an almost communistic attitude to society. Land reform – with a distribution to men and women on an equal basis – sought harmony: 'Cultivating land in common, eating rice in common, clothing ourselves in common, and using money in common, the people of every place will share equally and there will be no person who is not fully fed and warmly dressed.' What a difference from the corruption and inefficiency of the Manchu Empire! No wonder the European missionaries were split over Hung Hsiu-ch'uan's version of the Gospels; the Catholics saw him as a dangerous heretic, while the Protestants felt he led an unorthodox crusade against a decadent and pagan régime. To the European imperialist governments, of course, the T'ai P'ing revolutionary movement was an embarrassment, once the Second Opium War ended. The T'ai P'ing offer of free trade, except in tobacco, opium and wine, had no appeal now that they could develop the Treaty Ports and collect the customs dues against the indemnity. How hollow the British claim of intervening on behalf of international commerce really was can be judged by the fact that Nanking welcomed an average of thirty or more ships from Shanghai daily.

In 1860 the T'ai P'ings, overtures to the British at Shanghai proving fruitless, moved against the Manchu garrison in the port, hoping that a stratagem with members of the 'White Lotus' inside the city would win the day. To their surprise detachments of British and French troops were transferred from the foreign settlements to aid the imperial forces in a general defence. Dismayed by this unchristian invention, the T'ai P'ings withdrew, a misfortune for the Chinese inhabitants because the foreign soldiers then went on the rampage. The man responsible for British involvement was Rear Admiral James Hope of the naval station in Shanghai; he saw his duty as placing every obstacle in the way of the rebels, a pugnacity that in 1862 drew criticism from even the generally pro-government *Shanghai Times*. Reporting the rout and slaughter of an underarmed rebel column ten kilometres or so north of the port, the newspaper remonstrated:

> We believe that Admiral Hope is the first English officer of the present century who has adopted the unsoldierly practice of making war without

having declared war. Having recognised the T'ai P'ings as a Power, according to the usage of civilized nations, he ought to have given them the alternative of retreat, submission or butchery, before commencing the latter. This he did not – and if the code of honour has not changed since then, it has been grossly violated in the two recent attacks on the T'ai P'ings.

But Hope had his ear closer to the ground than the foreign residents of Shanghai appreciated. Within months there was an alliance between the British and Manchu governments to suppress the T'ai P'ings and foreign troops were dispatched up the Yang-tze River. The close season for shooting rebels had officially ended. Ning-po was also retaken from the T'ai P'ings, a considerable loss as large quantities of smuggled ammunition arrived there from Hong Kong and even Singapore, but the secondment of British officers, like General Gordon, to the imperial armies finally tipped the scales.

Hung Hsiu-ch'uan died in 1864, after a reign of thirteen years as Heavenly King. The leadership of the T'ai P'ing T'ien Kuo having long been divided on strategy, his death did nothing to improve matters. Aided and abetted by the 'Ocean Devils' – for the Europeans appeared to the rebels as 'the demons' and not fellow Christians in their cynical support of Peking – the Manchus gradually wore down resistance. Nanking was taken by the 'Hsiang Army'

General Gordon's bodyguard in the campaign against the T'ai P'ing Christians.

Manchu Bannermen. The guard assigned to the British Consul in Canton.

in 1854 and by the end of the ensuing year the last T'ai P'ing concentrations had been dispersed. Lord Palmerston had won a great victory though tales of wholesale massacre and dreadful sackings conducted by the imperial armies and their allies in the final stages of the conflict embarrassed him in Parliament that same year. For the mass of the Chinese people the betrayal was total, especially for those who had embraced Protestant Christianity, at a time when Taoism and Buddhism were losing their power, and had found spiritual succour as well as political direction in the T'ai P'ing movement.

ECONOMIC
DEVELOPMENTS

A by-product of the First Opium War was the beginning of Chinese curiosity about Europe. Lin Tse-hsu had ordered the translation of Western newspapers, and in 1844 he published, with another scholar, the *Hai-kuo T'u-chih*, or *Illustrated Record of Maritime Nations*, in twelve volumes. Contained in the book was information on paddle-boats, armaments and fortifications, for as the preface stated the aim was 'to increase knowledge and make preparation for practical purposes'. A similar motive possessed Tseng Kuo-fan after the T'ai P'ing rebellion, though this soldier-scholar considered that the purchase of adequate military equipment abroad would enable the Empire to resist England and France. The products of foreign technology rather than importation of the technology were preferred. A limited number of students went abroad to study and a few arsenals were established, one for naval forces near Shanghai in 1865, but there was no transformation akin to that experienced by Japan after the contemporary Meiji Restoration.

Why did China remain impervious to modernization before the foundation of the Republic? Why was the impact of the Treaty Ports on the economy of the Empire so limited? There are no easy answers to these questions and an analysis of economic developments during the last half-century of Manchu rule can do little more than sketch in the background to the entry of Chinese civilization into the twentieth-century world. As the imperial troops were to find to their cost in the disastrous Korean campaign of 1894–5, Japan was historically more open to foreign influences. Just as over two millennia it had been prepared to borrow culturally from the Chinese Empire, whose humiliating defeat in the Second Opium War served to underline the weakness of traditional oriental societies under siege by European guns, so in 1868 Japan turned to the modern world for a means of effective self-defence. The dissident aristocratic forces behind the Meiji Restoration swept away an inefficient feudalism in order to preserve Japan through selective westernization. Outside Japan, the colonial port cities – Calcutta, Bombay, Madras, Karachi, Colombo, Singapore, Batavia and Manila – created westernized Asian élites, for whom national independence was a goal that could be pursued without apology or a sense of contradiction. Not so in Shanghai or Tientsin, despite the interest of the 1898 reformers in the institutions of the Treaty Ports; K'ang Yu-wei remained steadfast in his belief of gradual amendment within the context of the Manchu Empire till as late as 1908. In contrast to colonial India, where foreign rule fostered a national consciousness as well as a belief in the value of Western models for government and administration, the Treaty Ports only sharpened the traditional Chinese insistence on a self-sufficient and self-satisfied identity. The intervention of soldiers from

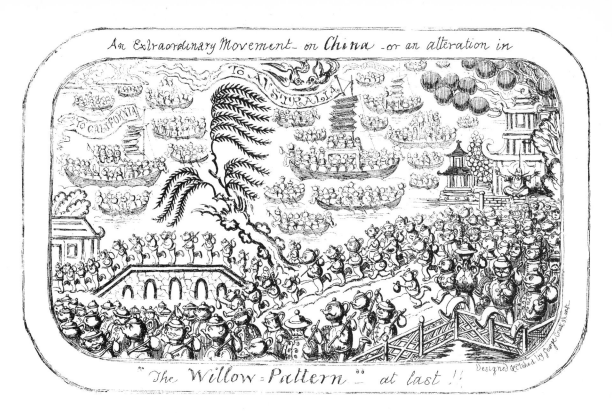

An Extraordinary Movement on China — or an alteration in

"The Willow = Pattern" at last!!

Cruikshank engraving on the subject of Chinese emigration overseas. It appeared in the *Comic Almanack*, 1853.

Shanghai in the T'ai P'ing rebellion impressed upon neither the *shih* nor the *nung* a consciousness of European superiority: they merely noted the better arms.

Other than shipping and armaments, there was a general reluctance on the part of the Chinese to purchase foreign manufactured goods, a disinclination not attributable to xenophobia. The disappointment of Lancashire mills – their anxiety over the smallness of exports to China stood behind the article that internal customs duties be controlled in the Treaty of Tientsin – resulted from a failure in competition with the native handicraft industry. A trade report of 1866 pointed out that:

> Cotton is grown extensively in China, and the people weave it into a coarse, strong cloth which is much better suited to the wants of the peasants and working men than the more showy but less substantial product of Foreign machinery. The customers of the British manufacturer in China are not the bulk of the people but only those who can afford to buy a better looking but less useful article.

The Empire was no backward economy. It had an elaborate system of production and distribution, which during the first half of the nineteenth century in *per capita* terms probably compared favourably with Europe. With no vacuum to fill, therefore, the foreign capitalists in the Treaty Ports discovered penetration of Chinese markets very difficult and the indigenous industry by virtue of its sheer size was able to cope with growing internal demand as well as exports. The Empire managed without technological innovation, the emperor shopping internationally for major items of manufacture and leaving external trade to the Treaty Ports. The political upheavals of the century from 1851 have blinded some historians to the resilience of the traditional economy, which in decline though it surely was, did not hit rock bottom till the late 1920s – the aftermath of the Warlord Era. Where, for instance, entirely new commodities were introduced into the economy, such as kerosene and cigarettes, the *shang* were quick to handle their distribution and in the case of the latter had by 1915 acquired a stake in the market as producers using Chinese raw materials.

The Treaty Ports were as isolated in China as the colony ports of the Portuguese had been earlier throughout Asia: they were peripheral. This does not imply that they were economically insignificant themselves. Their parasitic functions, as centres of financial speculation and international commerce, made them massive for the reason that the Empire was so vast and populous. Before the First Opium War, Shanghai, eventually the biggest city in China, handled a volume of shipping equal to that of London. Only Manchuria under the colonial rule of Japan experienced accelerated development. Eccentric and largely unoccupied prior to 1900, this province was a relative frontier, an area unlikely to hinder planned Japanese investment. The vehicle of change elsewhere was more indirect: modernization came through the educational activities of the missionary societies, not the businessmen, native or foreign, living in the Treaty Ports.

Despite the inveterate prejudice of officials against the 'barbarians' and the obstructionism of Dowager Empress Tz'u Hsi, a number of modern enterprises were started. Incorporated in 1873–4, the China Merchants Steam Navigation Company was the first marine venture to be owned and operated by the *shang*. Five steamers had been built in Chinese shipyards before the death of Tseng Kuo-fan in 1872 but there was to be no modernized navy available against the Japanese in Korea. New methods were introduced for mining and manufacturing textiles, whilst a national telegraph system linking principal cities helped to speed communications. Resistance to improved transport facilities outside Manchuria centred on the construction of railways. The first line in China, built in 1876 to connect Shanghai with Woosung, had to be torn up within two years on government instruction. The local inhabitants were distraught at the 'fire-carriages', fearing that their coming would disturb the natural harmony of the land.

Another economic development was migration overseas. To the adventurous or impoverished Chinese of Kwantung and Fukien the countries of South-east Asia, known as the Nanyang or 'Southern Ocean', offered an escape from an agricultural life at home that was being slowly but progressively lowered in standard by the pressure of increased population. Though there were Chinese settlers in Sumatra at the time of Cheng Ho, the main wave of migration overseas coincided with the nineteenth-century movement of people out of Europe. The two streams actually met in the gold-rushes, where the Boston *Bankers Magazine* reported in amazement that 'Chinamen, hitherto the most impassive and domestic creatures of the universe, have started into new life at the tidings of mines and have poured into California by the thousands'. One can only presume that in 1860 Boston had not heard about the T'ai P'ing rebellion; nor could there have been any knowledge of the Malayan tin-miners' wars, in which Chinese fought each other as well as Malays. But most settlers who braved imperial restrictions on travel abroad

Eighteenth-century porcelain figure of a goddess.

OVERLEAF Street scene before an open-air theatre. Stages were usually placed opposite temples.

天子萬年

were not engaged in mining: either they opened up new land for farming or started trading and manufactures in existing towns. Encouragement of Chinese settlement was the policy of the Brooke family, the 'White Rajahs' of Sarawak, a principality in Borneo obtained from the Sultan of Brunei. Sibu became known as 'New Foochow' because of the influx of farmers from Fukien. Large concentrations of migrants appeared earlier in the British Straits Settlements of Penang, Malacca and Singapore. When Stamford Raffles occupied Singapore in 1819 there were only one hundred and twenty Malays and thirty Chinese inhabiting an obscure fishing village. Two years later, the architect of British imperialism in the archipelago was gratified to observe that the Chinese population of the colony had risen to over one thousand, some of whom had come by sea direct from Amoy. The British belief in the presence of a large Chinese community as a proof of prosperity laid the basis of the present state of Singapore, with more than two million Chinese citizens. Though envied for their new-found prosperity by the local inhabitants, and even the object of savage persecution by the Spaniards in the Philippines, the Chinese migrants steered an independent course, maintaining their own culture and declining involvement in local politics. They still looked to China as their homeland and gave aid to Dr Sun Yat-sen, himself an overseas Chinese, in the struggle to overthrow the Manchus.

TZ'U HSI AND THE END OF THE IMPERIAL SYSTEM

No one did more than Dowager Empress Tz'u Hsi to delay a programme of modernization. Manchu supremacy and her own enjoyment of power informed the Machiavellian web of intrigue she so cleverly spun. A favourite concubine of Emperor Ch'ing Hsien-feng, she rose to be co-regent with Empress Tz'u An on the Emperor's death in 1862. With a single-minded ruthlessness that estranged even her own son, the child-emperor T'ung-chih, she liquidated rival princes and relegated Tz'u An to obscurity. Inspired by the memory of Empress Wu, who had interrupted the T'ang dynasty in 690 to become the only woman in Chinese history ever to don the yellow robe, the colour reserved for emperors, Tz'u Hsi and her eunuchs ruled the court at a time when the Empire was harassed by enemies without and vexed by increasing dislocation within. It could not have been worse: incompetence and obscurantist reaction typified the last years of the Ch'ing dynasty.

Relations between Emperor Ch'ing T'ung-chih and his dominating mother reached a climax in 1872 when the moment arrived for the imperial marriage. Tz'u Hsi prohibited her son from visiting his wife, a girl favoured by Tz'u An, and sought to interest him in her own candidate, whom she introduced as an imperial concubine. In disgust T'ung-chih abandoned all the ladies of the Purple Forbidden City and frequented the brothels of the capital, whence he contracted venereal disease and died two years later at the age of nineteen. As a replacement, Tz'u Hsi installed on the throne a three-year-old nephew, the Emperor Ch'ing Kuang-hsu. The death of Tz'u An in 1871 left her unrestricted scope for machination but she had to reckon with an unexpected vein of independence in the emperor, who responded to the national crisis following the Sino-Japanese War by embracing the reform movement led by K'ang Yu-wei.

Conflict between China and Japan had been brewing for several decades as

ABOVE Embroidered *ch'i-lin*, the Chinese unicorn. At the birth of Confucius one appeared and spat out a piece of jade on which it was written that the philosopher would be 'an uncrowned emperor'.

An imperial audience. The sign over the entrance reads 'Eternal Son of Heaven'. A late nineteenth-century illustration.

The would-be reformer, Emperor Ch'ing Kuang-hsu, and his brother.

OPPOSITE ABOVE
The Summer Palace, Peking. Funds intended for the navy were diverted by T'zu Hsi, with the result that at the battle of the Yalu River the Chinese sailors found themselves without adequate supplies of ammunition.

Tokyo, imitating the European powers, looked for territorial gains from the Manchu Empire. Two areas had a particular attraction for the Japanese: Taiwan and Korea. Anticipating pressure on the Manchu homeland if Korea fell under Japanese influence, the Ch'ing court drew its vassal, the Korean king, closer to China. In 1884 a mixed Chinese and Korean force, led by Yuan Shih-k'ai (1859–1916), defeated the pro-Japanese faction and dispersed Japanese troops secretly backing it. Not until 1894 did circumstances bestow on Tokyo the desired opportunity for large-scale intervention. When the Korean ruler, unable to suppress a rebellion, appealed to China for military aid, the Japanese swiftly seized Seoul and installed a new monarch. In the ensuing war, Japan won crushing victories on land and sea. All the ships in the small, but modern, imperial fleet were sunk by the Japanese at the battle of the Yalu River. This force, the lineal descendant of Tseng Kuo-fan's pioneer scheme, had been left with virtually no ammunition, and there was a public outcry once the news got about that funds intended for the navy had been diverted by Tz'u Hsi to build a new Summer Palace near Peking. It revealed that China had only been playing at modernization. Manchu halfheartedness towards naval power, so patently the tactical advantage of their European competitors, resulted from a distrust of the southern Chinese, who provided both ratings and officers. To Tz'u Hsi any change which might remotely threaten the Ch'ing dynasty had to be resisted, whatever the price. And for China the price was very high indeed. The harsh terms of the Treaty of Shimonoseki (1895) gave independence to Korea, a first stage towards formal annexation by Japan in 1910; ceded to Tokyo the Liao-tung peninsula and Taiwan; involved the payment of a huge indemnity, and accorded Japan the status of 'most-favoured-nation'.

Spectacular defeat should have been enough to convince the court that modernization was overdue. Japan, minute in comparison with the Empire,

K'ang Yu-wei, foremost intellectual and reformer at the end of the nineteenth century.

had shown its potency and there were scholars ready with constructive suggestions for innovation. Whilst the European powers, at Russia's behest, had combined to deny the Liao-tung peninsula to Japan, they had presented a fresh set of demands themselves. Germany secured the 'lease' of Tsing-tao, Britain Wei-hai-wei, France Kwangchow Bay, and Russia Dairen as well as the right to build the so-called Chinese Eastern Railway through Manchuria. From 1895 there was a continual succession of memorials pleading for modern studies and examination reform. By June 1898 Emperor Ch'ing Kuang-hsu considered it was safe to espouse change. He gave his confidence to K'ang Yu-wei and a series of imperial decrees announced the reform of the civil service examinations, the establishment of westernized schools, the modernization of the armed forces, and economic measures, including central planning, modern banks, the opening of mines and construction of railways. But the Hundred Days of Reform were more than Tz'u Hsi could stomach. Fearing that these policies would curtail her influence, she rallied the conservative elements, Manchu and Chinese alike, and plotted a *coup d'état*, which the emperor attempted to forestall by ordering Yuan Shih-k'ai, commander of a modernized army in the vicinity of Peking, to arrest the dowager empress. For reasons of his own, the general disobeyed: the reforming officials fled

abroad and it was Emperor Ch'ing Kuang-hsu who was imprisoned in one of the lake palaces adjacent to the Purple Forbidden City. Because of possible reaction from Western nations, who might have been sympathetic towards a reforming emperor, Tz'u Hsi did not dare to execute Kuang-hsu immediately, but thereafter it was obvious that the court would oppose any fundamental change in Chinese society and serious revolutionary activity concentrated on the extinction of both the Ch'ing dynasty and the imperial system. In place of K'ang Yu-wei's constitutional monarchy, the vision of the future was now Dr Sun Yat-sen's republic.

The height of folly was the encouragement Tz'u Hsi gave to the Boxers. About 1898, members of the secret society called the 'Righteous Harmony Fists' enlarged their sacred boxing to include attacks on Christian missions and foreign importations like telegraph lines. Originating in Shantung, a province where the concessions of Wei-hai-wei and Tsing-tao had just been granted, the Boxers spread their anti-foreign agitation to the capital, and, with the support of imperial troops, assaulted the Legation Quarter. One had no need of a crystal ball to foresee that the consequence of the Boxer Rebellion of 1900 would be a punitive expedition of soldiers drawn from all the countries with an embassy in Peking. The despoliation of the capital by the allied troops rivalled the atrocities of the Mongols, a testimony to the thoroughness of their commander-in-chief, Field-Marshal Count Von Waldersee, whose orders from the Kaiser were 'to give no quarter and to take no prisoners' so that 'no Chinese will ever again dare to look askance at a German'. Massive reparations, the punishment of war criminals, permanent garrisons of foreign soldiers in the capital, and a five per cent import tariff: these were the terms of capitulation and they underscored the utter bankruptcy of the Ch'ing dynasty. Had it not been for the American declaration of an open door policy, whereby China was to remain a free, open market, there is every reason to suppose that the spheres of influence of the various imperial competitors would have developed into colonial possessions. As it was, the Russians stayed on in Manchuria for five years, till total defeat in the Liao-tung peninsula during the Russo-Japanese War (1904–5) and revolution at home persuaded the Tsar that President Theodore Roosevelt was right in advocating non-intervention.

Again, modernized Japan had shown the way. Not only did the victory over Russia confer mastery of the sea in the region but more important it demonstrated that a properly equipped oriental country could beat an occidental one. Pressures for reform in China mounted and, in 1905, after nearly two millennia of service, the examination system was abolished. By 1911 there were one and a half million students in 52,000 modern schools, and another 100,000 students in Protestant mission schools. When Tz'u Hsi expired in 1908, having arranged for the captive Emperor Ch'ing Kuang-hsu to join her in death, there was a sudden vacuum at the centre of the Manchu Empire. The draft constitution of that year was more autocratic than its Japanese model, but with only a child-emperor on the throne the Manchus could not hold on to the privileged position their drafters had tried to secure. Conditions were suited to revolution and the accidental discovery of a plot in Hankow triggered a nation-wide uprising that swept away the Empire and allowed Dr Sun Yat-sen to be sworn in as the first president of the provisional government of the Chinese Republic at Nanking on 1 January 1912.

Part of the funeral procession of the Dowager Empress T'zu Hsi, who died in 1908.

Japanese torpedo-boat in action against Russian warships during the Russo–Japanese War of 1904–5. How the Japanese saw their technological triumph.

6

The Republic

In a dispatch published on 7 September 1909, the Peking correspondent of *The Times* lamented 'the deplorable weakness of the central government, where since the fall of Yuan Shih-k'ai, there seemed to be no man competent or willing to assume responsibility'. The regency of Prince Ch'un, the brother of the late emperor and the father of the child-emperor, Ch'ing Hsuan-t'ung, was unimpressive: his misreading of the political and economic situation caused dismay to reformers and republicans alike. He handled affairs of state clumsily and failed to curb the rampant corruption of the administration. Even the military reforms of Yuan Shih-k'ai were endangered by the sale of commissions and the neglect of training for new recruits in the Northern Army. Out of office, living in compulsory retirement since the death of Dowager Empress T'zu Hsi, the fifty-year-old general bided his time, for, as he was to advise a friendly commander sent against the revolutionaries in 1911, the best policy was: 'Go slowly and wait and see.' On his recall, Yuan Shih-k'ai wanted to ensure terms of appointment coincident with his own far-reaching ambitions.

The circumstances for this return to power were brought about by the activities of the Alliance Society, the 'T'ung-meng-hui' of Dr Sun Yat-sen. Its members staged ten revolts in South China and attempted seven assassinations before the incident at Hankow sparked off a general uprising. Most ominous for the Ch'ing court was the presence of disaffected officers and men belonging to modernized regiments among the Hankow revolutionaries. Fearing their example might be followed by other units of the Northern Army, which Yuan Shih-k'ai had created, the Manchus turned again to the retired general and entrusted him with supreme command against the rebels. But they hesitated over his demands for a national assembly, the formation of a responsible government, the legalization of political parties, and the guarantee of adequate funds for the armed forces. At a slow and deliberate pace Yuan Shih-k'ai reasserted imperial authority north of the Yang-tze River, eventually arranging a ceasefire with the rebels, now settled at Nanking. Frantic over the extent of sympathy for the insurrection in the provinces, the Ch'ing court made the commander-in-chief prime minister as well and allowed him to negotiate an end to the civil war. Yuan Shih-k'ai's moment had come. The agreement reached between the two sides was the establishment of a republic, Sun Yat-sen being sworn in as the first president of the provisional government in Nanking but prepared to step down in favour of Yuan Shih-k'ai, once the latter had secured the abdication of Emperor Ch'ing Hsuan-t'ung. When the commanders of the Northern Army urged by telegram the

THE WARLORD ERA
(1912–28)

Dr Sun Yat-sen and Chiang Kai-shek, who in 1923 was appointed as the first commandant of Whampoa Military Academy, near Canton.

President Yuan Shih-k'ai, dressed as the One Man, on his way to celebrate the winter solstice.

ending of the dynasty, the formal procedure for abdication was set in motion, and Yuan Shih-k'ai emerged as the sole authority in North China on 12 February 1912. Three days later, he replaced Sun Yat-sen as president of the Republic, after a unanimous vote by the provisional senate at Nanking.

The European powers again had at the helm of China the 'strong man' they preferred. It is ironical that they were so willing to recognize the Peking administration as well as float the enormous loans necessary to finance Yuan Shih-k'ai's armies, whereas in Nanking the revolutionaries were such uncritical admirers of Western democratic institutions. However, this was *La Belle Époque*, when a self-satisfied and optimistic Europe, sustained by industrial technology and world-wide colonial empires, felt certain of its superior judgement concerning the affairs of the deceased Chinese Empire. Even so, there existed at this time a belief among the 'T'ung-meng-hui' that Yuan Shih-k'ai was in sympathy with the republican ideal. Sun Yat-sen appreciated the general's administrative ability and his military power, but hoped that the new president would be constrained by the constitution and the transfer of the capital to Nanking. In the event Yuan Shih-k'ai was astute enough to retain Peking and out-manoeuvre politically the Kuomintang, as the party of Sun Yat-sen became known from 1912. The country lacked an understanding of what was involved in the working of democratic institutions, and as a result the advocates of republicanism found themselves without popular support. As a British observer of the 1913 election remarked:

The election of members, whether of the National Parliament or of provincial assemblies, is absolutely unreal. . . . In Newchang, which is a town of some 100,000 inhabitants, the election of a parliamentary representative took place while I was there. Thirty-five voters recorded their votes, and of those thirty-five the majority were employees in the office of the local administrator. The public took no part and exhibited no interest in the proceedings.

Between the republicans, who were led by overseas Chinese and men driven abroad by the Manchu authorities, and the majority of the Chinese people, there was only one point of agreement: the overthrow of the Ch'ing dynasty. Once the abdication had occurred, Yuan Shih-k'ai guessed that he could make a personal bid for the throne, though his title might have to be king rather than emperor.

To consolidate his position as chief warlord, he had to weaken the local militia under the Kuomintang's influence, prevent lesser warlords from ganging up on him, undermine the confidence of the political parties, and increase his own military strength. Liang Ch'i-ch'ao, who resigned as a minister at the end of 1915 to organize opposition against the growing power of the president, declared that in the methods he chose to employ Yuan Shih-k'ai did 'not know the difference between a man and a beast. All he knows about human beings is that they fear weapons and love gold, and it is by these two things he rules the country. For four years, there have been no politics in Peking except the ghostly shadows of a knife and a piece of gold. . . . By bribery and terror, he has enslaved our people.' The European powers remained silent when the president suspended parliamentary government and let it be known that he was to don the yellow robe – by public request. But Japan was hostile to such a scheme because a modernized China, whether unified as a kingdom or an empire, would curtail its own plans for continental expansion. In 1914 the Japanese had seized the German-leased territory of Tsing-tao and other adjoining areas, but the Allies, concerned to restrict the theatre of the First World War, obliged Yuan Shih-k'ai to acquiesce in the arrangement. Then, in January 1915, Japan presented the Twenty-One Demands, whose purpose was the reduction of China to a virtual protectorate. With no hope of support from the European powers, now locked in total war, Yuan Shih-k'ai was forced to accept the least offensive demands. Japanese warships stood off the coast of China and army units were put on alert in Manchuria, yet Tokyo, facing the likelihood of a violent reaction from Chinese of all classes, decided that the occasion for pressing all the demands had not come. 'Sad and humiliating', Yuan Shih-k'ai admitted the treaty was. To a large number of Chinese the agreement of the president was very much more: it seemed that Yuan Shih-k'ai was about to betray the nation, as he had Emperor Ch'ing Kuang-hsu (1898), the child-emperor, Ch'ing Hsuan-t'ung (1912), and the Republic (1914). In him the Confucian virtues of loyalty and righteousness appeared singularly lacking.

In an atmosphere of suspicion and resentment, therefore, Yuan Shih-k'ai claimed that the Mandate of Heaven had passed to him. On 15 January 1916, the new dynasty, the Hung-hsien or Grand Constitutional Era, was formally announced. But both his political skill and his luck had deserted him, for this usurpation of authority was opposed not only by the republicans but even more important by the other warlords. The words that K'ang Yu-wei, the leader of the 1898 reform government, addressed to Yuan Shih-k'ai summed up the general sentiment. He wrote: 'What law is there under your rule? You think that since the Republic was created by you, it can be abolished by you? You are a conjuror who regards the rest of us as ants and termites completely at your disposal. The changes in recent years have left no impression whatever on your conscience.' There can be no doubt too that Japanese agents and money influenced uncommitted military leaders, yet had not the would-be emperor himself shown the way of strategic disobedience? Though Yuan Shih-k'ai was quick to disclaim imperial pretentions, the game was up and he died in the following June after a nervous illness caused by disappointment. The closest he ever got to becoming the One Man was the celebration of the winter solstice in 1914, when, typically, the ambitious president was conveyed to and from the Temple of Heaven in an armoured car. His legacy to the ailing Republic was a host of warlords who were neither Confucian generals nor officers of a national army: these opportunists, whom he had nominated or accepted as the provincial authorities in order to reduce the influence of the Kuomintang, were able to tap local resources and act independently after the chief warlord disappeared. It was Yuan Shih-k'ai's personal eminence that had permitted a comparatively peaceful transition from Empire to Republic: the political revolution was contained within the continuity of the military establishment. The decade from 1916 revealed the actual extent to which the country had disintegrated.

Though the national government at Peking never controlled more than the immediate environs, it remained a prize for the rival warlords to fight over because of the refusal of the European powers to recognize any other régime as legitimate. Financial motives were behind this persistence, for foreign loans were financed by customs duties which the European powers collected in the name of Peking. In 1917 one general attempted to restore the ex-Manchu emperor, but the intervention of other warlords sent him back to retirement. All that this move and the later Japanese restoration of Ch'ing Hsuan-t'ung as ruler of the puppet state of Manchukuo achieved was to discredit still further the imperial system. With warlords, large and small, fighting for the resources of the provinces, conditions steadily deteriorated. The troops themselves were ruffians in uniform, not even the remnants of Yuan Shih-k'ai's Northern Army ever having seen action against a foreign foe; they were garrison troops whose commanders turned the garrison areas into private estates. They intercepted taxes earmarked for the central government, intimidated civilian officials, and co-operated with the agents of absentee landowners in fleecing the peasant-farmers. Drainage and irrigation schemes fell into disrepair and communications were dislocated. Trade was paralyzed and capital fled from the countryside, where it was urgently needed, to be buried in the Treaty Ports. The *shih* were powerless before rifles, and the old civil service disappeared: the *nung* plagued by bandits, soldiers and famine, suffered dreadfully. 'There are districts', a British commentator wrote in 1931, 'in which the position of the rural population is that of a man standing permanently up to the neck in water, so that even a ripple is sufficient to drown him.'

Military rule alienated both *shih* and *nung*; its callous disregard for basic human rights, unalleviated by any sense of responsibility for the welfare of the people in times of distress, outraged the historical sentiments of the Chinese; it prepared conditions for the second phase of the revolution, that of the peasants. For the scholars, however, there was a means of escape from the tyranny of soldiers. Ex-officials, scholars, and aspiring students turned to education for employment, particularly in the new universities established along modern lines. The *shih* succeeded in retaining status indirectly, the May Fourth Movement soon demonstrating the continued vitality of their influence on national affairs. At the centre of this patriotic agitation of 1919 were the students and staff of Peking University. When the Treaty of Versailles awarded Tsing-tao to Japan, three thousand demonstrators assembled in T'ien An Men Square and then burned down the houses of pro-Japanese ministers. Backed by a less than comprehending nation, the new, young *shih* compelled the Peking government to withdraw its delegation from Versailles without signing the peace treaty.

With the various warlords fighting among themselves and seizing each other's territories, Sun Yat-sen made attempts to found an independent government in Kwantung. But the European powers steadfastly refused him financial and diplomatic support, and the failure of an expedition against the northern warlords forced his resignation in 1922. It was during his retirement in Shanghai that he met an important emissary, Adolph Joffe, who represented the newly founded Soviet Union. Even to Sun Yat-sen, the admirer of the United States, it was clear that Western democracy could not be the solution to China's problems. The prestige of Europe had been greatly shaken by the carnage of the First World War and the transformation of Russia through the Bolsheviks from a grasping, reactionary enemy into a progressive, helpful friend made a profound impression on China. Something was required that would suit Chinese traditions and yet lead the Republic towards urgently needed stability and unity. As a result of the agreement between the ex-president and the Russian envoy, members of the Chinese Communist Party joined the Kuomintang as 'individuals' and, under the leadership of Sun Yat-sen, prepared a new revolution to crush the warlords and reunite the country as a socialist state.

The government and army was to be left in the hands of the Kuomintang, whilst the Communists concentrated on propaganda and mass organization. To increase the military efficiency of the revolutionary forces, Chiang Kai-shek (1887–1975) was sent to the Soviet Union for training and on his return he became first commandant of Whampoa Academy, near Canton. Previously trained in modern techniques both in China and Japan, the course of advanced studies with the Red Army enabled Chiang Kai-shek to train a generation of famous generals – Kuomintang and Communist. His appointment also gave him an opportunity to build up a following within the Kuomintang, so that after the death of Sun Yat-sen on 12 March 1925, he assumed leadership of the Northern Expedition against the warlords. An incident two months later set the scene for the next stage of the revolution. On 30 May 1925 a crowd of students, demonstrating against the foreign-controlled police of the International Settlement in Shanghai for brutalities perpetrated on striking workers in a Japanese-owned mill, were fired upon

Chou En-lai on the Long March (1935). Born in a family long established as *shih*, he encountered Communism as a student in Paris.

with some fatal casualties by a police detachment. Chinese sentiment was aroused, though the current military government in Peking wavered. A national boycott of Japanese and British goods started and the injustice of extra-territoriality in the Treaty Ports became a focus of indignation. Taking advantage of the feeling directed against the compliant military, Chiang Kai-shek launched the Northern Expedition early in 1926. Resistance in South China was slight, as provincial warlords found their armies melted away before the intense heat of revolutionary fury. By the summer he reached the Yang-tze River; Wuhan, Nanking and Shanghai were occupied: but the victory brought the Communists and the Kuomintang into open conflict. The landlord and merchant elements backing Chiang Kai-shek were terrified by the incipient social revolution, as Mao Tse-tung (1893–1976.) incited the *nung* against the landowners and Chou En-lai (1898–1976) directed the restless *kung* in Shanghai. On 26 March 1927 Chiang Kai-shek ordered Kuomintang troops to co-operate with underworld toughs in attacking the rebellious Shanghai workers. By a quirk of fate, Chou En-lai escaped the massacre. Other prominent Communists were not so lucky, and henceforth the two sides remained bitter enemies, despite the Japanese invasion of China which produced a second united front.

THE KUOMINTANG AND THE CHINESE COMMUNIST PARTY

In 1928 the Kuomintang armies entered Peking. Although the Japanese tried to obstruct the final stage of the Northern Expedition, Chiang Kai-shek's troops bypassed Shantung, following the route of the Peking–Hankow railway, and easily drove off the forces belonging to the last northern warlord, Chang Tso-lin. His assassination in Manchuria by the Japanese, who blew up the train in which he fled, may not have been so opportune for the Kuomintang as at first appeared. Eight years later it was his son, Chang Hsueh-liang, commander of the expedition operating against the Communists in Shensi, who devised the Sian Incident, when at the point of a gun Chiang Kai-shek agreed to a truce and a united front against Japan.

The capture of Peking and the formal transfer of the capital to Nanking obliged the European powers to acknowledge the Kuomintang régime, though fears that Chiang Kai-shek might be a Communist lingered for some time. The attitude of the British was not untypical. On one hand they accepted the international status of the Chinese Republic; on the other, there existed a strong desire to treat China as an unorganized or dependent territory. Thinking clung stubbornly to the gunboat policies of Palmerston. The Treaty of Tientsin had guaranteed treaty powers the right of their warships to visit inland ports and the Admiralty took full advantage of the possibility of stationing vessels nearly two thousand kilometres up the Yang-tze River. The last gunboat in the Yang-tze River Flotilla, HMS *Sandpiper*, was launched as late as 1933. If a British firm had labour troubles or passport holders were in jeopardy, a gunboat would be sent to the area as a precautionary measure. To overawe the native Chinese it was customary for ships of the Royal Navy to salute each other with seventeen or twenty-one gun salvoes. A commander-in-chief once boasted to the Shanghai Chamber of Commerce that the officers and men in the Yang-tze River Flotilla exceeded the total number of fellow countrymen employed in trade pursuits on that river. In September 1926 some of these sailors took part in a bombardment which left between fifty and two thousand inhabitants dead at Wanhsien. Britain's ambivalence about the Chinese Republic was adroitly used by Japan to lend a degree of respectability to its own aggression.

Whilst Chiang Kai-shek was ready to press the European nations on the vexed issue of extra-territoriality, which the Foreign Office in London thought it advisable to concede, he avoided offering direct resistance to the increasing Japanese threat. Instead, he concentrated on 'extermination drives' against the Chinese Communist Party. To British observers in China the Generalissimo, as Chiang Kai-shek was styled, seemed a stronger and more consistent Yuan Shih-k'ai; he had ended the chaotic conditions of the Warlord Era, a return to which, business interests argued, would bring irrevocable ruin to trade and endanger the substantial investments already made in the Chinese economy. The fascist dictatorship favoured by the Generalissimo was recognized as such, but autocracy might prove to be the most effective means of developing China. They chose to overlook the uglier aspects of Kuomintang rule. Scant notice was taken of the political terrorism of the Blue Shirt Society, whose fanatical members swore personal allegiance to the Generalissimo, and the spoils of office, the vast fortunes amassed by Kuomintang leaders, went unremarked, even though it was known that Chiang Kai-shek personally used the craft of the Opium Suppression Superintendance Bureau to traffic in the drug. What Sun Yat-sen had striven to prevent most of all had happened – the Kuomintang military, like a more presentable set of warlords, had become the dominant force in the Republic, so that corruption was again endemic.

The three principles of Sun Yat-sen – nationalism, the people's livelihood and democracy – were not transformed into an inspiring ideology for the Nationalists, as the followers of the Generalissimo were called. Chiang Kai-shek embraced Christianity in 1927, yet his régime was not Christian: he admired Tseng Kuo-fan and quoted the precepts of the Confucian canon, though he repudiated the imperial system. Once Ch'iang Kai-shek had become the supreme leader, *ling-hsiu*, he expected unconditional loyalty from his followers. To what end he led them, to what kind of future, few could be certain. Worst still, nationalism alone seemed inadequate, especially when it meant in practice appeasement of the Japanese. Internecine conflict, first with rival generals, then with the Communists, consumed the Republic's strength and depleted its scarce resources: of the total expenditure of the Nationalist government in 1929, forty-eight per cent was spent on war. Chiang Kai-shek, the son of a well-to-do farmer, outdid all his military contemporaries in the most turbulent period of late Chinese civilization.

Five different offensives, each one more massive than the one preceding, were launched by Chiang Kai-shek against the Communist base areas in Hunan, Kiangsi, Hupeh and Kwantung, before Mao Tse-tung and his rural agitators had to break out on their famous Long March. The first two, launched in 1930 and early 1931, employing three hundred thousand troops, two hundred heavy guns and one hundred aeroplanes, were repulsed by a guerrilla strategy then being developed by Mao Tse-tung. The third encirclement, directed by the Generalissimo himself, was interrupted by the Mukden Incident, when in September 1931 Japan took advantage of local friction to seize the province of Manchuria and install the ex-Manchu emperor, Ch'ing

Chairman Mao. A renowned early portrait.

Hsuan-t'ung, as puppet ruler of a new state, called Manchukuo. Chiang Kai-shek resigned in December 1931, only to return with greater power shortly afterwards. Despite increased Japanese pressure, such as the attack on Shanghai and the infiltration of the provinces south of the Great Wall, the Nationalists consistently regarded the Chinese Communist Party as their principal foe. Responding to a boycott of Japanese goods, on 29 January 1932, Tokyo had sent into Shanghai via the International Settlement an expeditionary force of four thousand marines. To the general amazement of China and the world, the Nationalist forces stationed in the city were still fighting the invaders a month later, by which time the Japanese had committed thirty thousand men. After thirty-four days of indiscriminate bombing and atrocity, Japan obliged the Nationalists to accede to a humiliating peace, whereby they agreed to stop anti-Japanese agitation, which had become nation-wide.

'The history of modern China', wrote Mao Tse-tung a few years afterwards, 'is the history of imperialist aggression.' The continued siege of China *was* the prerequisite historical condition for the success of the Communist Revolution. In this perception of the unusualness of the Chinese situation Mao Tse-tung parted company with Marxism-Leninism as propagated by Moscow. To understand such a fundamental divergence of view it is necessary to look back several years. Mao Tse-tung has remarked,

> From the time of China's defeat in the Opium War of 1840, Chinese progressives went through untold hardships in their quest for truth from the Western countries. . . . Chinese who then sought progress would read any book containing the new knowledge from the West. . . . In my youth, I too engaged in such studies. . . . Yet imperialist aggression shattered the fond dreams of the Chinese about learning from the West. It was very odd – why were the teachers always committing aggression against their pupil?

The country had become a 'joint colony', declared the 1922 Manifesto of the Second Congress of the Chinese Communist Party, because foreign powers 'not only occupy their broad territories, islands, protectorates and new colonies, but have robbed China of many important harbours in order to create foreign settlements; and finally have divided China into several spheres of influence in order to realize their monopolistic exploitation.'

The first cells of the Chinese Communist Party had come into existence during 1920 at Shanghai, Peking and Ch'ang-sha. The leader of the latter group was a poor Hunanese school teacher named Mao Tse-tung. Perhaps the lack of a European language prevented him from going abroad under the Work-study Scheme, a venture sponsored by a group of leading *shih* for those who wished to study in France. Others avid for Western knowledge saved the fare to France, where they combined employment in factories with part-time education. Perhaps an instinct advised Mao Tse-tung to remain at home. Later he told Edgar Snow, the first Westerner to receive an interview: 'I felt I did not know enough about my own country, and that my time could be more profitably spent in China.' His decision to stay helped to shape his original outlook on the world: it led to his understanding of peasant problems and the revolutionary dynamic inherent in the great agrarian revolts of the past. Mao

Tse-tung came to argue that the impoverished peasantry would be able to wage protracted war from revolutionary bases situated in remote areas because it was at places where the control of the Nationalists was weakest that the sparks of revolution could be lit. 'A single spark can start a prairie fire.'

This unique development of Marxism–Leninism was not a sudden revelation. The May Thirtieth Movement of 1925, its strikes, boycotts and agitation, helped the Chinese Communist Party; membership rose in six months from about one thousand to ten thousand, excluding youth members; and even the Kuomintang purge in Shanghai failed to deter confidence in urban risings. The Chinese Communist Party, following Moscow's directions, attempted in 1927 to seize large southern cities, such as Canton, Nan-ch'ang and Ch'ang-sha, but were defeated with heavy loss.

Because of Mao Tse-tung's experience with peasant organization – he had been in charge of a training college of organizers for the peasant movement near Canton in 1925 – his task was planning and directing the Autumn Harvest Rebellion in Hunan and Kiangsi. The autumn was chosen as the time that peasant farmers were most likely to support any rebellion, since it was during the autumn harvest that taxes were collected, even though in some places they had already paid five years in advance. The rebellious *nung* were expected to assist the proletarian *kung* in the capture of Ch'ang-sha. On the day, the city workers remained lukewarm and Mao Tse-tung retreated with the remnants of his column, about one thousand men, to the mountainous terrain of Chingkangshan. There he joined forces with the survivors of the 'Red Army', mutinous units of the Nationalist garrison at Nan-ch'ang, and with their commander, Chu Teh (1886–1976), set up a revolutionary base area. Their programme redistributed land according to the size of a family and established representative councils of workers, peasants and soldiers, a method of government tried by the Bolsheviks. Unauthorized by Comintern, these 'soviets' were condemned by the Central Committee of the Chinese Communist Party in Shanghai as 'rightist', not least for the reason that Mao Tse-tung appeared to regard the industrial workers, the sacred proletariat, as auxiliaries of the peasants.

In spite of protests from Mao Tse-tung, the Chinese Communists accepted Stalin's instructions for renewed activities among the urban population. The year 1930 witnessed another series of disasters. Unwilling to condone the waste of revolutionaries in premature assaults on the cities, Mao Tse-tung decided to withdraw to the Juichin base area in Kiangsi, eastwards from threatened Chingkangshan. He was now convinced that the only strategy was 'encircling the cities with the countryside'. The city remained the instrument of control for the central government, as it had always been from the reign of the Emperor Ch'in Shih Huang-ti. Looking back on these difficult years in 1939, Mao Tse-tung concluded: 'the ruthless economic exploitation and political oppression of the peasants by the landlord class forced them into numerous uprisings against its rule. . . . It was the class struggles of the peasants, the peasant uprisings and the peasant wars that constituted the real motive force of historical development in Chinese feudal society.' What the Chinese Communist Party had to do was lead the peasant masses in their historic mission: the democratic forces of the countryside would rise to overthrow the bureaucratic feudalism supported by the cities, be it imperial or republican.

After the lifting of the fourth Nationalist encirclement of the Juichin base area in 1933, a victory the Kiangsi revolutionaries had gained by conventional rather than guerrilla tactics, the commanders of the reorganized 'Red Army' viewed as obsolete Mao Tse-tung's idea of prolonged rural struggle. The flight of the Central Committee from Shanghai to Juichin also served to strengthen this belief. As a result the Communists engaged in positional warfare during the fifth Nationalist offensive, and at the end of 1934 total defeat stared them in the face. Breaking out of the closing trap was the only resort.

On 16 October 1934 began the Long March, an epic of human endurance. In 370 days the Communists covered 6,000 miles: of the 80,000 men who broke out from the fifth encirclement only 20,000 survived the march. It was force of circumstances rather than deliberate planning that made the journey so long. A withdrawal to north-east Kweichow was the first objective, but it soon became clear that they needed an overall strategy. This was devised at the Tsunyi Conference in January 1935, when Chairman Mao emerged as the undisputed leader of the Chinese Communist Party. The Conference adopted the slogan 'Go north and fight the Japanese', an aim that made sense to the rank and file of the 'Red Army'. Summing up the Long March from the new base area at Yenan, in Shensi, Mao Tse-tung said on 27 December 1935:

> We say that the Long March is the first of its kind ever recorded in history, that it is a manifesto, an agitation corps, and a seeding-machine. . . . For twelve months we were under daily reconnaissance and bombing from the air by scores of planes; we were encircled, pursued, obstructed and inter-cepted on the ground by a big force of several hundred thousand men; we encountered untold difficulties and great obstacles on the way, but by keeping our two feet going we swept across a distance of more than 20,000 *li* through the length and breadth of eleven provinces. Well, has there ever been in a history a long march like ours? No, never. The Long March is also a manifesto. It proclaims to the world that the Red Army is an army of heroes and that the imperialists and their jackals, Chiang Kai-shek and his like, are perfect nonentities. It announces the bankruptcy of the encircle-ment, pursuit, obstruction and interception attempted by the imperialists and Chiang Kai-shek. The Long March is also an agitation corps. It declares to approximately two hundred million people of eleven provinces that only the road of the Red Army leads to their liberation. Without the Long March, how could the broad masses have known so quickly that there are such great ideas in the world as are upheld by the Red Army? The Long March is also a seeding-machine. It has sown many seeds in eleven provinces, which will sprout, grow leaves, blossom into flowers, bear fruit and yield a crop in future. To sum up, the Long March ended with our victory and the enemy's defeat.

The Generalissimo could not accept such a verdict, and Nationalist forces, largely Manchurian recruits, moved against the Yenan base area. In Sian and Lanchow arrangements were made to accommodate over one hundred bombers. Tons of bombs arrived. Rumour had it that a large proportion con-tained poison gas. This campaign, Chiang Kai-shek asserted, would be the final encirclement.

1938: a People's
University in Yenan.
The speaker may be
Mao Tse-tung.

The expeditionary commander, however, was less certain. Chang Hsueh-liang disliked the general trend of Nationalist policies. His men could hardly be expected to welcome a fierce guerrilla campaign in Shensi when Japanese armies were looting and raping their native provinces. Nor could he understand the Generalissimo's readiness to oblige Japan in suppressing outbursts of Nationalist feeling. When Chang Hsueh-liang was unable to secure the release of prominent leaders of the National Salvation Movement, arrested for anti-Japanese sentiments by the Nationalist police, he told Chiang Kai-shek that his 'cruelty in dealing with the patriotic movement of the people is exactly the same as that of Yuan Shih-k'ai'. But the Generalissimo underestimated the depth of feeling throughout the northern armies and arrived at campaign headquarters in Sian determined to expedite the war. On 12 December 1936 Chiang Kai-shek found himself the prisoner of Chang Hsueh-liang and Yang Hu-ch'eng, commander of the Shensi army. Two events had tipped the scales towards military insurrection. The first was the signing of the German-Japanese anti-Communist agreement, which Italy

Devastated Nanking railway station, after a Japanese air-raid in November 1937.

tacitly supported. As a result the Italians established diplomatic relations with Manchukuo, and, infuriated, Chang Hsueh-liang told his officers: 'This is absolutely the end of the Fascist movement in China!' Secondly, the army of Hu Tsung-nan, the only Nationalist forces actively engaged in attacking the Yenan base area, suffered a severe defeat from the Communists at Holienwan. 'Chinese should not fight Chinese' propaganda by Communist agents and effective guerrilla tactics were responsible for the startling reverse.

The Chinese Communist Party immediately offered to support Chang Hsueh-liang against the Japanese. Chou En-lai arrived in Sian with a negotiating team and at last the Generalissimo was persuaded to end his harassment of the Communists: the second united front had come into existence. Chairman Mao first initiated new proposals for co-operation with the Nationalists against Japan in the previous year. Apart from genuinely

Japanese bombing of Shanghai, August 1937.

wishing to rid China of Japanese aggression, the Chinese Communist Party desired war with Japan as a part of its plan for the ultimate triumph of the revolution. The technological superiority of the Japanese armies would ensure Nationalist defeats in positional warfare and their loss of control over many provinces. Though the Japanese might set up puppet administrations, they could not garrison the countryside and still have troops to conquer all China. Even in the already occupied north-eastern areas, the Japanese units were only at garrison strength in the towns and along the chief lines of communication. The villages, the focus of Mao Tse-tung's revolutionary agitation, would be left alone. Whilst Chiang Kai-shek might have to concede defeat in conventional operations, the Chinese Communists, who had ten years' experience of guerrilla warfare behind them, could be sure of being able to outlast the Japanese invasion. Chairman Mao noted in 1938:

> The richest source of power to wage war lies in the masses of the people. It is mainly because of the unorganised state of the Chinese masses that Japan dares to bully us. When this defect is remedied, then the Japanese aggression, like a mad bull crashing into a ring of flames, will be surrounded by hundreds of millions of our people standing upright, the mere sound of their voices will strike terror into him, and he will be burned to death.

When the people's guerrillas had gnawed away the invader's morale and fighting spirit as well as his military efficiency, the moment for a triumphant counter-attack would have come.

The Sian Incident enhanced the reputation of Chiang Kai-shek: he was acclaimed as the leader of national resistance to Japan. Within seven months

OVERLEAF The people, the victims of the Sino–Japanese War (1937–45).

another incident, this time an exchange of fire between Chinese and Japanese troops at the Marco Polo Bridge outside Peking, confirmed him in this unsought role. Instead of conducting negotiations, the Nanking Government had to acknowledge the hostilities as the beginning of the Sino-Japanese War. Peking fell in July 1937 and with the arrival of Japanese troopships at Tsing-tao and Shanghai heavy fighting became general. The Western powers stood aloof. With a war imminent in Europe, the British tolerated the Japanese violation of their treaty rights and even maintained a stiff upper lip when the British Ambassador's car was machine-gunned from the air. Japanese forces advanced rapidly up the Yang-tze River, sacking Nanking for a whole week. By the end of 1938 the Japanese held most of the coastline, the middle and lower Yang-tze valley, as well as north-eastern China. Resistance was stiff – a Japanese army met defeat in Shantung – and the determination of the Chinese clearly shown in breaching the Yellow River dykes. Millions died in the flooding but these 'scorched earth' tactics slowed the invader's progress.

The Imperial Japanese Army had never bothered to keep Tokyo fully informed about its actions in China. The military, heirs to the war-like traditions of the Samurai, dominated political life in Japan, especially after a significant number of civilian members of the government were assassinated in the early 1930s. The invasion of China was looked upon as a great adventure, an opportunity for a sweeping victory over a poorly equipped and trained enemy. The shock of not obtaining a complete surrender stunned the Japanese General Staff Headquarters. The Nationalists had retreated into the interior; established at Chungking, they remained far out of reach. The Communists had infiltrated the occupied zones, where they planted new revolutionary bases; though behind the front line, their sudden forays undermined Japanese authority because not enough soldiers were available for guard duties. China was too vast to occupy and her lack of industrial centres ruled out any vital blow: Japan could defeat conventional Chinese armies, but could never conquer China. In the face of Chinese resistance and the prospect of a long war, the Japanese military were relieved to discover the alternative theatres presented to them by the outbreak of the Second World War. The fall of France and Holland, the isolation of embattled Britain, and the distance of the United States from Japan, encouraged the belief that their rich possessions in East Asia could be easily captured. On 7 December 1941 the raid on Pearl Harbor crippled the American Pacific Fleet, and within twelve months Japanese forces threatened India and Australia. Western rule in East Asia disappeared: it was the end of a colonial era. Japan had underestimated the capacity of American industry as well as the strength of outraged American opinion; it had overestimated the ability of the Imperial Army and Navy to cope adequately with far-flung gains; but the sight of Western power crumbling in 1941 was never forgotten. 'The First World War,' Mao Tse-tung commented, 'was followed by the birth of the Soviet Union with a population of 200 millions. The Second World War was followed by the emergence of the socialist camp with a combined population of 900 millions.'

When in 1945 the dropping of the atomic bombs on Hiroshima and Nagasaki caused the surrender of Japan, the Nationalists were bottled up in the west and the Communists controlled the north, apart from the cities and large towns with Japanese garrisons. To whom these soldiers should surrender

'Scorched earth' tactics. Bridges, dykes and other facilities were destroyed by the retreating Chinese forces. Here a Japanese train crosses over a temporary bridge in 1939.

proved an immediate point of dispute. Though from 1938 onwards the Nationalists had remained inactive at Chungking, much to the embarrassment of their American advisers, Chiang Kai-shek, insisting that he was head of state as well as zone commander-in-chief of all Allied forces, demanded and obtained American air and naval assistance to transport five hundred thousand of his troops to the cities of Manchuria and North China. During the war with Japan the Generalissimo had maintained that he was only waiting for the right moment to strike, yet it soon became obvious that his equipment and military supplies, accumulating via the Burma Road and airlifts from India, were intended for later use against the Communists, not the invader. In addition to transport facilities, some fifty-three thousand US marines took up positions at strategic centres in Hopei and Shantung. According to the Assistant Secretary of State Dean Acheson, these were in China 'not for the purpose of any Chinese faction or group'. But to many people mediation looked oddly like intervention, especially once civil war was joined. Also the misconduct of American servicemen in Peking, where the rape of a girl student caused nation-wide protests, served to increase suspicions. An even more galling aspect of Nationalist policy was liaison with the supposedly vanquished Japanese. This is how an American diplomat recorded his bewilderment in a diary entry for 27 December, 1945:

> I still don't understand about the Japanese. Officially they are disarmed, but the fact is they never seem to be. In Shanghai fifteen thousand still walk the streets with full equipment. In Nanking the high Japanese generals are bosom buddies of the Chinese. In the north tens of thousands of Japanese soldiers are used to guard railroads and warehouses and to fight Communists. If you ask what all this is about the answer is either a denial or in more candid moments a 'Shhh, we don't talk about that.'

The contrast between the opposing sides, the Nationalists and the Communists, was very pronounced.

The Nationalists emerged from their long, self-elected isolation in the western provinces a spent force. They were even more reactionary and corrupted: out of touch with the contemporary situation, the officials seemed bent solely on recovering their former positions and prerogatives; efficiency and morale frittered away in idleness, the troops were unprepared for civil war, however modern their weapons. 'When marching through Shanghai', an American Consul noted in 1947, 'recruits have to be roped together. There have been repeated incidents . . . where groups brought here attempted to escape and were machine-gunned by guards with resultant killings.'

The Communists stepped up their activities in the countryside as soon as Japan surrendered. Columns moved beyond the Great Wall and entered Manchuria, which Russia had occupied in August 1945. The Soviet Union could have handed over its resources to the Chinese Communist Party, but the Russians waited for the arrival of the Nationalists in April 1946 before they dismantled and carted away most of the province's industrial plant. Large quantities of Japanese war material, however, did find their way into Communist hands. Stalin was at this time encouraging the Yenan Government to try coalition, and Mao Tse-tung even offered to visit the United States, when the intractability of Chiang Kai-shek threatened to sabotage every peace negotiation. Surfeited with surplus American arms, the Generalissimo misjudged his opponent's strength as well as the mood of the Chinese people. When in late 1946 large-scale battles restarted, the triumph of Communism was assured.

Mao Tse-tung's strategy of 'encircling the cities with the countryside' had its reward. In September 1948 he ordered Lin Piao (1908–71) to attack Mukden and the city fell on 2 November. The Nationalist collapse elsewhere in North China was swift. The 'Red Army', the instrument of the Chinese Communist Party, proved irresistible. The force was economically self-sufficient, burdening no one and receiving no pay as such. Like the military agriculturalists of Ts'ao Ts'ao, the Later Han general, each soldier was given a piece of land to cultivate, which was tilled by others when he was away fighting. Democratic in organization, the 'Red Army' was never allowed to

Chu Teh and Mao Tse-tung, the original Chingkangshan revolutionaries, confer during the civil war.

repeat the excesses of other contemporary armies. 'Our principle', said Mao Tse-tung, 'is that the Party commands the gun, and the gun will never be allowed to command the Party.' Relations with the people were therefore excellent, a unique experience for Chinese civilization, while in Nationalist-held areas racketeering and suppression prevailed. On 20 April 1949 the Communists swept across the Yang-tze River, their artillery near Nanking crippling the British frigate HMS *Amethyst* for 'a violation of Chinese waters'. It was the close of the gunboat era, though Chiang Kai-shek's refuge in Formosa was to enjoy the belated protection of the United States Seventh Fleet. As the same American diplomat had already noted in the reports he received on 'the vast countryside . . . another world; the Communists, perhaps as much through necessity as wisdom, are penetrating the villages and finding a response where for a long time no one has cared what happened or who thought what'.

CULTURAL
REVOLUTION
The abolition of the imperial examination system in 1905 was a trauma for the *shih*. Though the case for educational reform had been overwhelmingly made and accepted, the discontinuation of the ancient method of selection for public office represented more than a critical break with past traditions.

It compelled intellectuals to reconsider the role of the artist and thinker in the context of twentieth-century China. By 1922 the objectives of the new education system were listed as adaptation to a changing society; the promotion of democracy; the development of individuality; the economic advancement of the average citizen; and the achievement of universal education, while allowing flexibility to suit local circumstances. These liberal goals, a feature of growing American influence in educational thinking, replaced the authoritarian pattern copied in 1912 from Japan, a country which favoured the German aim of achieving power through education. But there were Western friends of China who still hoped that a strong man would set right not only the curriculum of the schools but even more the medium of instruction, the language itself. In 1928 Turkey was able to replace its archaic Arabic script with a simple Latinized system of writing as a result of forceful measures undertaken by Mustapha Kemal. When in the same year the Nationalist Government gave a half-hearted acceptance to the 'National Language Romanization' proposals, a Western supporter of language reform said: 'If China had a Kemal Pasha, we should probably see this system replace the characters in daily life.' Such an opinion grossly underestimated the difficulties in transcribing the Chinese language and overlooked the differences between Turkish and Chinese nationalism. Yet the debate on language reform – a contentious issue among Communists today – reveals how wide and deep was the cultural revolution of the early Republic.

The crusade for literary and language reform started with an article by Hu Shih (1891–1962). While a student at Columbia University in 1917, he sent 'Suggestions for a Reform of Literature' to *Hsin Ch'in Nien*, or *New Youth*, a magazine founded in 1915 that was to become the mouthpiece of the younger intellectuals. He advocated the adoption of *pai-hua*, or vernacular Chinese, as the national medium of communication and told writers that they should not hesitate to use colloquial words and expressions. 'In the history of change in speech and writing', he asserted, 'generally the common people are the reformers and the scholars and writers are the conservatives.' His target was the literary style associated with the imperial examination system, the preserve of the *shih*, whose official speech, the *kuan hua*, had served as the *lingua franca* of administration. On his return to China later in 1917 Hu Shih was appointed professor of philosophy at Peking University, where together with a number of like-minded teachers he strove to advance the vernacular, despite accusations by offended colleagues that the reformers used the 'cant of street vendours and rickshaw pullers.' Hu Shih countered with the argument that the general trend of Chinese literature has been its periodic appropriation of subliterary forms of popular entertainment: folk song, drama and fiction. In his studies on the heritage of vernacular literature and the future of *pai-hua* he recommended as subjects for the new writer: 'factory workers of both sexes, rickshaw pullers, inland farmers . . . domestic tragedies, marital sorrows, the position of women, the unsuitability of educational practices.' This view of literature as a mode of social criticism stood midway between the traditionalists, who urged the authorities to suppress publications in *pai-hua* because they expressed views harmful to the nation, and radicals, like Ch'ien Hsuan-t'ung (1887–1939), who demanded the destruction of the Chinese written language. Official resistance was overcome by the patriotic agitation

Modern China

SOVIET UNION

Chita

EASTERN CHINESE RAILWAY

MONGOLIA

Ulan
Bator

MANCHUKUO

Vladivostok

JAPAN

Tokyo

Hami

Mukden

KOREA

Tun-huang

Great Wall

Great Wall

Peking

Seoul

YENAN
BASE
AREA

Tientsin

Dairen

Lanchow

Pao-chi

Sian

Tsing-tao

Loyang

Ch'eng-tu

Wanhsien

Wuhan

Shanghai

Nanking

Hangchow

Ning-po

Chungking

Ch'ang-sha

Amoy

Taipei

Nan-ch'ang

TAIWAN

CHINGKANGSHAN
BASE AREA

Canton

Kunming

North

Hanoi

BURMA

LAOS

VIETNAM

	Burma Road
	Long March of 1934-5
	Grand Canal
	greatest extent of Japanese power before 1945
	major rail links
	international frontiers

0   300   600

km

of the May Fourth Movement, since following the demonstrations there appeared a growing number of magazines printed in the colloquial style and stating the case for Chinese Nationalism.

Outstanding as a modern Chinese novelist and social critic was Lu Hsun (1881–1936) who came from a scholarly family and whose real name was Chou Shen-jen. Described by Mao Tse-tung as 'the greatest and bravest standard-bearer of this new cultural army', Lu Hsun has received wide acclaim in the People's Republic. He was highly respected in his own lifetime, especially for his astringent essays and satirical stories on officialdom or outmoded custom, but his elevation as a national hero has occurred after 1949. After a classical Chinese education and a course in Western medicine in Japan,

Lu Hsun decided to concentrate on writing. Fame came from 'The True Story of Ah Q', which appeared in 1923 among a selection of pieces entitled *The Outcry*. Though perhaps overpraised artistically, the tale is a caustic commentary on the failings of contemporary society. Ah Q, a bone-headed odd-job man, envies his superiors and emulates their worst behaviour. His insignificance makes swanking difficult: as the village butt, he cannot find a victim to bully himself and he retreats into a make-believe world of 'spiritual victories'. The epitome of the ineffectiveness of China and the well-to-do people running the Republic, Ah Q's progress of self-deception and deceit struck chords in many readers. The supreme irony is the execution of Ah Q with foreign bullets. Expelled from his employer's household for amorous advances towards a maidservant, he leaves the district to join a band of robbers. When he returns to sell stolen goods, his desire for extra prestige leads him to pretend revolutionary ardour. Arrested by genuine revolutionaries who occupy the village and ally themselves with the local gentry, Ah Q is condemned for a crime of which he is innocent. The story concludes:

> As for any discussion of the event, no question was raised in Weichang. Naturally all agreed that Ah Q had been a bad man, the proof being that he had been shot; for if he had not been bad, how could he have been shot? But the consensus of opinion in town was unfavourable. Most people were dissatisfied, because a shooting was not such a fine spectacle as a decapitation; and what a ridiculous culprit he had been too, to pass through so many streets without singing a single line from an opera. They had followed him for nothing.

The machine-gun execution is entwined with the failure of the revolution to improve the lot of the poor. Lu Hsun's horror was the moral bankruptcy of the Republic, a characteristic of the period which eventually caused his embrace of Communism along with a large number of writers.

Early in 1924 Sun Yat-sen gave a series of lectures to Kuomintang members in Canton. These lectures, later published as *San Min Chu-yi* or *Three Principles of the People*, were an attempt to impress a social commitment on the nationalist movement. Sun Yat-sen seemed determined to take precautions against either embryonic Chinese capitalism getting the whip hand or the new leadership going into an alliance with landlord families. 'The land problem', he frankly admits, 'has not yet had any satisfactory solution in Europe and America. If we want to solve it we have to do it now. It would be too late if we should wait until our industry and commerce were developed. By that time the difference in wealth would be too great. . . . The best solution is the equalisation of land-ownership.' China needed to recover its ancient custom of rural co-operation, but with every family owning a share of land: a modern 'equal field' system. Had this aspect of his principle of the people's livelihood attracted support from the Kuomintang and the poverty of the countryside not been abandoned to the care of Mao Tse-tung, there is a possibility that modern Chinese history might have turned out differently. As it was, the pessimism of Lu Hsun was justified and in their daily life ordinary people suffered for decades the uncertainties of Ah Q.

No less riven by the twentieth century was the Chinese painter, though in the visual arts the challenge of the West arose more slowly and seems to have

A scroll painted by Ch'i Pai-shih (1863–1957).

been more readily absorbed within the native tradition. To Chinese unable to visit Paris the little Quartier Latin founded in Shanghai by returned artists was a sanctuary. It formed the nucleus of the European movement in the Republic, where conversation touched upon Surrealism and the Western *avant-garde*. But these artists were hopelessly isolated: at a distance from contemporary developments in Europe, their isolation from the mass of the Chinese people was underscored by their only patrons, the new commercial families who only sought flattering portraits or ornamental sculpture. With the growing threat from Japan and the bitter rivalry between the Nationalists and the Communists, the internationally minded artists belonging to the '*Société des Deux Mondes*' (1929–32) found their position becoming more and more untenable. And it was the outbreak of the Sino-Japanese War that dispersed these painters as well as the intellectuals and writers living in the coastal cities.

A major revival of traditional painting was stimulated by the patriotic response to this external pressure. Most significant was Huang Pin-hung (1864–1955), who received a classical Chinese education and worked as an editor in a publishing house. His style was not widely appreciated, and it is only since his death that his full stature as perhaps the last of the great painters in the *wen-jen* tradition has been generally realized. More unconventional and admired were the works of Ch'i Pai-shih (1863–1957). Lacking a formal education, he started life as a carpenter and turned to painting with few preconceptions. Individualistic and daring, his treatment of insects, birds and flowers, or scenery has delighted an audience both inside and outside China. The third distinguished traditional painter is Chang Ta-ch'ien (born 1899), renowned for his skill in imitating old masters. During the Sino-Japanese War he spent two years making an intensive study of the Buddhist cave paintings at Tun-huang. He now lives in Brazil.

7

The People's Republic

On 1 October 1949 Mao Tse-tung formally announced the creation of the People's Republic of China. The Mandate of Heaven had passed to the Communists, whose authority was only challenged in Hainan, Tibet, Taiwan and a few offshore islands. The failure of General Marshall's peace mission in 1946–7 should be seen as part of the Nationalist inability to recognize that the writing was already on the wall. Once General Marshall appreciated that he could no longer make any impression on the Generalissimo as to his military prospects, despite reports of the tenuous hold of Nationalist garrisons on the northern cities, he decided that further American mediation was foolhardy. Civil war and a Communist victory had become inevitable, providing in the meantime the Nationalist Government did not collapse through its own efforts, as unchecked inflation eroded the economy and destroyed Chinese currency on the foreign exchange market. Between the end of the Second World War and departure of General Marshall the official exchange rate between Chinese and American dollars increased from 20:1 to 73,000:1. When in September 1948 the American Embassy purchased a house in Nanking for 60,000 US dollars, the Central Bank of China did not have enough cash on hand to exchange the draft and the seller had to wait two days for more to be printed. By that time his money had depreciated twenty-five per cent. To print a Chinese note now cost more than the face value it bore.

Blame for the defeat of the Nationalists was firmly pinned on their own 'corruption and incompetence' in the American *White Paper* issued by the State Department during the summer of 1949. The document, a scathing attack on the Nationalist record, rested, Dean Acheson explained in an accompanying letter, on

> the unfortunate but inescapable fact . . . that the ominous result of the civil war in China was beyond the control of the government of the United States. Nothing that this country did or could have done within the reasonable limits of its capabilities could have changed the result; nothing that was left undone by this country has contributed to it. It was the product of internal Chinese forces, forces which this country tried to influence but could not.

Neither the Nationalists nor the Communists subscribed to the democratic ideal of the 1911 revolutionaries, yet it had to be admitted that the Chinese Communist Party alone understood the needs of the people. Mao Tse-tung took full account of the peasant-farmers' desire for land reform, honest and efficient administration, reasonable levels of taxation, and freedom from the

Answering to the people. A woodcut by Chen Wang entitled 'A slacker being criticized' (1951).

greed of the military. His writings too had an appeal for the educated classes; during the Yenan years Chairman Mao transformed the ideology of the Chinese Communist Party into something distinctly Chinese. The Mandate of Heaven belonged to the Hunanese schoolteacher and peasant leader who had never been abroad nor learnt a foreign language: Mao Tse-tung had achieved the successful combination of *nung* and *shih*, but unlike the first Ming emperor, he was not prepared to give the scholars a privileged position. From the outset he made it plain that their skills should be used for 'serving the people'.

The attitude of the United States to the People's Republic was 'waiting for the dust to settle'. The future of the Nationalists on Taiwan looked bleak. An army of three hundred thousand and a few naval vessels seemed a frail defence, especially during the spring of 1950 when the Communists developed their capability for amphibious operations in the capture of small off-shore islands held by the Nationalists. Even the return to power of Chiang Kai-shek, who resumed the presidency yet again in March, could not rally the political exiles. Then in June, North Korea invaded South Korea, and for 'security reasons' the United States espoused Taiwan, without reference to the United Nations, and sent the Seventh Fleet to shield the island from any attack. Was not Chiang Kai-shek still the legal head of state? Were not the Communists

Chiang Kai-shek as the President of the Republic of China (Taiwan). Behind is a portrait of Sun Yat-sen, whom the leaders of the People's Republic of China also consider the founding ancestor.

Chinese civil war.
A Communist attack on
a city during 1948
in North China.

usurpers of a properly constituted republic? Was not Mao Tse-tung a tool of the Russians? Were not the Nationalists on Taiwan manning a bastion of the Free World? Such arguments accommodated this shift in American policy, which culminated in the signing of a mutual defence treaty late in 1954. That the Ming partisans on Formosa had not been able to reconquer China in the seventeenth century was an historical fact both parties chose to forget. That the Western notion of legality had no counterpart in the Chinese political thinking likewise disturbed neither of them. It suited Washington and Taipei to ignore the rejection of the Nationalists by the mainland Chinese. Although the United Kingdom recognized the People's Republic, moves initiated by the Soviet Union and India to have the United Nations unseat Taiwan came to nothing. Possibly the Americans would have reconsidered their position after the Korean War had they not become deeply involved in Vietnam; for the United States inherited the strategic problems of the Japanese Empire and over two decades it struggled as ineffectively to reach a military solution. Meanwhile, Chiang Kai-shek with two million exiles was allowed to misgovern nine million Taiwanese; and Mao Tse-tung, Chairman of the People's Republic, succeeded in founding a new social and economic order, which began to win international acceptance.

In February 1947 Chou En-lai told an American reporter that 'the Chinese Communists will henceforth work out their own problems without mediation by the Soviet Union, Great Britain, the US or any other foreign country'. The Chinese Communist Party's exasperation with Russian conduct in Manchuria was only matched by its anger at the ineptitude of General Marshall in combining mediation between the belligerents in the civil war with physical support for the Generalissimo in the form of transportation facilities, lend-lease materials, surplus equipment and technical services. The Russians had occupied Manchuria during the final days of the Second World War, and were thus in a position to give control of the province, the most industrially developed part of China, to the Chinese Communist Party, whose forces under Lin Piao's command were then predominant in the countryside. This did not occur. At the request of Chiang Kai-shek, the Russians remained in occupation of Manchurian cities until Nationalist forces were flown in to take their place. When the Soviet forces pulled out of the province in April 1946, they systematically stripped factories of all movable equipment, thereby sabotaging the industrial potential of China.

Several explanations of Russian policy in Manchuria are advanced. It may be that Stalin was preoccupied with the recovery of Russian privileges in East Asia, lost through the Russo–Japanese War of 1904–5. At the Yalta Conference in February 1945 Churchill and Roosevelt had accepted the great power claims of Russia without consulting Chiang Kai-shek. Another possibility, that Moscow understood conditions in China as little as did Washington and London, has the historical evidence of Stalin's persistent urging of a Communist-Nationalist coalition government. Moscow seemed to cling to a view of Chinese politics more suited to the late 1920s: no account was taken of the Yenan experience of the Chinese Communist Party, nor the extent of

Nationalist disintegration during the idle years in Chungking. As Stalin saw it, the Chinese Communists, though they controlled considerable rural areas, had no chance of carrying the revolution from the country to the city and of overthrowing the Nationalists. 'He looked upon Mao', Issac Deutscher has remarked, 'as upon a queer pawn on his chessboard, placed in one of its less important corners.' The decision to loot factories would have been reached in the expectation of a stalemate in China. Anxious that the Nationalists, allies of the United States, should be denied the industrial power built up by the Japanese in Manchuria, Stalin may have seen the issue as one of security for the Pacific states of the Soviet Union.

There is, however, another explanation which credits Stalin with a dog-in-the-manger attitude towards the Chinese Communist Party. Moscow was aware of the doctrinal aberration of Mao Tse-tung's thinking, a fundamental divergence of view on revolutionary potentiality in the non-industrial world dating from before the days of the Chingkangshan Soviet. Though Mao Tse-tung had been careful not to antagonize Moscow, the Chinese Communist Party received no assistance in its struggle against the Japanese and the Nationalists. When on 3 February 1949 the People's Liberation Army marched into Peking, foreign observers in the Legation Quarter, through which the Communists deliberately routed their triumphal entry, were surprised, even disappointed to find that the column contained neither Russian weapons nor Russian advisers. The price for future aid, financial and technical, could have been envisaged in Moscow as less independence in Marxist-Leninist ideology, since it was highly unlikely that any other foreign power would help in restarting Chinese industry.

It was not easy for the People's Republic to achieve a close alliance with the Soviet Union. Apart from the different revolutionary experiences of the two countries and the Stalinist emphasis on ideological orthodoxy, there was the desire of the Russians to re-establish their predominance in Manchuria, where they held the Chinese Eastern Railway and Port Arthur. However, in 1949 neither Stalin nor Mao Tse-tung could afford to fall out publicly. Moscow intended that heterodox Yugoslavia should find no allies within the socialist bloc and so the request of Peking for assistance with its socialist revolution did not fall on deaf ears. After two months in the Russian capital Mao Tse-tung secured in February 1950 the Sino-Soviet Treaty of Friendship and Alliance. Overshadowing this period of world history, we should remember, was the threat of atomic warfare. Hiroshima and Nagasaki were uncomfortably close to the People's Republic and in the West Churchill in his Fulton speech had praised the Lord for entrusting thermo-nuclear weapons to the United States rather than to 'some communist or neo-fascist state'. Later Chou En-lai recalled: 'Many were frightened by the atomic bomb. At that time even Stalin was mentally shocked, and was worried about the outbreak of World War III.' To counter such pessimism Chairman Mao had told Anna Louis Strong, an American reporter visiting Yenan in 1946, that 'the atomic bomb is a paper tiger used by the US reactionaries to scare people. It looks terrible, but in fact it isn't. Of course, the atom bomb is a weapon of mass slaughter, but the outcome of a war is decided by the people, not by one or two new weapons.' This point of view was to be used by the Russians after the estrangement between Moscow and Peking as an accusation that the Chinese were willing to run the risk of a world nuclear war because of an expectation that they more than others would survive it. Mao Tse-tung's view of the international situation, however, was quite separate, since he rejected Stalin's fear that local wars in East Asia would increase political tension to such an extent that general conflict must result. Relations between the Soviet Union and the United States could accommodate liberation movements in the Third World. The events of the last quarter-century have proved Chairman Mao right, just as the socialist model developed in the People's Republic has become in the eyes of some countries an alternative to the Russian one.

Mao Tse-tung argued that contradictions within the West itself were sufficient to prevent an alignment of all capitalist countries against the Soviet Union. These contradictions arose from class differences within each country as well as from the rivalry and competition which necessarily existed between the capitalist countries themselves. Although he was aware of the commitment of the United States to preservation of the *status quo* in East Asia, Mao Tse-tung foresaw that even its vast resources could not sustain indefinitely client régimes engulfed by 'a people's war'. China was, of course, dissatisfied with the post-war world. In return for the recognition of the Mongolian People's Republic, a region only incorporated in the Empire by the Ch'ing dynasty, the Chinese obtained from the Russians abandonment of their special rights in the Liao-tung peninsula and over the Eastern Chinese Railways. When these formally terminated in 1954, after the Korean War, the People's Republic achieved on the northern frontier the end to a century-old process of encroachment, an achievement which had eluded the last Ch'ing rulers, northern warlords, and the Republic. But it was unfortunate for relations with the West that elsewhere the Americans, as successors to the Japanese, were in occupation of areas which China traditionally controlled or possessed. Unperceived in contemporary Western thinking was the pattern of relations in East Asia. China, the most ancient, populous and developed country of East Asia, had always been the centre of authority and culture. The tributary system may have been largely nominal for the more distant nations, and even have represented in the exchange of gifts rather a method of official trading in valuable commodities, but it was an historical fact prior to the arrival of the Europeans. For countries like Vietnam and Korea, contact with Chinese civilization remained intimate as late as the nineteenth century. The presence of American forces in a ring of bases around the People's Republic was seen in Peking as the continuation of foreign imperialism and a positive threat to national integrity. Thus, intervention in the Korean War by Chinese 'volunteers' represented a dual response towards perceived aggression and the Allied drive on the Manchurian frontier.

North Korea was brought into existence by Russian occupation after the Japanese surrender. Stalin did not consult with the Chinese Communist Party over the creation of the Democratic Republic of Korea as a separate state, nor does he appear to have warned Peking of the surprise attack on the Republic of Korea mounted by North Korean troops in 1950. When United States and South Korean forces counter-attacked across the 38th parallel and drove northwards towards the Yalu River, Peking felt that it could stand aloof no longer. General MacArthur, commander-in-chief of the United Nations armies, consistently ignored instructions to contain the fighting and it was his all-out northern assault that brought three hundred thousand Chinese People's Volunteers into the war. Under American pressure the General Assembly had belatedly approved the United Nations' advance into North Korea, despite Chinese warnings. Mao Tse-tung was by no means certain about the wisdom of intervention: the economy had not recovered from the protracted struggle with Japan and there was no guarantee that Chinese soldiers would hold their own against the superior equipment of the United Nations force. Yet for the first time Chinese arms matched those of the West. This success was expensive, and Peking sighed with relief on the commencement of negotiations for a peace settlement in June 1951, though they dragged on for two years. By limiting the supply of weapons the Soviet Union brought about a military equilibrium in Korea, but once the People's Republic had intervened it was clear in Moscow that Peking again dominated international affairs in East Asia.

'Resist America, Aid Korea': this was the slogan of the Chinese People's Volunteers. The Korean War cost the People's Republic its seat at the United Nations, since the General Assembly passed a resolution condemning the intervention of 'volunteers' as 'aggression', and the clash with American soldiers on the battlefield led to a permanent stalemate in the Chinese civil war, for the US Seventh Fleet became the shield of Taiwan. Soviet military aid, however, re-equipped the People's Liberation Army and in 1953, shortly after Stalin's death, backing was forthcoming for China's First Five-Year Plan. The Russians committed themselves to assistance with 211 major projects, and ten thousand experts were seconded to the Chinese. Loans of 430,000,000 US dollars, together with an unspecified sum for military equipment, were repaid to the Soviet Union over a decade, from China's growing trade surplus.

Differences between Moscow and Peking could not be hidden forever. The People's Republic had emerged as a world power: China participated in the Geneva Conference of July 1954, persuading Hanoi to temper its demands; and in the ensuing year, at the Bandung Conference of Asian and African States, Chou En-lai advocated the principles of peaceful coexistence, though the People's Republic still viewed as all important 'the struggle against colonialism'. Chinese foreign policy was less strident and less insistent on armed struggle. Whilst there could be no doubt about the need to concentrate on domestic reconstruction, the growth of US-sponsored collective security agreements like the South-East Asia Treaty Organization underscored the importance of military preparedness. Both the Soviet Union and the People's Republic supplied economic and military aid to the Democratic Republic of Vietnam, but Mao Tse-tung made it quite clear that Chinese troops would not intervene as in Korea unless North Vietnam should be invaded.

At the Twentieth Party Congress in Moscow, Khrushchev's attack on Stalin and his revision of several fundamentals of Marxism-Leninism displeased Peking. The Chinese Communist Party had not been consulted: the opinion of Chairman Mao, the peer of Stalin, ought to have been taken into full account. The Hungarian Uprising that autumn was a warning, the *People's Daily* announced on 29 December, 1956, that the 'anti-doctrinaire tide' sweeping the socialist world might degenerate into revisionism. Mao Tse-tung commented:

Certain people in our country were delighted when the Hungarian events took place. They hoped that something similar would happen in China, that thousands upon thousands of people would demonstrate in the streets against the People's Government. Such hopes ran counter to the interests of the masses and therefore could not possibly get their support. In Hungary, a section of the people, deceived by domestic and foreign counter-revolutionaries, made the mistake of resorting to acts of violence against the people's government, with the result that both the state and the people suffered for it. . . .

Khrushchev's advocacy of peaceful coexistence with the West and his belief that industrial capitalist societies could achieve a peaceful transition to socialism were particularly unhelpful to China. In East Asia the chief enemy of the People's Republic was the United States, then underwriting any and all anti-Communist régimes. The Suez crisis too had cast doubt on the acquiescence of Great Britain and France in their diminished world role. More serious in Chinese eyes was that the Soviet Union's orientation towards the industrial part of the world blinded its leadership to the value of Chairman Mao's model for revolution amongst the underdeveloped nations. This ideological rift widened in 1958 when the People's Republic launched the Great Leap Forward, claiming that the people's communes were a short-cut to full Communism. But it was the reluctance of Moscow, despite intercontinental ballistic missile capability, to sustain Peking during the second 'offshore island' crisis of the same year, when Communist artillery bombarded the Nationalist-held islands of Quemoy and Matsu, that brought painfully home to the Chinese Communist Party its isolation in the world. In 1960 the possibility of an arms control agreement between Moscow and Washington led in Peking to an attack on Khruschev for 'revising, emasculating, and betraying' Marxism-Leninism. It behoved world socialism to recognize henceforth the Thought of Mao Tse-tung as the guiding light.

The Hundred Flowers campaign of 1956–7 was Chairman Mao's method of handling dissatisfaction with Communist rule. In order to avoid an outburst similar to that in Hungary, which he regarded as a symptom of the bureaucratism and repression tolerated by the Hungarian leadership, it was essential for the Chinese Communist Party to listen to the wisdom of the people. Through the free expression would come a tremendous release of latent energy and enthusiasm, forces the Party could harness to accelerate China's economic development. The period of relaxation known as the Hundred Flowers was the first public instance of Mao Tse-tung's belief in the necessity of a permanent or continuing revolution. When he urged the people to 'let the Hundred Schools contend, let the Hundred Flowers bloom', a reference to the Hundred Schools of philosophy of the Classical Age, his chief target was the intellectuals, the *shih*.

THE HUNDRED FLOWERS AND THE GREAT LEAP

After the abandonment of the imperial examination system in 1905, there occurred a massive expansion of education with the founding of thousands of higher middle schools, so that the new *shih* may have numbered around five millions by 1957. These scholars had received their education in the

Scene from a modern ballet performance in Peking celebrating the revolution. Villagers are being freed from oppression by the People's Liberation Army. A didactic emphasis was not unusual in traditional Chinese theatre, too.

'bourgeois' Republic, and much of their learning rested on the assumptions of Western capitalist society. Not every person had had the privilege of attending people's colleges in Yenan. Changes were taking place in the People's Republic, as society moved along a socialist path, but the need to reunify the country obliged the Chinese Communist Party to revive the non-hereditary bureaucracy of the Empire. Since the pre-republican era also possessed a tradition of public rather than private enterprise, there existed a danger that the scholars might swing back towards a Confucian scale of values, with loyalty to the family rather than the state. Unless a 'proletarian viewpoint' emerged as a standard for judgment, the intellectuals running the apparatus of the state and the growing industrial sector could be tempted into Western capitalist thinking, or they could slip back into the élitist attitudes of the traditional scholar–bureaucrat.

While we stand for freedom with leadership and democracy under centralized guidance [wrote Chairman Mao], in no sense do we mean that coercive measures should be taken to settle ideological matters and questions involving the distinction between right and wrong among the

The People's Republic

people. Any attempt to deal with ideological matters or questions involving right and wrong by administrative orders or coercive measures will be not only ineffective but harmful. . . . Administrative orders issued for the maintenance of social order must be accompanied by persuasion and education. . . . Contradictions in a socialist society are fundamentally different from contradictions in old societies, such as capitalist society. Contradictions in capitalist society find expression in acute antagonisms and conflicts, in sharp class struggle, which cannot be resolved by the capitalist system itself, but only by socialist revolution. But contradictions in socialist society are not antagonistic and can be resolved one after another by the socialist system itself. [They are] those between the relations of production and the productive forces, and between the superstructure and the economic base.

Contained in this statement is the key concept of Mao Tse-tung's strategy for the achievement of a true People's Republic. Neither blind obedience nor uncomprehending acquiescence is enough: the Party must correctly handle the contradictions within Chinese society 'to enable socialist culture to thrive in our land'. Only in such a situation will the essential goodness of the individual shine forth, like Chu Hsi's famous analogy of a pearl lifted from a bowl of dirty water. No matter how disruptive and inexplicable the upheavals of the Hundred Flowers campaign, the Great Leap Forward, the Great Proletarian Cultural Revolution or the campaign against the philosophy of Confucius may appear to us as outsiders, we should deceive ourselves if we

BELOW Peking. Cycle rickshaw transporting a heavy load of paper, a Chinese invention.

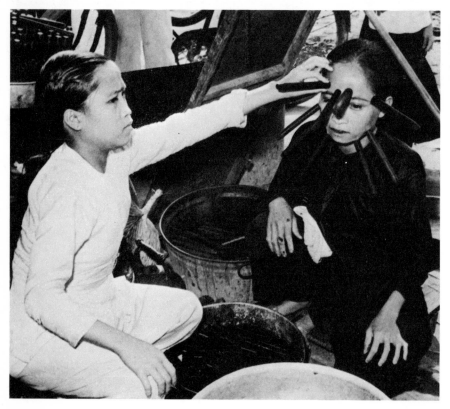

LEFT Medicine in the countryside.

ever regard them as aberrations. For Mao Tse-tung insisted: 'that which is correct always develops in the course of struggling against that which is wrong. . . . As mankind in general rejects an untruth and accepts a truth, a new truth will be struggling with new erroneous ideas. Such struggles will never end. This is the law of development of Marxism.'

Nevertheless, the extent and pointedness of criticism during the Hundred Flowers campaign did seem to take the Party by surprise. Wall posters appeared objecting to the one-party system and the arrogance of Party members. Student protests broke out in major cities, prefiguring the events of the Cultural Revolution a decade later. On 8 June the licence to criticize was abruptly withdrawn. 'Rightists' went to the rural areas for re-education and misguided intellectuals received the benefit of demotion or a reduction in salary. Unlike Soviet Russia, there was neither mass transportation to labour camps nor executions on any scale. The death penalty was reserved for a few active counter-revolutionaries in Wuhan. But the abrupt termination of the Hundred Flowers campaign remains a mystery. Did the Party launch the criticism to identify its hidden enemies? Was Mao Tse-tung's confidence in the progress of the People's Republic misplaced? Or, perhaps, were his opponents in the Party seeking to nip in the bud a permanent revolutionary struggle? From this cultural upheaval the People's Republic of China turned a year later to the economic revolution of the Great Leap.

Notwithstanding the industrial development achieved during the First Five-Year Plan, especially in heavy industry, the Chinese economy was in poor shape through the relative stagnation of the countryside, where handicrafts and traditional agricultural techniques predominated. Production of foodstuffs had expanded, but the improved diet of the *nung* accounted for most of this increase and the amount of grain delivered to the state, through taxes and compulsory purchase, remained almost stationary. The need to stimulate the rural economy was made pressing by the rise in the urban population. A limited return to free-market conditions was unthinkable, not least for the reason that it would encourage a rich-peasant mentality, something the Chinese Communist Party wished to avoid. Chairman Mao was steady in his belief that the establishment of a socialist system of relationships was fundamental to economic reconstruction. It was a principle echoed by Liu Shao-chi, when he said: 'The present task is to effect a thorough and systematic readjustment in the relationships between people, rooting out the capitalist and feudal survivals of bygone days and building new socialist relationships.' So private plots were banned, communes formed and the Great Leap Forward began.

By late 1958 the rural co-operatives had been merged into twenty-five thousand communes, each with a population of around twenty thousand people, as compared with three thousand in the average co-operative. The basic aim of the commune movement was to provide investment funds for industrial development by making use of economies of scale and obtaining greater output by improved rural organization. The area of a commune was often coincidental with that of the *hsiang*, or county; thus any contradiction between the economic and the administrative unit disappeared. Apart from better communal facilities such as canteens, nurseries and homes for the aged, which released women to productive tasks, enlarged resources and manpower gave the commune an advantage over the co-operative in handling schemes for water conservation, irrigation or afforestation. The commune was nothing less than the recreation of rural co-operation, the ideal of the country-side time out of mind in China, but founded for the first occasion on the leader-ship of the *nung* themselves. For the individual peasant-farmer, recently harassed by famine and insecurity, membership offered the chance to help in a team dedicated to building a solid basis for rural development.

The under-employed masses of rural China were mobilized in a modern version of the corvée. Over one hundred million of them undertook immense hydraulic engineering projects, and brought more land under irrigation in eighteen months than in the whole of China's early history. This part of the Great Leap certainly blunted the impact of the drought years in the early 1960s. Though the People's Republic was obliged to import food grains, the situation could not stand in more marked contrast to that prevailing in contemporary India, where thousands of people die of hunger even after good harvests. Another aspect of decentralization, of movement away from Soviet planning methods, was the production of pig iron in 'backyard' blast furnaces. The declared aim of the Soviet Union to overtake the economy of the United States seemed a near-reality in October 1958 on the launching of the Sputnik artificial satellite; not to be out of the race, Mao Tse-tung announced that in fifteen years the Chinese economy would surpass Britain's. Iron and steel production may well have doubled in 1958, but the claim of the Chinese Communist Party for the achievement of a significant industrial breakthrough soon had to be played down, because a considerable proportion of 'backyard' iron was of such low quality as to be useless. A victim of this sudden upsurge of industrial activity was the railways, as trains hauled the pig iron from the rural areas to the industrial centres.

In January 1960 the Great Leap Forward was suspended. It had become apparent to the Chinese Communist Party that radical economic policies would lead to disaster. Overdevelopment in certain sectors of industry, such as the manufacture of machine-tools, overloading of the transportation system, and over-hasty collectivization of the rural population contributed to a sharp drop in both agricultural and industrial output. Two other factors encouraged this decline: inclement weather and the withdrawal of Russian technical aid. Droughts, floods and typhoons afflicted the People's Republic during the period 1959–61, but no less damaging than these natural calamities was the dispute with the Soviet Union. In July 1960 Khrushchev cancelled all economic aid and recalled all Soviet specialists, technicians and engineers. Projects were left incomplete, even blueprints and plans vanished overnight. Moscow could not have chosen a more difficult moment for Peking: Khrushchev expected to bring Chairman Mao to heel. The reverse happened. The Chinese Communist Party decided to reshape its policy for development, switching from heavy industry to agriculture. The new slogan was 'Agriculture as the base of the national economy with industry as the leading factor'. In contrast to the Great Leap, the new policy was one of caution and gradualism. It was argued that the economy required a period to recuperate, but without letting any capitalist tendencies develop. What the Sino-Soviet split brought about was the 'self-reliance' philosophy of the People's Republic. As René Dumont observes:

Omnipresent Chairman Mao on a gateway of the Purple Forbidden City. The notice reads 'Long live the unity of the world proletariat.'

China demonstrates to us that *internal efforts alone are necessary for development*; that *one must count first on oneself* and not on foreign aid. The latter brings in its train dependence and can always prove lacking at the moment it is most needed. It makes possible permanent blackmail: that of the USSR on China, that of Europe on Africa or that of the USA on the western hemisphere.

THE GREAT PROLETARIAN CULTURAL REVOLUTION (1966–9)

Although the Great Leap Forward was abandoned as a shortcut to full economic development and the realization of the communist ideal, and at the end of 1958 Mao Tse-tung stepped down as head of the government in favour of Liu Shao-ch'i, there was by no means a decisive swing away from the kind of revolutionary course envisaged by the chairman of the Chinese Communist Party. Mao Tse-tung's authority was slightly diminished and he disliked the tendency of policies introduced between 1959 and 1962, but the radical turn of events known as the Great Proletarian Cultural Revolution partly resulted from the unfolding of his own thought. He was one of those rare individuals who seem to reverse the usual effects of growing old – that is, he became more revolutionary as the years passed. Nor is it astonishing that the ideas of this old man should have appealed to students who, in their transient situation, were still malleable and receptive. Whatever is ultimately concluded

about the Cultural Revolution, in this one respect it remains unique. For it was essentially a movement of the young, an upsurge of revolutionary fervour from below. Sensing the frustrations of young people, Chairman Mao guided their revolt into an attack on the complacency of their parents as expressed through the Party. Grandfather and grandchildren opposed the 'rightist' tendencies of the middle-aged officials.

In 1971 the *People's Daily* recalled that the Great Proletarian Cultural Revolution was 'the second Chinese revolution', subsequent statements have amplified the necessity of further upheavals, and the leadership of the masses is now accepted as the touchstone of ideology in China. This divergence from Soviet traditions represents a very deep philosophical difference of opinion. What Mao Tse-tung believed was that the seizure of power by the Communist Party, while necessary for the transition to socialist society, was not enough to guarantee it. Only a continuing revolution of the masses would ensure there was equality and an end to the social division of labour. The material progress sought in the Great Leap Forward has been replaced with an emphasis on discovery of a 'socialist path' which can lead straight from underdevelopment. The People's Republic has not been prepared to await modernization before embarking on revolutionary changes in society.

The genesis of Mao Tse-tung's ideas on revolution in an underdeveloped country was, of course, his appreciation of peasant problems. He had had no apprenticeship to Communist theory in Europe. His views on organization and strategy were derived from first-hand experience in rural 'soviets'. Unlike the Bolsheviks, who were theorists before suddenly coming to power in 1917, the Chinese Communists controlled large areas, however inaccessible, and for two decades before 1949, under revolutionary conditions, they had coped with the difficulties of administration, land reform, education and warfare. Policies were tried and mistakes admitted. Ever since Mao Tse-tung assumed the chairmanship in 1935, the Chinese Communist Party has made its discussion public knowledge, once an agreement has been reached. Because contradictions within a socialist context were held to be non-antagonist, there was never any reason to pretend that the Party was either monolithic or infallible. The existence of a great explosive revolutionary force in the peasantry, a bottomless well of inspiration and understanding, allowed a dialogue between the Party and the people. Only after convincing the people that they were going in the direction wanted could its members put themselves at the head of the movement. 'It is not the authoritarian approach of telling people what their destiny will be,' commented Owen Lattimore, 'but helping people see the way in which they want to settle their own destiny.' Perhaps Mao Tse-tung was unconsciously drawing upon Taoist tradition when he encouraged the people to question the Party. As Lao-tzu hinted, 'men are wiser than they know'.

It is interesting to note that discussion of the social teachings of Confucius in university circles called forth a directive from Chairman Mao in December 1963, when he said that there should be less talk about personalities of the past and more about the current situation. A year later, he told a Nepalese delegation that China's education system was 'fraught with problems, the most important of which is dogmatism. . . . The school years are too long, courses too many, and various methods of teaching unsatis-

Interior of a department store in Peking. The signs overhead are not commercial advertisements, but exhortations about the Thought of Chairman Mao and the glories of the People's Republic.

factory. The children learn textbooks and concepts which remain merely textbooks and concepts: they know nothing else. . . .' When in 1969 he labelled the Ministry of Culture the 'Ministry for Alien Personalities of Outworn Times', Mao Tse-tung, once a teacher himself, was also aiming at the educational reverence of the past. In his mind were probably the views of Communist officials like Chou Yang, the Deputy Director of the Central Committee's Propaganda Department, who had declared in 1960: 'We must stress writing: writing the characters correctly without making errors, and understanding grammar. It is also necessary to advocate the reciting of books, which is a Chinese tradition.' Though the correct writing of characters was not unimportant, the implied emphasis on calligraphy as well as the advice about recitation ran contrary to the Yenan way of learning as a collaborative process between tutor and student. It was an anachronism: a didactic method whereby the status of the *shih* was preserved, albeit in his modern metamorphosis as the bourgeois intellectual. To alter this situation Chairman Mao had secured in 1962 Party commitment to a 'socialist education' campaign, whose culmination in the Cultural Revolution of 1966–9 was a struggle to overcome the class forces opposing the transformation of a bourgeois culture into a proletarian one. Only in the middle of this revolutionary struggle did it become apparent that these opponents were to be found in the Party itself.

In 1963 cadres began to take part in manual labour. These functionaries held positions of leadership within the Party, administration, armed forces and communes: according to Liu Shao-ch'i they were 'the nucleus of the Party organization and of the Chinese revolution'. Alongside the introduction of cadres to physical work, the 'socialist education' campaign launched a barrage of anti-hierarchical slogans and encouraged criticism of the teaching system. Yet Mao Tse-tung's attention was also fixed on the People's Liberation Army, always a mass movement solidly rooted in the population. In picturesque language, he had described its relationship to the people as that of a fish to water.

> But only a profoundly democratic and egalitarian army [the deputy editor of the *People's Daily* has reportedly said], can stay close to the people, helping them in their labours and living with them. The threat that hangs over our country has increased recently as a result of American aggression in Vietnam and the treason of modern revisionists. A great debate was therefore organized in our army, and after several months of discussion at all levels the decision was made to strengthen even further the bonds between the army and the people by abolishing rank and giving soldiers an even more intensive political education.

On 1 June 1965, all the ranks in the People's Liberation Army, introduced in 1955, were done away with. Responsibility for this reversion to the Yenan model was due to Lin Piao, who had succeeded P'eng Teh-huai as minister of defence at the time of the Great Leap Forward. Moreover, he took care of the political education of the military, by issuing the *Little Red Book*, with a foreword that boldly asserted:

> Comrade Mao Tse-tung is the greatest Marxist-Leninist of our era. He has inherited, defended and developed Marxism-Leninism with genius, creatively and comprehensively and has brought it to a higher and completely new stage. Mao Tse-tung's thought . . . is a powerful ideological weapon for opposing revision and dogmatism . . . [and] is the guiding principle for all the work of the Party, the army and the country.

That Mao Tse-tung had chosen to bypass the Party could be doubted no longer. Not only did he designate 'people within the Party who are in authority and are taking the capitalist road' as the target of the 'socialist education movement', but even more he urged 'all communes and brigades to learn from the People's Liberation Army four great democratic attitudes, and to practise democracy in politics, democracy in production, democracy in financial affairs, and democracy in military affairs'. The heroic days of Chingkangshan and Yenan had returned: once again the Red soldier was extolled as the embodiment of virtue. The ideological battle-lines were drawn.

On 10 November 1965 the first shot was fired in the form of an article directed at Wu Han, a historian and deputy major of Peking. It was alleged that though an historical play by Wu Han entitled *Hai Jai Dismissed from Office* contained a defence of the retired P'eng Teh-huai and the hierarchical position he represented, the Ministry of Culture turned a blind eye to this assault on socialist values. Various officials lost their jobs but the strength of Mao Tse-tung's opponents in the Party obliged him to organize the Red Guards.

His chief antagonist was Liu Shao-ch'i, who announced that Party work

The ethereal beauty of the mountains overshadows the intensive agriculture in the valleys of Kwangsi.

OVERLEAF Red Guards in a study session prior to a Peking rally. They are reading the *Little Red Book*.

teams would be sent into the main universities and colleges to replace inadequate cadres and assist the students to form their own committees for the Cultural Revolution. By this action the head of the government hoped to avert fundamental criticism of the Party or its leading members. Liu Shao-ch'i was the 'Chinese Khrushchev'. Although he was not a particular enthusiast of the Soviet Union, he agreed with P'eng Teh-huai concerning the necessity of co-operation with the Russians in the face of the American threat then escalating annually in the Vietnam War. The People's Republic should be strong and modernized, even if this meant concessions to Moscow and the emergence of a technological élite. This chasm between Mao Tse-tung and Liu Shao-ch'i was swiftly perceived by the university students, who responded in a manner worthy of the May Fourth Movement. Student agitation increased and spread into factories and on to farms, revolutionary activities which received ideological sanction in Mao Tse-tung's *ta tzu pao*, or wall poster in big characters, entitled 'Bombard the Headquarters' and displayed on 5 August 1966. Two weeks later he received in T'ien An Men Square the first of the eight gigantic meetings that brought, within three months, eleven million Red Guards to Peking in order to exchange experiences. Chiang Ch'ing, Chairman Mao's wife, acted as their stage manager.

Although classes and formal education stopped by mid-1966, schools, colleges and universities stayed open as centres of discussion and political activity. The students, whose title of Red Guards had been dignified by Chairman Mao's adoption of their armband in August, undertook pilgrimages to Yenan as well as Peking. Thousands of town students joined the *hsia-fang* movement: they went into the countryside to help with farm work and discuss the Cultural Revolution with the *nung*. Throughout their ascendancy the Red Guards challenged 'feudalism, capitalism, and revisionism'. In moments of excessive enthusiasm they destroyed traditional cultural objects and harassed persons with Western-style clothes or possessions, a xenophobia reminiscent of the Boxers. They called upon Party officials to acknowledge their objectives, and make self-criticism. On 6 January 1967, over a million workers in Shanghai attended a mass meeting at which prominent functionaries were denounced. During the same month local 'reactionaries' in Nanking engaged the Red Guards in street fighting, which left fifty dead and several hundred injured. At this point Chairman Mao called for the establishment of 'Revolutionary Committees' to replace local committees of the Party. Their membership was based on the 'three-in-one combination' of Red Guards and revolutionary workers, Party officials and cadres, and the People's Liberation Army. The latter was used to set up the new committees; it also intervened to support the Red Guards in local conflict as well as check revolutionary outrages. The burning of diplomatic offices in Peking, a mass response to the imprisonment of nineteen 'patriotic' Chinese journalists by the British authorities in Hong Kong, alerted Mao Tse-tung to the danger of a violent swing to the 'ultra-Left'. His resolution must have been strengthened by a talk with Chou En-lai, who related how the Red Guards had interrogated him for a gruelling forty-eight hours. That a consummate politician who had managed to arrange compromise administrations in the provinces, save officials from unjust attack and maintain production in the factories, felt there was a crisis at hand must have given Mao reason to pause.

ABOVE Public portraits of Mao Tse-tung in Peking.

Chairman Mao. Revolutionary grandfather with revolutionary grandchildren.

At the beginning of October, two months after the firing of the British Chancery, Mao Tse-tung issued a long report on the progress of the Cultural Revolution in the provinces, which he had toured during the summer. He cautioned prudence. 'We are at the very moment when the little Red Guard generals run the risk of making mistakes; they must learn from the experiences of those among them who have made errors in the past.' The spontaneous upsurge of proletarian revolutionary consciousness was endangered by factionalism. This point he hammered home a year later, when he told the Red Guards to accept the leadership of the working classes. In December 1968, Mao Tse-tung stated: 'It is necessary for educated young people to go to the countryside to be re-educated by the poor and lower-middle peasants. Cadres and other people in the cities should be persuaded to send their sons and daughters who have finished junior or senior middle school, college or university to the countryside.' The group warfare of the Red Guards – bitter feuds between rival factions jockeying for position – contributed to neither the welfare of education nor the country. In reality, a former Red Guard admitted in 1971, 'We were too arrogant; we did not know how to submit our petit-bourgeois outlook to proletarian ideology.' The Cultural Revolution thus closed with an admission of the sagacity of the people and their army.

Today, our perspective on the revolutionary turmoil of 1966–9 is a short one. It is difficult to trace out all the implications of the changes brought about in those three traumatic years. Yet there are a number that cannot be overlooked. First, the fact that the supremacy of the Party is no longer taken for granted indicates a singular departure from the traditions of the Communist movement. Chairman Mao did not cast aside the Party, but he did alter its relation to the Chinese revolution. Besides ending the political career of Liu Shao-ch'i, breaking the power of Party bureaucrats and destroying respect for the special knowledge of the expert, the Cultural Revolution asserted that the true repository of wisdom remains with the people, now more politically aware than ever before. Through their mass organizations, they have acquired a political education. Second, the People's Liberation Army appears to have returned to its Yenan roots. The Russian model adopted after the Korean War has vanished, along with some of the danger that military leaders might pose to the future of the People's Republic. Mao Tse-tung's subsequent revival of Party committees in the provinces and the fall of Lin Piao – he was reported killed in an air crash *en route* for the Soviet Union on 12 September 1971 – can be seen as a consolidation of the civil revolutionary movement.

The third change is perhaps the most far-reaching one. In order to delegate power to the masses it was necessary to have a strong consensus on aims and alternative organization. The *Little Red Book* provided this ideological framework, and incidentally led to the canonization of Mao Tse-tung. The Cultural Revolution may have shaken up the whole Chinese people – an event which heartened the advocate of continuing revolution – but an unforeseen legacy could be the cult of the chairman. That there will be need for future upheavals Mao Tse-tung has left no one in doubt. The question is, of course, the effective handling of their contradictions now he is dead. He was involved in the anti-Confucius campaign of 1974, a renewed assault on the hierarchical principle, and in 1976 engineered the defeat of Ten Hsiao-ping, the rehabilitated associate of Liu Shao-ch'i and heir-apparent to Chou En-lai.

AN END TO INTERNATIONAL ISOLATION 'Force is the only thing the Russians understand.' This view of President Truman was the epitome of American foreign policy in the 1950s. The State Department may have been less hardbitten in its approach to the Soviet Union once the latter had acquired an atomic armoury, but belief in the effectiveness of the thermo-nuclear threat when dealing with the socialist bloc died hard. A case in point was the Communist shelling of Quemoy and Matsu; these off-shore islands received their first bombardment in 1954–5. Washington encouraged Taipei to hold out, though as Nehru, the Prime Minister of India, declared it was 'almost generally recognized that those islands should immediately be evacuated and taken possession of by the Government of the mainland'. An intransigent John Foster Dulles, the American Secretary of State, threatened a preventive nuclear strike on the People's Republic. The 'Domino Theory' required the defence of a handful of islands within a few miles of coast. Otherwise, it was argued in Washington, Taiwan would fall along with all the other countries of South-east Asia, because they were like a row of dominoes. If one fell it would knock down the next in line, which then would knock down the one after, and so on, until none were left standing. This simple analogy has proved a fallacy: it has worked, if at all, in reverse. 'The greater the outside pressure upon China, the "containment" policy,' C. P. Fitzgerald commented, 'the more was China stimulated by traditional fear of Western agression to expand her influence so as to forestall or frustrate that of the powerful nation, the United States, which had shown such clear signs of hostility.' At the cost of immense human suffering and the waste of untold resources, the Americans unsuccessfully intervened in Vietnam, Laos and Cambodia. They understood neither the political aspirations of South-east Asia nor the historical experience of the Chinese. Their B-52 bombers were merely a modern version of gunboat

Red Guards walking to Shanghai from the rural areas in 1967.

高举毛泽东思想的

无产阶级革命造反派

青松不老毛

用鲜血和生命保卫毛主席

彻底粉碎刘邓反动路线炉轰国防工办火烧李富春

以王黑旗为首的七机部党委交权是大阴谋！碎工役制制度

机院东方红造一机部革命造反联合委员会的后就是

打倒拘西金勃刘日涅夫

打倒混蛋透顶的苏修领导集团

出红色造

Wall posters on a gateway in Peking.

diplomacy. Yet a more lethal one: during the twelve days of the Paris peace talks in 1972 they dropped forty thousand tonnes of bombs on the population of Hanoi.

Hemmed in and threatened by US-sponsored collective security agreements, such as the South-east Asia Treaty Organization, the People's Republic urged the Soviet Union to pursue a firmer anti-Western policy. Khrushchev disagreed with Chairman Mao's view that 'the East wind prevails over the West wind' in world affairs; he disliked the ideological implications of the Great Leap Forward, especially the Chinese assertion that people's communes represented an advance on the other socialist models; and not least, he thought that 'peaceful co-existence' with the West was the correct policy because in advanced societies the transition from capitalism to a socialist society could be accomplished peacefully. The lukewarmness of the Soviet Union meant that the People's Republic could no longer rely on it as an ally. In 1959 the Russians withdrew from the Chinese nuclear programme, and a year later they were engaged in discussions with the United States, Britain and France on the limitation of nuclear weapons, a diplomatic move which eventually led to *détente* in the 1970s. The Cuban missile crisis of 1962 was the exception to the rule of peaceful co-existence: it may have even brought Washington and Moscow closer together. 'The hot line' never reached Peking. Yet the Chinese detonated their first nuclear device on 16 October 1964 and launched a space satellite on 24 April 1970. And it is likely that they have an intercontinental ballistic missile. One consequence of these developments has been

While the *Little Red Book* is raised aloft by soldiers in Peking, Chairman Mao acknowledges the salute and reveals his personal weakness, chain-smoking. Behind him Lin Piao joins in the general acclamation; he disappeared from the political scene shortly after this photograph was taken.

the recent appreciation of China's place in the world. Mao Tse-tung had answered the famous rejoinder of Khrushchev that paper tigers have nuclear claws: there was now even less likelihood that the West would dare to use them.

Although the international status of the People's Republic as a super power was recognized on 25 October 1971, when the United Nations awarded China's seat to Peking and ousted Taipei, there is still a legacy of thorny problems in foreign affairs.

President Nixon's visit to the People's Republic was a remarkable reversal of American policy, not least because in the joint communiqué issued at Shanghai the United States accepted in principle the future withdrawal of its forces from Taiwan. This was nothing less than the tacit acceptance of China's sphere of influence in East Asia: it was the equivalent of American acquiescence in Russian authority over Eastern Europe. The 'paper tiger' nature of 'US imperialism' was to the Chinese at last revealed. However, the enmity between Russia and China is not so easily resolved. Since 1964 there have been border clashes on the Amur River, where Russian troops have behaved, according to the Chinese, like 'anti-socialists': that is to say imperialists. It needs to be recalled that, though in the nineteenth century Tsarist Russia stripped the Ch'ing Empire of vast territories here and farther west, the People's Republic was prepared to accept the 'unequal treaties' as a basis for settlement, at least until the more serious incidents from 1969 onwards. The new understanding between Peking and Washington reflects Chinese worry about Russian intentions.

Another unsettled border dispute exists in the Himalayas, where the People's Republic disavows the MacMahon line. Annoyed that India would not admit that its northern frontier resulted from British aggression and anxious to improve overland communications between Tibet and Sinkiang, the Chinese built a road across the Aksai Chin plateau in 1956–7. When New Delhi finally awoke to what was happening in this very remote area, vigorous protests were made to Peking. The Sino-Indian War of 1962 ensued: the Indian border forces suffered a heavy reverse at the hands of the People's Liberation Army, despite the fighter aircraft supplied to India by the Soviet Union. The Chinese quickly evacuated most of the territory seized, the conflict having underlined adequately the strength of their arms in Central Asia. After the Tibetan rebellion of 1959 the Dalai Lama had taken sanctuary in India, and for a time there were notions of a restoration. The military events of 1962 put an end to both intrigue and speculation. Elsewhere the People's Republic concluded border treaties with neighbouring states, so that causes for local friction disappeared. How different the situation is from the condition of China over the previous century, the period after the First Opium War. Perhaps the most symbolic gesture which marked the end of isolation is renewed Chinese interest in Africa. Instead of the rolls of silk and the sets of porcelain offered by the Ming ambassador-admiral Cheng Ho, the modern leaders of East Africa are pleased to receive railways as gifts.

8

China, the Modern Miracle

The philosophical blueprint of present-day China is the Thought of Mao Tse-tung. After the Cultural Revolution had destroyed the Party bureaucracy and the People's Liberation Army stepped in as a new balancing and unifying force in Chinese society, the *Little Red Book* was elevated as the yardstick for individual behaviour and the standard text of education. The massiveness of this unprecedented exercise in communications can be gauged by the national paper shortage it caused. The impact on the country was immense. A Japanese visitor remarked in 1971 that 'in place of our advertisement hoardings, political slogans are plastered over the walls in all the towns and villages, and even the theatre and exhibitions always carry a political implication. . . . Few societies are so advanced in the general political awareness.' The Chinese are now preoccupied with public, not private, affairs. Nothing like this mass participation exists in any other country, capitalist or socialist, developed or underdeveloped. One of the reasons for such a vast difference between the People's Republic and the rest of the world is the unparalleled course taken by its socialist revolution, whose mainspring was the *nung*. Inheritors of the immemorial traditions of the countryside's opposition to the town – the seat of the scholar-bureaucrat and refuge of the landlord class – these peasant-farmers formed a ready instrument for Mao Tse-tung's successful assault on the Republic. They permitted his strategy of 'encircling the cities with the countryside'. Their revolutionary determination contained the two characteristics typical of Chinese peasant rebellion: it had, Owen Lattimore points out, 'a political thrust to overthrow authority and a social thrust which has always been anti-Confucian and against the accepted ethic of the state. This means that even something as modern as Marxism and Communism found in China what Marxism and Communism require, that is a potential of political revolution borne on a tide of social revolution.'

A second reason connects with the recent history of China: the Long March to Yenan and the Sino-Japanese War of 1937–45. The Chinese Communist Party arose in response to Japanese aggression and gained the military advantage in China despite every effort of the Nationalists. The Tsunyi Conference of 1935 was a decisive watershed: the delegates adopted Mao Tse-tung as leader and 'Go north and fight the Japanese' as a slogan. The Yenan years were more than the nostalgic memory Liu Shao-ch'i declared them to be in the early 1960s: they witnessed the forging of the revolution in daily politics, education, administration, warfare and production. Unlike Lenin, Mao Tse-tung had in Yenan laboratory conditions for socialist experi-

THE THOUGHT OF
CHAIRMAN MAO

Public art on a gigantic scale. Its purpose was to draw attention to the new era of the world inaugurated by the Thought of Chairman Mao. Interestingly, this triumphal arch was erected in Macao, the Portuguese colony adjacent to Hong Kong.

mentation, and these trial and error preparations for the ultimate takeover of the country were conducted amongst the *nung*. The millions living in the base areas shaped his own thinking and provided in the development of Party goals the final reason for the uniqueness of China today. In Yenan Mao Tse-tung started to modify and adapt Marxism-Leninism so that the Western ideology was suited to Chinese circumstances. A result of this sinicization, a parallel to the previous absorption of the Buddhist faith, was the Sino-Soviet dispute.

'Mao Tse-tung's great accomplishment,' said Liu Shao-ch'i in 1946, 'has been to change Marxism from a European to an Asiatic form. . . . The basic principles of Marxism are undoubtedly adaptable to all countries, but to apply their general truth to concrete revolutionary practice in China is a difficult task. . . . He is the first that has succeeded in doing so.' As Joseph Needham remarked: 'What may have been an important factor in the rallying of the Chinese intellectuals to the Communist point of view is the fact that Neo-Confucianism was closely related to dialectical materialism.' Eight years earlier, Chairman Mao had talked of 'the Sinification of Marxism' and laid emphasis on the need to avoid dogmatism by the discussion of politics in a manner of speech accessible to the average Chinese. His acute sense of the learning capabilities of the peasantry never left him: he remained at bottom a teacher of common men. It was never too late to learn. Nor was it ever impossible for the people of any country to find their own path to socialism, once they have perceived that they must solve the problems of revolution themselves, and along the way admit their errors as well as their successes. This belief on the part of Mao Tse-tung should be held in mind when looking at the changes inaugurated by the Cultural Revolution. Otherwise the significance of the *Little Red Book* will be obscured. On one hand, there is the public discussion of revolutionary progress and the loss of the Party's privileged social position: on the other, the Thought of Chairman Mao has graduated from 'the application of the universal truths of Marxism-Leninism . . . in the concrete practice of the Chinese revolution' to become 'Marxism-Leninism – Mao Tsetung Thought'. Peking's dropping of the hyphen in the English spelling indicates grammatically his new equality with Marx and Lenin. It has yet to be seen if democratic socialism and the primacy of Chairman Mao can be permanently combined; or if, no less crucial an outcome, industrialization and economic power will square with an ideology which originated in the fastness of Yenan.

Some commentators would discern in the veneration of the Thought of Mao Tse-tung all the trappings of a religion, and compare him with Hung Hsiu-ch'uan, the T'ai P'ing leader. They draw attention to the ritual of carrying and raising aloft the *Little Red Book*, so prominent during the years of the Cultural Revolution. They note that the most central experience of Maoism is conversion, whether it is the initial insight of the bourgeois convert or the confession of incorrect ideas by the Party official. And they close their case with the argument that in his lifetime Mao Tse-tung became a miracle-worker, the declared cause of success in such diverse projects as hydraulic engineering and archaeological excavation. Whilst there can be no denial of religious elements in the mass response to the Thought of Chairman Mao, though a moderation of the personality cult was evident in his final years, it

At the beginning of the Great Proletarian Cultural Revolution members of the People's Liberation Army receive copies of the *Little Red Book*.

would be absurd to suggest that a sense of numinous awe is dominant. On the contrary, the thrust of the last decade has been against feudal superstition; temples were closed and ancestor worship proscribed by the Red Guards. A humanistic temper has been typical of Chinese intellectuals for the past millennium and, notwithstanding the young Mao Tse-tung's anarchism and sympathy with Taoist subversion, his ideology placed emphasis firmly upon pragmatism. He was above all else modern China's most accomplished military strategist and political leader: in his life and work we find the rare combination of authority over both the gun and the theoretical essay. It was a singular achievement for one man within a lifetime and it did provide encouragement for hero-worship as the One Man.

To some extent Maoist ideology is a lineal descendant of nineteenth-century attempts at borrowing 'Western learning' for use within the Chinese context. Mao Tse-tung stated that it was necessary to absorb Marxism-Leninism, not merely for use but as the foundation on which Chinese civilization could be restored. He told the Chinese Communist Party in 1938,

> Today's China is an outgrowth of historic China. We are Marxist historicists; we must not mutilate history. From Confucius to Sun Yat-sen we must sum it up critically, and we must constitute ourselves as the heirs of all that is precious in the past. Conversely, the assimilation of this heritage itself turns out to be a kind of methodology that is of great help in the guidance of the revolutionary movement. A communist is a Marxist internationalist, but Marxism must take on a national form before it can be applied.

Keeping fit in a traditional manner, *tai-chi*. This old man takes his exercise in one of the courtyards of the Purple Forbidden City, Peking.

In the process of this revolutionary application, however, China has gone beyond straightforward restoration as the People's Republic and claims once again a central place in world affairs. Chinese diplomacy in the Third World suspiciously recalls the inscription on the Galle stele, which Cheng Ho set up long ago in Sri Lanka: 'Of late we have dispatched missions to announce our Mandate to foreign nations.' The Mandate, of course, belongs properly to the Thought of Mao Tse-tung. The institutions charged with responsibility for carrying out these teachings on behalf of the people are several: the Party, the cadres outside the Party, the People's Liberation Army, and the Red Guards. Their inter-relationship has not been constant, since Chairman Mao's desire for flexibility and relative openness to changing conditions was expressed in permanent revolution. The Cultural Revolution was an effective reassertion of his leadership in state affairs and ideology, but what happened to Confucianism under the Manchus may have been a nightmare that haunted him. Could 'Marxism-Leninism-Mao Tsetung Thought' become just as inflexible and out of touch with daily reality now that Chairman Mao is dead?

Notwithstanding the amazing economic, military and diplomatic restoration of China since 1949, one question remains unanswered. How are the Chinese people to continue to revolutionize their society now that political power has been won? The Cultural Revolution addressed itself to this problem and encountered difficulties: it was found impossible to abolish immediately the

THE PARTY AND
THE PEOPLE'S
LIBERATION ARMY

RIGHT An old woman crosses into Hong Kong on her traditionally bound feet. Lord Macartney had noticed the fashion in 1793, but reflected that it was 'not so many years ago that in England thread-paper waists, steel stays, and tight lacing were in high fashion, and ladies' shapes were so tapered down from bosom to hips that there was some danger of breaking off in the middle upon any exertion'.

social division of labour without running the risk of completely destroying the apparatus of production; nor did the 'Revolutionary Committees', whose 'three-in-one combination' of Red Guards and revolutionary workers, Party officials and cadres, and members of the People's Liberation Army, succeed in heading off factionalism amongst the revolutionary groups. Even in the middle of the turmoil Chairman Mao had to remind the nation of the leadership role of the Party. A directive of early 1968 blandly stated:

> In the conditions of socialism, the great Cultural Revolution is basically a great political revolution made by the proletariat against the bourgeoisie and all other exploiting classes; it is the continuation of the struggle which for many years has set the Chinese Communist Party and the broad popular masses, under its leadership, against the Kuomintang reactionaries; it is the continuation of the class struggle between the proletariat and the bourgeoisie.

One of its targets was Yang Ch'eng-wu, the former chief of the army general staff. An old associate of Lin Piao – he had been political commissar to his forces – Yang Ch'eng-wu was retired in the previous year for 'ultra-Left' activities. He appears to have formed an alliance with the most extreme factions of the Red Guards in order to rehabilitate his more radical associates already condemned for 'anti-Mao tendencies'. Possibly a plot involving troops from the Peking garrison misfired on 8 March 1967. The upshot was his condemnation as an unprincipled careerist by Lin Piao, after consultations between the Minister of Defence and Chairman Mao. Although Lin Piao managed to put a respectable distance between himself and Yang Ch'eng-wu, his announcement was an indication that even the *Little Red Book* could not prevent dissension within the People's Liberation Army.

The fall of Lin Piao himself in September 1971 underlines the paradox. No longer were the military to be regarded as political exemplars: the 'four great democratic attitudes' had paled before a movement of the broad popular masses, under the leadership of the Party. The exact fate of the Minister of Defence remains uncertain. He may have been killed in an aircrash while fleeing to the Soviet Union, which is the official version; or, if still alive, he may be under arrest. Whatever the details of his fall from the exalted position of heir-apparent to Chairman Mao, there is enough evidence of a profound difference of opinion between the two men stemming from the revival of Party committees in the provinces. It was in the course of Mao Tse-tung's tour around the country in autumn 1971 that mass organizations were superseded. Lin Piao was opposed to the termination of the various committees established during the Cultural Revolution and, though 'Chairman Mao intended to return to Peking and meet with Vice-Chairman Lin Piao in order to persuade him to renounce his errors, on the principle of saving the sick man and curing the sickness', he took flight. Chou En-lai must have also played a part in the struggle. The premier was the central figure in China's emergence from the Cultural Revolution: internally, he had kept the administrative machine working and prevented a breakdown of production; externally, his moderating influence brought about the relaxation of tension that led to President Nixon's visit and the seating of Peking at the United Nations. Loyal to Chairman Mao from the time of the Tsunyi Conference, where he was noticeably ready to endorse the ideologue's election, Chou En-lai has always stood apart from the Party hierarchy. The bureaucratic ideal represented by Liu Shao-ch'i, the dominant one in the period before 1966, never seemed to appeal to his political temperament. A skilled negotiator and tactician, Chou En-lai stayed at the very centre of revolutionary politics until his death from cancer in 1976, at the age of seventy-eight. Evidently his last triumph on behalf of Mao Tse-tung was outwitting Lin Piao.

The relationship between Mao Tse-tung and Chou En-lai was the enigma of modern Chinese history. It illustrated the unusualness of China's revolution and the changes in fortune of both the Party and the People's Liberation Army. Throughout his long and distinguished public career, Chou En-lai has been credited with a belief in moderation and a concern for the protection of the economy. Yet he led the anti-Rightist drive after the Hundred Flowers campaign and he did not draw back from the fray during the Cultural Revolution. Whilst Chairman Mao may have always harboured the slightest distrust of this *shih*'s son, whose years abroad in the early 1920s could have qualified his commitment to the Yenan way, there can be no question of Chou En-lai's loyalty, his *chung*. He kept the country going whenever ideology required a major upheaval, even though Mao Tse-tung would have been prepared to shake the premier's own position if it were necessary to keep on a revolutionary course. But he outlasted Liu Shao-ch'i, the Party bureaucrat, and Lin Piao, the revolutionary general, leaving the political stage only a few months before Chairman Mao himself.

'It is contrary to the will of the people,' wrote Mao Tse-tung in the *People's Daily* on 10 March 1976, 'to revise previous verdicts.' This personal intervention in the issue of Teng Hsiao-ping's suitability for high office meant that the revisionist predilections of Party officials were becoming again the chief target of criticism. It was the familiar argument over material incentives: the unequal rewards that encourage enterprises to compete for materials and markets and allow technical and political bureaucracies to enrich themselves – at the expense of the people. The argument, however, could never be quite the same as the debates before the Cultural Revolution. The inexorable rise of Party membership after the foundation of the People's Republic – from 1.2 million in 1945 to 17 millions in 1961 – necessitated in Chairman Mao's eyes a renewal of revolutionary vigour, lest the new recruits took for granted their social leadership. Partnership with the Red Guards and the People's Liberation Army in the Cultural Revolution shattered delusions of grandeur. Moreover, the questioning and the reorganization of the education system has changed the balance of power in society, liberating to a greater extent than was thought possible the aspirations of the overwhelming rural population, and not least the young. On these masses it was obvious that Chairman Mao pinned his hopes for the future. The Cultural Revolution was illuminating: a popular movement, it began at the bottom.

Throughout the history of Chinese civilization there has been an awareness of the difficulty involved in mastering ideographic script. In a comparison of Sanskritic and Chinese writing made by Cheng Ch'iao, a well-known encyclopaedist of the Two Sungs period (960–1279), it was recognized that the foreign script was 'very simple' because it could represent an endless number of sounds by a few single hooks and curves. But his conclusion was very Chinese in the preference expressed for calligraphy. 'The world is of the opinion', he asserted, 'that people who know ideographs are wise and worthy, whereas those who do not know ideographs are simple and stupid.' Praise for such restrictive practice was never echoed by the Chinese Communist Party, which found its aim of universal literacy thwarted by the writing system. To deal with this hindrance to cultural aspirations, Mao Tse-tung declared in 1951 that 'the written language must be reformed; it should

OVERLEAF *Hsia-fang*: town-dwellers seeking refreshment in rural work and ideological discussion. Here, in 1967, teachers and students of the Peking Aeronautical Engineering Institute assist in the harvesting of wheat on a commune near the capital.

follow the common direction of phoneticization which has been taken by the world's languages.' It needed to reflect standard Chinese as spoken and record the sounds in a simple script. This appeared the prerequisite for a system of popular education: it alone would ensure that the literary monopoly of the *shih* was abolished and that the *nung* and the *kung* were able to make a significant contribution to the social organization. In reality, adopting the Roman alphabet has proved too complicated. Monosyllabic Chinese relies heavily on tone for the differentiation of meaning and the transcription of these closely related sounds into Roman letters produced unintelligible writing. When it was realized that the demise of the ideographic script would also mean the end of written unity between dialects, effectively cutting off from standard Mandarin as many as one hundred million southerners, language reform turned to the simplification of existing characters, though a 'Chinese Phonetic Alphabet' officially remains the long-term aim. Chou En-lai favoured both. 'It is clear', he wrote in 1958, 'that the simplified characters are easier to learn and to write than the characters in their original forms. It is, therefore, natural that the masses, including the workers, peasants, school pupils and school teachers, enthusiastically receive the simplified characters. . . . From the standpoint of the people, we should affirm definitely that the work of simplification is a good thing.' As for anxiety about the brush, he recalls that 'calligraphy is an art; it will not be restricted by the simplification. We cannot compel everybody to write according to the scheme. . . . At the same time, we should welcome the writing of simplified characters by our calligraphers so that these simplified forms will appear more artistic.'

Adult education in the Yenan period was given greater prominence than the education of children. Mao Tse-tung's emphasis on mass support for all policies – a support obtainable only when the masses are reached by propaganda and by information transmitted through mass media – caused literacy to be regarded as a basic political necessity. After the Cultural Revolution there has been a reassertion of this educational priority, with secondary-school students not going straight into higher education. Instead they go to a factory, a commune, or a unit of the People's Liberation Army. The corollary is that universities and colleges enrol students from among workers, peasants and soldiers who have practical experience. More extreme, Peking University in 1975 was largely abandoning its campus for new teaching quarters in factories and communes, so that it could directly serve the interests of the people and contribute to economic development. The model for this move was Chaoyang Agricultural College in Liaoning. Its students, who were *nung*, trained for three years before returning to their villages with their newly acquired skills. Their courses combined science with work and research in the field: they were able to raise the standard of agricultural technique in the immediate countryside and act as a living link between education and society. Moreover, the assault on examinations during the Cultural Revolution has resulted in the eclipse of their predictive function. They are not used for selection as much as a guide for teachers and students as to their success in coping with the curriculum. 'The method of examination', Chairman Mao had remarked in 1964, 'tackles the students as enemies and launches surprise attacks against them.' Education is now regarded as a process continuing throughout life and for many work teams the *People's Daily* provides the text for daily discussion. The *shih* should be replaced by a new proletarian intelligentsia because of the new unity of theory and practice in teaching. An example is the arithmetic lesson conducted by an old peasant under the title of 'A Debt of Blood and Tears'. It is reported how a class wept and shouted when he showed the method of calculating the rate of interest paid to a landlord over a number of years.

The anti-Confucius campaign was, however, directed at the military leadership as much as the intellectuals. Commanders were just as likely to exploit their positions and look down upon manual labour. According to the *People's Daily* on 2 February 1974, Lin Piao was a revisionist guilty of revering the teachings of the ancient and reactionary philosopher. This campaign had the appearance of one directed from the top, with Chairman Mao personally involved; yet the references to the outrage felt by 'workers, peasants and soldiers' were factual. The People's Liberation Army is very different from other armies. A Japanese observer noted,

> it is usual to see Chinese soldiers working in fields and factories alongside other workers. There is no arrogance in their attitude and no sign on their faces that they are aware of possessing any special powers. Historically speaking, the Chinese army sprang from the peasant revolution and the armed resistance movement against the Japanese. Its original purpose was to work with, not against, the people and even now this tradition of easy co-existence still persists.

COMMUNES VERSUS CITIES

Self-denial is the expected pattern of social behaviour today in China. The diligent peasant-farmer and the industrious factory worker are the twin ideals. Frugality and foresight, always the fundamental qualities of the best *nung*, have become watchwords in the service of the people. But austerity is tolerable when it goes hand in hand with effective social and economic reconstruction. The recovery of the economy under the Chinese Communist Party has been little short of miraculous. Though it has been in effect isolated from world-wide inflation, economic development has had to square with ideology and the concept of permanent revolution. This remains no mean achievement in itself, but for those Chinese who lived through the final years of Nationalist misgovernment it is a matter of profound relief. They remember only too well the galloping inflation, the unchecked speculation in basic commodities, and the shortages of everything except war materials. By mid-1948 the retail price index in Shanghai, from a 1937 base of 100, had reached 287,700,000.

After his visit to the People's Republic in 1972, John Kenneth Galbraith described the reconstruction in these terms:

> There can be now no serious doubt that China is devising a highly effective economic system. Development is from a very low level of per capita production, and that product is still low. With the liberation, decades of national and civil war, endemic pillage and public anarchy came to an end. Under almost any economic system this would have led to economic gains. Law, order and honest government are very productive. But there is massive evidence of great continued movement – new housing, new

industrial plants, new buildings at old plants, the impressive figures on the increase in local industrial and agricultural production and employment, the supply of basic staples in markets and shops, the people thronging through to buy them and the estimates of relative or percentage increases in production of agricultural and some industrial products. . . . The Chinese economic system would not please most Americans or Europeans but it is not used by them. It does strike me as better adapted to its particular circumstances – more flexible, practical and dynamic and with a strikingly more successful protection of quality – than that of the socialist cum Communist states of the West.

Fundamental to this success has been the role of the commune. The name comes from the Paris Commune of 1871, an institution that Engels cited for the bourgeoisie as an example of the dictatorship of the proletariat. It had witnessed the abolition of the social division of labour, the perennial stumbling block of the transition to socialism. In the People's Republic the first communes were set up as part of the Great Leap Forward of 1958. Experience over the next two or three years demonstrated that some of these twenty-five thousand communes were too large; many were in consequence subdivided to give a more manageable size and to correspond with the local pattern of trading. By 1966 there were seventy-eight thousand communes, each one approximately equated with the *hsiang*, or county. Some range in the size of communes is to be expected in a country of such variegated geography and climate. Even in 1958 the largest communes were situated on the North China Plain, where the average population was forty thousand. This contrasted with average figures for the climatically marginal areas of the north-west: Kansu had sixteen thousand and Sinkiang only fourteen thousand.

216

'Long live Chairman Mao', the flash cards proclaimed on the twenty-first anniversary of the People's Republic. Ever since the demonstrations in the May Fourth Movement of 1919, the great square of T'ien An Men outside the Purple Forbidden City has held a peculiar fascination for modern Chinese. Here it was that the Red Guards assembled for their mass rallies during the Cultural Revolution.

The trend towards smaller units continues in frontier regions, though elsewhere a degree of stability and equilibrium has become apparent.

The commune is a collective unit of production and of ownership of land and other resources. It also functions as the unit of local government responsible for education, welfare, security, justice, finance, trade and communications. It is in fact the channel through which the peasant-farmers deal with higher authorities for planning production, sales, purchases and taxation. Within the commune there are work teams of between twenty and thirty families to whom an allocation of land has been made. The family remains the smallest constituent group as well as the basis of economic life, and a parcel of family land usually exists for the supply of household vegetables, fruit and meat. But the commune movement is a radical departure from the pocket-handkerchief farms of the past; it is a concerted attempt to build a sound foundation for technological and social advance. Chou En-lai told the National People's Congress in 1975 that raising the backward parts of the countryside to a reasonable level, through better fertilizer, farm machinery and irrigation, filling in the blank spots in industry, and extending the railway network, were the first stages in the plan to modernize China. By 1980 the economy should be strong enough for the launch that will put the People's Republic 'in the front rank of the world' by the year 2000.

In line with the policy of 'walking on two legs' the education system aims in the countryside at combining theory with practice. Commune primary schools are locally run but receive a subsidy from central funds. *Hsia-fang*, the periodic migration of town dwellers to the rural areas for physical and ideological refreshment in labour and discussion, has penetrated the sectors of secondary and higher education, with students we have noticed spending their formative years in agriculture. The countryside now is less isolated than

217

at any time in Chinese history, and the belief in the rural population as the wellspring of wisdom and truth has its influence on the cities. An anti-urban temper can be discerned in the policies of the Chinese Communist Party. It has been suggested that Mao Tse-tung's distaste for cities might have been due to the historical experience of the Treaty Ports. Certainly industrial development after 1949 has followed a conspicuously different course, as new centres have been planned and opened away from the coastline: they are sited in cities like Changchun, Loyang, Kunming, Chungking and Lanchow. The recently constructed railway line joining Cheng-tu and Kunming forms an integral part of this interior policy. Of its total length of nearly eight hundred kilometres, over a third comprises bridges and tunnels. Where the terrain is extremely rugged the stations have been built in the tunnels themselves. A major feat of engineering, this railway track give access to the western provinces and links strategically important Yunnan and Singkiang.

The fate of Shanghai, the premier Treaty Port, is instructive. Despite its possession of a skilled workforce, a developed local business structure, special services, and satellite industries, the Chinese Communist Party has prevented further growth in population and industrial output. No longer does Shanghai dominate commercial activities: before 1949 the city and its environs contained forty-three per cent of all registered companies. Shanghai was the exploding city of the early twentieth century – a place of abode for the fabulously rich and the desperately poor who were sucked into its wretched and overcrowded slums by the possibility of relief from destitution in the villages. Brothels, banks and brutal working conditions in factories' were standard. The political power of secret societies was flaunted for every one to see, as were their activities in racketeering and vice. Shanghai, the adventurer's paradise, had been always outside the control of the Chinese authorities. The result of Communist rule on the city is dramatic change.

> Shanghai today [Neville Maxwell said in 1974] is a city transformed, even a city re-born, even if it is still overcrowded. Nevertheless there is a feeling of order, even of space. It is brisk, clean, and purposeful, a working city, not an agglomeration of individuals, most of them wretched, but a huge community made up of an infinite number of small communities. It appears as a working democracy, in the sense that the people are involved, through a structure of neighbourhood and street committees, with decisions that affect their everyday lives. There is full employment, there are no beggars, and the look and feel of the society seem to confirm the Chinese statement that there is no prostitution. There is a network of community-run health services, with hygiene being the responsibility of neighbourhood and street groups rather than the city or the state. Furthermore with a birth rate beginning to decline under the impact of the family planning programme (the city authorities report that in the past few years it has fallen from 2 per cent to 0.7 per cent), and the effects of the relocation of industries and the emigration of 'educated youngsters' to the countryside, the population of about 10 millions has begun to decline by about 100,000 a year.

This amazing transformation was of course interrelated with progress in the countryside. By choosing a rural model for national renewal the Chinese Communists ended the drift of landless peasants to the cities. It is a feature of

Shanghai, a city now reclaimed by the Chinese.

A commune bazaar in South China.

the People's Republic that greatly interests the Third World. But there is a policy of urban rehabilitation too. Old cities were repaired and brought back into economic use. The long years of war, coming after the collapse of the imperial system, had taken their toll of public and private buildings. Wherever practicable there was put in train a process of decentralization, with factories being resited beyond the city limits, outside the ring of communes that undertake intensive agriculture in order to feed each city. One of the aims of Chinese planning is to avoid the re-emergence of a sharp dichotomy between the urban and industrial sector and the rural sector of the economy. Since the development of the commune, industry has become increasingly diffused into the countryside so that industrial activities are an important source of employment and wealth in many communes. As early as 1966 in Kwantung certain communes derived forty-five per cent of their total income from industry. The problems of rural underemployment and urban overcrowding are thus solved at the same time. The city population too has a surprisingly large rural element, because urban boundaries include much of the surrounding countryside.

Membership of a factory is not unlike membership of a commune. For the city dweller the factory incorporates politics, education and welfare services, besides a livelihood. It is 'a place where illiterate workers learn how to read and write, and where employees can and do improve their work skills and develop new ones through education and training. It is a place where housing, schools, recreational facilities, roads, shops, and offices are often constructed or remodelled by factory employees. It is also a place from which employees go out into the fields and help the peasants with their harvesting.' Although the two cells of national growth are the factory and the commune, the primacy of the latter is unchallenged. In city streets visitors report military and civilian trucks transporting people and goods to the rural areas. Others travel to farms on bicycles or on foot. Exhortation by the Party and popular enthusiasm accounts for this movement of people in a direction singular to the People's Republic. Most significant of all is the willingness of young participants, the heirs to the Cultural Revolution. They will help to ensure that there is no growing apart of city and countryside, so that China avoids a new breed of town-based bureaucrats cut off from the daily life of the people, the country's most inexhaustible resource. Talking of the strenuous efforts of a very poor village at the beginning of the People's Republic, Chairman Mao said: 'I think the situation is the same as regards our whole nation. In a few decades, why can't 600 million paupers, by their own efforts, create a socialist country, rich and strong?' In the late 1970s most Chinese can answer this in the affirmative. Such optimism is perhaps one of his greatest bequests.

'LET THE PAST SERVE THE PRESENT'
The art of Tun-huang, its strength and simple vigorous style, excited traditional Chinese painters as well as those who had received a Western training. Here was a striking mixture of West and Central Asian influences within a Chinese tradition of painting. The exhibition of Chang Ta-ch'ien's 'restored' copies at Ch'eng-tu, and their publication in Shanghai after the Second World War, served as a reminder to Chinese artists that there were untapped sources of inspiration and technique from the past. Social realism on the Russian model is pursued by many artists working with cartoon or wood-cut techniques, and indeed large-scale poster art is dominant in public life, but there exists a strong current of attraction towards the artistic heritage of China. It is part of the People's Republic's strange love–hate relationship with the past. Chairman Mao had told the people not to dismiss history but make it serve the present. Only then will the country be able to 'separate all the rotten things of the ancient feudal ruling class from the fine ancient popular culture that is more or less democratic and revolutionary in character'. Specimens of Mao Tse-tung's own poetry have appeared on paintings in the traditional style, and a great deal of money is spent on exhibiting and reproducing such works. Nor has any ideological objection ever been raised against Chi'i Pai-shih.

Where the past can eminently serve the present is in archaeology. An Institute of Archaeology was founded in 1949 and the degree of official support given to archaeological excavation is unmatched in the world. Early activists like Kuo Mo-jo (born 1892), who in 1930 had enrolled Lu Hsun in the All-China League of Left-Writers, had been fascinated by archaeology and the detailed investigation of China's past. 'The demands of society,' Kuo Mo-jo said, 'did not permit us to remain enclosed within ivory towers. We sensed the need for change but had no power to enforce it.' Yet one of the motives for the interest of the Party in archaeology may be the relative neutrality of finds. Because excavations turn up artifacts from ancient cultural periods and shed light on the material life of generations long ago, rather than directly interpret the imperial history of the recent past, it has been suggested that ideology has little reason to intrude. A Shang bronze can stand remote and alone.

Antiquarian study arose early in China. The first comprehensive history of the country, the *Historical Records* of Ssu-ma Ch'ien, dates from 100 BC and deals with the knowable past. Typical of Chinese historians was his reluctance to speculate or comment upon the beginnings of life. Ssu-ma Ch'ien was quite content with the fact that mankind existed long before his own narrative took up the thread of politics and society. Yet at the beginning of this century there was some scepticism amongst Western historians concerning aspects of Chinese historical tradition. The discovery of Peking Man in the 1920s and the Shang capitals at Anyang in the 1930s perforce changed attitudes, but it is a tribute to the pioneer work of present-day Chinese archaeologists that the world confidently anticipates that other marvels will be unearthed. The 1973 Chinese Exhibition in London was the show-case of the People's Republic. Not a few of the pieces on display, including the jade funeral suit of the Han Princess Tou Wan, had been excavated during the Cultural Revolution. Of central importance to palaeontology and the prehistory of China were the fossil remains of Lan-t'ien Man, a primitive relation of Peking Man found near Sian in 1963 and 1964. From the comparative thickness of the skull and the restricted cranial capacity it has been deduced that *Sinanthropus lantienensis* dates from about 600,000 BC. The find in 'the land within the passes' shows that there was a wide distribution of ancient ape-men on the North China plain and furnishes evidence to sustain Chinese historical traditions of the great antiquity of the human race in the Yellow River valley. Other discoveries of later inhabitants – specimens of Neanderthal Man from sites throughout the People's Republic and *Homo Sapiens* notably from Tzu-yang in Kwangsi – have confirmed the belief that Chinese civilization is the end-product of a continuous historical process stretching back to remotest times.

The connection between these fossil remains of the Old Stone Age and the sites of the New Stone Age is still obscure, though the excavation of Pan-p'o, an advanced Yang-shao culture site also situated near Sian, was a landmark in the investigation of the Neolithic of East Asia as a whole. The 1962 report on the village of Pan-p'o, with its detailed descriptions of all the finds, impressed archaeologists around the world. Today this prehistoric community, whose population at its height was five or six hundred people, is a museum to which thousands of visitors come and look at the partially reconstructed houses and kilns of the early *nung*. It antedates the massive drainage and flood prevention schemes of Yu the Great Engineer, the traditional founder of feudalism, but this separation from Chinese myth concerning the origins of social organization should not divert us from the main implication of contemporary archaeology: nothing has been discovered in the systematic investigation under the People's Republic that would question the view that sees Chinese civilization as always predominantly agricultural. And the prestige which archaeology now enjoys will ensure that there is no repetition of the tomb robbery and destruction of ancient sites which occurred during the Republic, when road and railway construction did more to enrich the antique trade than the national economy.

A rare coincidence of archaeology and ideology was the discovery in Shensi of a buried army of ceramic figures close by the mound marking the tomb of 'the First Emperor', Ch'in Shih Huang-ti. In 1974 peasant-farmers sinking a series of wells were surprised to encounter underground chambers containing life-size warriors, horses and chariots made out of pottery. So far archaeologists have unearthed only several hundred statues of amazing workmanship out of an estimated total of six thousand. But the pleasure this unexpected find has given the Party is transparent. Mao Tse-tung had always been particularly fascinated by Ch'in Shih Huang-ti, who was credited with the attempted destruction of feudalism and the reactionary teachings of Confucius which underpinned it. Peking Radio has sought to rehabilitate the memory of this ruler, traditionally known as the scourge of the scholars and the initiator of vast schemes that oppressed the people. Broadcasts have described the building of the Great Wall as 'the wisdom and creative power of the working masses', forgetting the human cost of reducing everything 'in a uniform manner'. The anti-Confucian campaign was thus strengthened by the recovery of the buried army of Ch'in, since prior to 1974 there was no archaeological evidence to refute the traditional Chinese view – that of Confucian historians – that 'the First Emperor' was an utter barbarian lacking in aesthetic sense.

Archaeologists at work on artifacts recovered from ancient tombs.

The fear that the Chinese Communist Party intended to undermine and finally destroy traditional culture has been allayed as much by the treatment of religion as the status accorded to archaeology. Dislike of Christian missionary activity is neither new nor specifically Communist. Ever since the Jesuit controversy on the rites of ancestor worship in the reign of Emperor Ch'ing K'ang-hsi, who did his utmost to comprehend the theological grounds of the bitter dispute with Rome, there has been an impatience on the part of the authorities and the educated classes with Western evangelism. The T'ai P'ing revolutionary movement was the last chance for mass conversion to Christianity in China. Its defeat and the disappointment of the popular aspirations which it stimulated, by the Ch'ing dynasty and the European powers, an unholy alliance if there ever was one, shifted the focus of intellectual and emotional excitement from religion to politics. Modern Chinese Christians are regarded as the possessors of a 'bourgeois ideology', but the degree of interference they suffer depends upon the extent to which their opinions politically diverge from Communist orthodoxy. At the Bandung Conference in 1955 Chou En-lai announced a policy of toleration, but unlike the Confucian scholar-bureaucrat of imperial days the Party member cannot ignore superstitions because they beguile the people. Christianity is too closely bound up with capitalism, or rather the West, for any relaxation of vigilance to occur. As for Taoism and Buddhism, these faiths have been in retreat for centuries, they remain a part of the social

Wooden figurines recently found in a Han tomb dating from about 100 BC.

224

landscape, but as on previous occasions in Chinese history their property and personnel have come under official control. The People's Republic could be described as a multi-religious community in which 'Marxism–Leninism–Mao Tsetung Thought' is the standard of moral behaviour, the state orthodoxy in place of Confucianism. Pressure will be exerted on religious convictions, as on any other 'backward attitude', whenever there is an acceleration of the permanent revolution. Yet the humanitarian outlook of the educated from Chu Hsi onwards should keep the people's respect for the memory of Chairman Mao in decent bounds. Indeed, the rational, organicist philosophy of Neo-Confucianism is by no means dead. The modern Communist is awed but not unintelligent: his touchstone is the people and his guide is dialectical materialism. Chairman Mao once said,

> While we recognize that in the general development of history the material determines the mental, and social being becomes social consciousness, we also – and indeed must – recognize the reaction of mental on material things, of social consciousness on social being and of the superstructure on the economic base. This does not go against materialism; on the contrary, it avoids mechanical materialism and firmly upholds dialectical materialism.

China *is* in transition. A new, distinct 'proletarian' culture may soon emerge, but whatever the transformation might be, it would appear that it can be managed without an abrupt severance from the past.

'A KEY FACTOR IN THE WORLD SITUATION'

'The Chinese revolution is a key factor in the world situation, and its victory is heartily anticipated by the people of every country, especially by the toiling masses of the colonial countries. When the Chinese revolution comes into full power, the masses of many colonial countries will follow the example of China and win a similar victory of their own.' Thus Mao Tse-tung in 1936 affirmed the centrality of events in China to the modern world. Once again the Chinese saw themselves at the centre of international affairs: they inhabited the Middle Kingdom of the Communist movement in the Third World. The events of the past forty years have modified this perception but in no way has the belief of the Chinese Communist Party in its innovatory role been dimmed. 'Marxism–Leninism–Mao Tsetung Thought' remains the pattern of the future.

Ideology apart, the re-emergence of China as a great power makes it a key factor in the world situation. In November 1971, at the first meeting of the United Nations after the admission of the People's Republic, its representative said that Peking would act as a protector of the Third World against the 'super-powerism' of the United States and the Soviet Union. In this role the People's Republic hopes that it will be supported by the combined weight of the countries belonging to the European Economic Community, an expectation which helps to explain the cordial reception given in Peking to pro-Common Market politicians from Western Europe. The economic influence of the European Economic Community has never been underestimated by the Chinese. At the same time the anti-Confucius campaign was not merely an attack on élitism among the intelligentsia. It was an aspect of the ideological education aimed at the new technological class and the leaders of the People's

Liberation Army: it was a preventative against the possibility of Western influences which might arise from the more relaxed relationship with the West and the import of Western technology. Perhaps the determination of the Chinese to sort out their own difficulties largely without reference to the rest of the world is the most unusual feature of the People's Republic, though this inwardness is in accord with a long tradition of isolation and exclusion. China possesses considerable natural resources and over the past two years has become an oil exporter, but its own programme of economic and social reconstruction is the focus of world attention.

Ever since Malthus noticed the expansion of population at the beginning of the nineteenth century there has been a vociferous school of alarmists warning about the 'yellow peril'. It was argued that China's population was so large and expanding at so rapid a rate, and her resources so limited, that internal pressure would lead either to an overflow into Siberia or into the countries of South-east Asia. With the advantage of hindsight we can now appreciate that the precarious population – food balance prior to the establishment of the People's Republic was as much a symptom of institutional decay as demographic change. There are tensions within present-day China but the overall population density is lower than that of many European countries. The impression of overpopulation derives from the uneven distribution of the Chinese people, especially the heavy concentrations in the Huai and Yang-tze river valleys. The regeneration of the countryside and the development of the interior are the means by which the Chinese Communist Party intend to feed one-quarter of the world's population. Since 1949 the progress made by the People's Republic has been unprecedented – the contrast with India is unavoidable. The natural increase of today's population of eight hundred millions may add another twenty-five per cent to the total by the year 2000. However, late marriages and smaller families, now recommended by the government, could bring about a stable figure somewhat above one thousand millions during the early part of the twenty-first century.

Another twenty millions reside at the moment outside the People's Republic: these are the overseas Chinese, the majority of whom live in South-east Asia. At the Bandung Conference of Asian States in 1955 Chou En-lai reversed what had been Nationalist policy towards the overseas Chinese by declaring that no longer would all persons of Chinese descent be automatically citizens of the People's Republic. Henceforth, persons should normally and naturally be citizens of the country in which they were born. Though for a variety of reasons this initiative was suspected to be a trick by many of the delegates, a machination of the international Communist conspiracy, the newly independent countries of South-east Asia have realized subsequently the commonsense behind the change in attitude and responded accordingly. For the People's Republic the overseas Chinese are not a subversive force, but rather a problem. Far beyond the control of Peking, they possess their own press and education system; they are often essential parts of local capitalism, acting as bankers, merchants or manufacturers; and their sympathy may be with Taiwan. Even the overseas Chinese who are stirred by events on the mainland – the poorer immigrants or the students in middle schools – can be counter-productive to a successful revolutionary movement, since their activities tend to unite the native peoples behind the existing régimes. In

Indonesia, Thailand and the Philippines the acquisition of local nationality still leaves the Chinese underprivileged politically. In Malaysia, the Chinese are too numerous to permit the introduction of severe discriminatory legislation, though the riots of 1969 in Kuala Lumpur were an instance of Malay frustration at the clear economic lead of the Chinese. During the Cultural Revolution there was pressure for a more active diplomatic role on behalf of the overseas Chinese affected by new laws in Indonesia, but the policy of the People's Republic remains assimilation or repatriation. China's failure to save the Indonesian Communist Party in 1965 is evidence of the continued inability, or unwillingness, to undertake overseas interventions. The 'Domino Theory' was invented in Washington, not Peking. And there is on South-east Asia's own doorstep the record of the government of Lee Kuan Yew over the treatment of minority communities. Not without blame, Singapore does stand out as a country scrupulous to avoid policies which seem to favour the Chinese majority.

The People's Republic has not solved the problem of the 'Two Chinas'; but it would be unrealistic to doubt that the eventual outcome of relations between Peking and Taipei will be the absorption of the island. Its twenty years of independence are but a brief span in Chinese history, and the current reconstruction on the mainland should ensure that China does not succumb again to foreign pressures. Like the two remaining European colonies of Hong Kong and Macao, Taiwan will return to China when the appropriate moment arrives. The presence of a renewed and vigorous stage in the evolution of late Chinese civilization is a fact of life for East Asia, and the world.

Epilogue:
China after Chairman Mao

The death of Mao Tse-tung, who was eighty-two years old, on 10 September 1976 was an event of world-wide interest. As the tributes flowed into Peking from foreign heads of government and internationally known politicians, it was clear perhaps for the first time how significant Chairman Mao had been for China, and how far 'Marxism–Leninism–Mao Tsetung Thought' had penetrated the consciousness of the world. Few people indeed were ignorant of his name, an accolade shared previously by no Chinese person. Only from Taipei came a discordant note when an official statement denounced Mao Tse-tung as a 'despotic leader'. Yet Hua Kuo-feng (born *c.* 1920), the successor of Chou En-lai as well as of Mao Tse-tung, might have adapted the words spoken in 960 by the first Sung Emperor and in reply asked of Macao, Hong Kong and Taiwan: 'What wrong have your people done to be excluded from China?' For the Chinese view of the world has not fundamentally changed: it has been adjusted to take account of the modern world, but only so far as to permit China to retain its central place. 'Marxism–Leninism–Mao Tsetung Thought' is considered to be as universal as ever were the teachings of Confucius. China, not Russia, is the repository of Communist wisdom.

The re-emergence of China as a major power was the work of Mao Tse-tung, who gave his country what it longed for after a century of chaos and uncertainty – the revolutionary leadership, the strategy, the institutional framework, and, above all else, the ideology that could inspire its regeneration. Unlike other revolutionary leaders, he did not venture abroad and his origins within the peasant life of the provinces were not even grasped by his Chinese comrades at first. The rebellious son of a 'rich peasant', he was unique in his understanding of the land problem which so had worried Sun Yat-sen. Once Mao Tse-tung discovered Marxist theory he was able to use it, and adapt it, in his analysis of the contradictions of China and the outside world. We have already traced the successful evolution of both his thinking and his strategy, but it should never be forgotten when observing the events in China after his death that he was acutely aware of the limitations of his own achievement. The triumph of 1949, which united the country as it had not been for centuries, was only perceived as the beginning of revolutionary development, for as soon as China had room to manoeuvre Chairman Mao resumed the search begun in Yenan for a distinctly Chinese path to socialism. Just as the Great Leap Forward shook up the countryside through the commune movement, so the impact on the cities of the Great Proletarian Cultural Revolution was intended to liberate revolutionary energies and purify official dogma. According to Chairman Mao, there had been eleven important struggles against

Chairman Mao lying in state in the Purple Forbidden City, Peking. His widow, Chiang Ch'ing, looks on from the centre. Her fall from political eminence started two months after this photograph was taken.

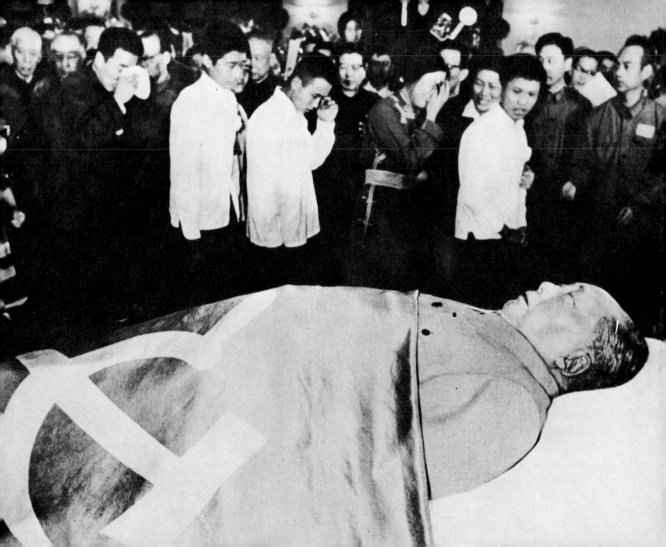

'enemies' within the Party since its inception, the last one being the campaign against Teng Hsiao-ping.

It remains to be seen whether or not the People's Republic stays on its singular revolutionary course now that Mao Tse-tung has died. So far there is little evidence to suggest that the ideologue's ideas have not been taken up enthusiastically by the mass of the people: revolutionary ardour is not waning. The gap between town and countryside has been greatly narrowed; education is no longer the preserve of the few and the assault on bureaucrats has lowered the status of the non-manual worker; there is a stable currency, no inflation, and freedom from foreign interference – these are outstanding bequests. What Chairman Mao could not provide was an heir, but such was the scope of his activities that those who are in power will have to go on from where he stopped. Though Hua Kuo-feng has been designated as his successor, it seems likely that some kind of coalition between the Party and the People's

Hua Kuo-feng, the successor of Mao Tse-tung and Chou En-lai.

Liberation Army will prevail for several years to come. The Tangshan earthquake, which killed as many as 200,000 people in July 1976 and may be viewed by superstitious Chinese today as a natural premonition of Chairman Mao's death, did help to confirm the authority of Hua Kuo-feng, simply for the reason that the scale of the disaster compelled resolute and united action. Under his careful direction the Party will probably cling to the 'anti-revisionist' line and avoid close ties with the Soviet Union. The Central Committee in the official obituary specifically mentioned its duties in this respect, since Chairman Mao

> led our party, our army and the people of our country in using people's war to overthrow the reactionary rule of imperialism, feudalism and bureaucratic-capitalism, winning the great victory of the new democratic revolution and founding the People's Republic of China. The victory of the Chinese people's revolution led by Chairman Mao changed the situation in the East and the world and blazed a new trail for the cause of liberation of the oppressed nations and oppressed peoples.

Mao Tse-tung himself once told Edgar Snow he simply wished to be remembered 'as a teacher'. But he always reminded his followers that 'one must be a pupil of the masses before one can become their teacher'.

The lessons of the Chinese people are still to be learned. The period of national decline is over and a quarter of mankind has taken a great leap from the Middle Ages into the modern world. The People's Republic, which maintains an annual trade surplus, could be drawn into the world economy, or, as they have chosen to do on previous occasions, the Chinese might decide to isolate themselves again. This time their atomic armoury ought to prove a better deterrent than the terrifying head-dresses that Manchu bannermen hoped would scare British soldiers during the Opium Wars.

In *Chinese Civilization* we have attempted to show the underlying continuity of a great contemporary civilization. The People's Republic is not a total break with the past. Interest in archaeology indicates exactly the complex love–hate relationship every Chinese has with the magnificent heritage of China. It was Mao Tse-tung's role to set the country once again at the centre of world affairs. Perhaps the future holds for it an era of splendour reminiscent of the T'ang or the Two Sungs, but even today China has become as fascinating a country as ever Cathay was to Marco Polo.

Chronology

from the Yuan dynasty to the present day

MONGOL INVASION   Yuan dynasty 1279–1368

Kubilai Khan 1260–90
Chu Yuan-chang born 1328
Death of Bayan 1340

CHINESE RECOVERY   Ming dynasty 1368–1644

Ming Hung-wu 1368–98
Ming Yung-lo 1402–28
Peking built 1402–7
Cheng Ho's first voyage 1405–7
Portuguese at Canton 1514
Nurhachu born 1559
Matteo Ricci at Peking 1598

MANCHU CONQUEST   Ch'ing dynasty 1644–1912

Ch'ing K'ang-hsi 1661–1722
Ch'ing Yung-cheng 1722–35
Ch'ing Ch'ien-lung 1735–95
Trade restricted to Canton 1757
Lord Macartney's embassy 1793–4
First Opium War 1839–42
Second Opium War 1858–60
T'ai P'ing rebellion ends 1866
Sun Yat-sen born 1866
Chiang Kai-shek born 1887
Mao Tse-tung born 1893
Sino–Japanese War 1894–5
100 Days of Reform 1898
Boxer Rebellion 1900
Death of Empress T'zu Hsi 1908

END OF IMPERIAL ERA   Chinese Republic 1912–49

                                                      Sun Yat-sen president 1911
                                                      Warlord Period 1912–28
                                                      Death of Yuan Shih-k'ai 1916
                                                      May Fourth Movement 1919
                                                      Chinese Communist Party formed
                                                        1920–1
                                                      Death of Sun Yat-sen 1925
                                                      May Thirtieth Movement 1925
                                                      Long March 1934–5
                                                      Sian Incident 1936
                                                      Sino–Japanese War starts 1937
                                                      Pearl Harbor 1941
                                                      Hiroshima and Nagasaki bombed
                                                        1945
                                                      Lin Piao captures Mukden 1948

COMMUNISM TRIUMPHS   People's Republic 1949 onwards

                                                      Sino–Soviet Treaty signed 1950
                                                      Korean War 1950–3
                                                      Great Leap Forward 1958
                                                      Russia recalls advisers 1960
                                                      A-bomb exploded 1964
                                                      Cultural Revolution 1966–9
                                                      Admission to United Nations 1971
                                                      President Nixon's visit 1972
                                                      Death of Chiang Kai-shek 1975
                                                      Death of Chou En-lai 1976
                                                      Death of Mao Tse-tung 1976

Notes and References

Names of authors listed below are always followed by a number in brackets corresponding to the full reference in the bibliography, e.g. Needham (1)'. When a translation made by a previous author is used without change in the text, the reference is given thus: 'tr. Waley'. As far as is practical, the exact source of the Chinese original is indicated in front of such a citation. When a translation has been made by the author, the ascription is: 'tr. auct.'. The references and notes are identified by folio and paragraph numbers.

INTRODUCTION

14.2 STABILITY OF CHINESE CIVILIZATION: Elvin (1), p. 17.

15.2 THE FOUR ESTATES: See Cotterell (1), pp. 42–6, 82–3, 122–3, 148–9, 195.

16.2 YU THE GREAT ENGINEER: *Ibid.*, p. 24.

17.1 LOESS SOIL: Chi Ch'ao-Ting (1), p. 24.

17.2 'WHEN THE CANAL . . . FEUDAL STATES': *Shih Chi*, ch. 29, p. 31; tr. auct.

21.2 'AN EMPIRICAL RATIONALISM . . .': Needham (1), pp. 137–8.

22.3 'THE PRODUCT . . . TWO ENVIRONMENTS': Lattimore (1), p. 25.

23.1 'WHICH THE GREAT KHAN . . . BY SEA': Marsden (1), bk. II, ch. LXIV.

I MING: THE CHINESE RECOVERY 1386–1644

24.1 'AS FOR THE CHINESE . . . PEOPLE': Ch'uan Heng, *Keng-shen wai-shih*, 41-b; tr. Dardess (1), p. 62.

27.2 'WAS IN HEIGHT . . . COVERED WITH IRON': Quoted by Dreyer, E. L., 'The Poyang Campaign, 1363: Inland Naval Warfare in the Founding of the Ming Dynasty', in Kierman and Fairbank (1), p. 209.

29.1 CORPORAL PUNISHMENT: Hucker (1), p. 48. 'What was most humiliating of all was that officials could be seized in open-court assembly, stripped naked, and flogged with bamboo poles, sometimes to death. In short, the long-prevalent Western view that the persons of Chinese civil officials were inviolate is simply unfounded in fact, so far as the Ming period is concerned.'

31.2 CHINESE CONTACT WITH AUSTRALIA: It is not unreasonable to expect that Chinese junks which call regularly at Timor, only just over four hundred miles from Port Darwin, sailed on to reconnoitre the northern extremities of the Australian coastline. A Taoist statuette, discovered near the shore at Port Darwin in 1897, could be a clue; the find was made beneath the roots of a banyan tree at least two hundred years old. Another tantalizing piece of evidence found in 1943, if we can presume its authenticity, is an ancient map of Australia, compiled by the captain of a Chinese vessel in 1426. It was lost again in Peking, and recent enquiries have failed to disclose the present whereabouts of the map. Needham (6), pp. 536–40, reviews the state of current opinion on Australia; considers relations with pre-Columbian America, pp. 540–53; and probable Chinese voyages into the Atlantic around the Cape of Good Hope, pp. 501–3.

31.3 'WATER BENEFITS': Chi Ch'ao-Ting (1), pp. 143–4.

31.3 SUNG LI AND THE GRAND CANAL: Needham (6), pp. 315–16.

32.1 CH'EN PANG-KO'S MEMORIAL: *Ming Shih*, ch. 84. p. 12a, b; tr. Needham (6), p. 336. In Cotterell (1) pp. 53–5 it was noted that because of the size and variation in the flow of China's rivers the traditional policy was co-operation with Nature rather than any attempt to contain the rush of water. Prince Huan of Ch'i, head of the feudal state astride the flood plains of the Yellow River, had come to grief when sometime before 600 BC he attempted to concentrate the nine streams of the delta into one. Therefore hydraulic engineers took to heart the motto of Li Ping, the Ch'in governor of Szechuan, a province he made prosperous in 316 BC, through an extensive irrigation scheme on the Ch'engtu plain: his advice was 'Dig the channel deep, and keep the dykes low.'

33.1 EDUCATION: Imperial interest in education was long-standing in China, scholars always being exempt from land revenue tax, but it was the period of the Two Sungs that witnessed the evolution of a national system. Block-printed editions of the Confucian classics were published just before the Northern Sung dynasty, though it was the invention of movable type around 1040 which allowed large-scale government sponsorship of manuals on agricultural method for the peasant-farmers. See Cotterell (1), p. 188.

33.3 BUILDING ACTIVITIES: Goodrich (2), p. 193.

33.3 POPULATION CHANGES: 'The Chinese population under the Northern Sung was well over one hundred millions. By 1580 it was at least half as big again, say somewhere between 160 and 250 millions. . . . The general demographic pattern is . . . the Chinese population reached a high point in the twelfth century, fell until the later fourteenth century, recovered to a new high point in the later sixteenth century, collapsed abruptly from then to about

1650, then grew until the end of the pre-modern period in 1850 . . . [when the figure was] over 400 millions,' Elvin (1), pp. 129, 309–10.

35.1 DISAPPEARANCE OF RURAL ADMINISTRATORS: *Ibid.*, pp. 260–5. He also writes that 'during the Ming dynasty (1368–1644) and the earlier part of the Ch'ing (or Manchu) dynasty, the manorial order with serfdom and a serf-like tenancy continued to dominate the countryside, though with diminishing vigour as time passed. In the course of the eighteenth century they finally disappeared, and a new and distinctive rural order took shape. The landlord and pawn-broker took the place of the manorial lord; financial relationships displaced those of status. The members of the gentry who ran rural projects now did so as professional managers, and not owners of land directly interested in the outcome of their labours. Class consciousness and social mobility among the peasantry increased; and society became restless, fragmented and fiercely competitive,' pp. 23–5.

35.2 'THE SECRET OF THE ALCHEMISTS': Marsden (1), bk. II, ch. XVIII.

35.3 WANG AN-SHIH'S ECONOMIC REFORMS: See Cotterell (1), pp. 181–6.

36.3 OIRAT-CHINESE TRADE: Mote, F. W., 'The T'u-mu Incident of 1449', in Kierman and Fairbank (1), p. 253. There can be little doubt concerning the motives of Wang Chen in his interference with the tributary system. He repeatedly refused the request to establish border trading posts at which there could be regular exchanges on the basis of fair dealing for the reason that his eunuch agents would then be unable to continue cheating the Mongols. Yet the restriction of trade with the tribes of the steppe was a policy of the Ming government which had the support of the *shih*. The officials were worried about the flow of Chinese armour, swords, crossbows and guns across the northern border; this was the military technology on which the security of the Empire depended. The embargo on firearms broke down towards the close of the Ming period, when knowledge of gunpowder and gun-making had spread into all the bordering territories.

41.3 CHINESE FIREARMS: Elvin (1), p. 95. The substitution of hard wood for metal in anti-cavalry bombards was justified by Ming commentators in terms of convenience; they became light enough for one man to haul. The imperial armies remained well equipped, though as Elvin suggests the true picture of the late Ming is technological standstill.

42.4 'YOUR HUMBLE SERVANT . . . A FULL STOMACH': *Jih-chih lu*, roll 10; tr. Li (1), p. 299.

45.2 THE WESTWARD ROUTE TO ASIA: This was the idea of the Florentine astronomer Toscanelli, an adviser of the Portuguese court with whom Columbus corresponded. Toscanelli was aware of the extent of China, his first-hand information coming from an oriental visitor to Pope Eugenius IV (1431–7). Although Columbus carried with him a letter from the King of Spain to the 'Great Khan', it is not unlikely that backing for the expedition was available because it was thought that the spice islands of 'the Indies' were closer to Europe than the coast of East Asia. In the event, as is well known, landfall occurred in America. See Hudson (1), ch. VII.

45.3 PORTUGUESE FORTIFICATIONS: The absence of strong navies in Asian waters gave the Portuguese their chance. After the victory of Din in 1509 they were able to concentrate their slender forces either in the narrow channels through which trading vessels sailed or near the small areas where the spices were produced. Hence, the strategic value of the Malacca base, and the ruthlessness of the Portuguese during its siege and capture. Privateering and imperialism were of course closely allied amongst European seafaring nations, the notable English official pirate captain being Sir Francis Drake. See Parry (1), ch, XI, XII.

46.2 'THEY HAVE FOUND . . . WERE FARRE OFF': De Mendoza (1), p. 92.

47.1 'WITH FIVE THOUSAND . . . IN THE WORLD': Quoted in Hudson (1), p. 249. See also Needham (6), p. 534.

47.2 'THIS COUNTRIE . . . ALTOGETHER': See Dawson (1).

2 THE MING REVIVAL

49.1 'THE CITY . . . WITH EYES TO SEE': *Mémories concernant les Chinois 'par les missionaires de Pekin'* (Paris: Nyon, 1776–1814), vol. 8, pp. 217–19; tr. Elvin and Skinner (1), pp. 1–2; slightly adapted. Jean-Joseph-Marie Amiot (1718–93) was a Jesuit in service at the court of the Emperor Ch'ing Ch'ien-lung. He wrote a number of books on China, including a grammar of the Manchu language.

50.2 'WHEN YUNG-LO . . . NINE GATES': Sirén (2), p. 43. The height and width measurements vary slightly from place to place; an average would be the western city wall near the P'ing-tzu Gate – its height is outside 10.30 metres, inside 10.10 metres, its width, at the top 11.50 metres, at the base 14.80 metres.

50.3 TZU CHIN CH'ENG AND THE TZU WEI HSING (*pole-star*): Sirén (3), p. 5. Elsewhere he has expanded the argument concerning the cosmological significance of Chinese buildings. In Sirén (5), Vol. 4, p. 1, we find: 'The development of architecture in China has since the earliest times been largely determined by intimate contact with nature, which to the Chinese, as to many ancient peoples, was ensouled. They planned their buildings with reference to the spirits of the earth, the water and the winds, they built palaces according to heavenly constellations and they dedicated their earliest sanctuaries, which were simply open-air altars, to the gods of the soil. Their activity as builders just as well as their religious ideas reflect a search for co-ordination with nature which has been of great importance for obtaining artistically successful results.

'The beauty and interest of Chinese buildings cannot always be appreciated from a strictly architectural point of view; they are often very simple and lacking in these elements of solidity and constructive proportions which we are used to connect with great architecture, but they have a charm of their own, born, so to say, out of a harmonious co-operation with nature. The wooden pillars rise above the supporting terraces, which often reach considerable heights, like tall trees on the mounds and hillocks. The lines of the far-projecting curving roof suggest the long wavering branches of the cryptomerias, and if there are any walls, they disappear almost in the play of light and shade produced by the broad eaves, the open galleries, the lattice-work of the windows, and the balustrades.

'It was, however, less by the suggestion of external forms than by the endeavour to interpret their purpose and meaning that the Chinese learned from nature. One may trace in their architectural activity as well as their pictorial and decorative arts a striving to express something of the life-impetus, the movement or the creative forces (*Yin* and *Yang*) which they found everywhere, though such endeavours are, indeed, modified by practical and constructual ideas.

'It should furthermore be remembered that there are few elements in Chinese architecture which did not originally have a symbolic meaning, even if in the course of time it has been forgotten or blurred by more practical considerations . . . Not only has the constructive system remained unchanged in principle during the centuries, but also the orientation of the buildings, their relation to their surroundings, and their external appearances.'

50.4 THE MERIDIAN GATE: Murphy, H. K., 'Architecture', in McNair (1), p. 365. Although the present structure dates from 1647, the restoration of 1801 being little more than a renewal of surfaces and decayed parts of the pavilions, it is most likely that the Ch'ing architects rebuilt the Wu Men in close correspondence with the earlier Ming gateway.

52.1 'THE SPLENDID EXTERIOR . . . OF THE PALACE CITY': Sirén (3), p. 20. He continues on p. 21: 'The labyrinth of walls and courts and colonnades and roofs is one great work of art, not of an individual creation but the result of a gradual growth (and decay) in accordance with architectural principles and the ancient traditions of might and splendour, which have prevailed in the construction of all the great Imperial Palaces of China.'

54.3 'HER MAJESTY'S THRONE ROOM . . . THE DULL BRONZE': Carl (1), pp. 204–5. Miss Carl was commissioned to paint a portrait of the Empress Dowager T'zu Hsi for the St Louis Exposition of 1904. On presentation at court the American artist found it 'impossible . . . to realize that this kindly looking lady, so remarkably young-looking, with so winning a smile, could be the so-called cruel, implacable tyrant, the redoubtable "old" Empress Dowager, whose name had been on the lips of the world since 1900'. In fact, Miss Carl's account of her unique residence was an attempt to correct the misimpression of T'zu Hsi's character in the West as well as to disclaim some of the unfavourable opinions attributed to herself.

58.1 GREEN MOUNT: Marsden (1), bk. II, ch. VI. The large Indian pagoda of white marble was built by Emperor Ch'ing Shun-chih in 1652 in commemoration of the first visit of the Dalai Lama to Peking.

59.2 THE SUNG IMPERIAL NAVY: A strong naval policy had been called for by many Sung officials in order to resist attacks by Kin, and later Mongol, forces penetrating the Yang-tze River valley. Lo (1), p. 491, writes: 'Built upon the remains of the provincial navy of Northern Sung and favoured by contemporary technological advances in the art of navigation, naval architecture, and the manufacture and use of firearms, the Southern Sung navy reached a high degree of efficiency. It won victories when the army suffered setbacks . . . [and it] had the distinction of being the first national navy to be established on a permanent basis and to

function as an independent service. In 1130 the Chinese navy already numbered 11 squadrons with 3,000 men. This led to the establishment, two years later, of the Imperial Commissioner's office for Control and Organization of the Coastal Areas, with its headquarters at Ting-hai, one of the islands of the Chusan group. By 1174 there were 15 squadrons with 21,000 men, and in 1237 the navy could boast a combat force of 20 squadrons with about 52,000 men. The most important naval base was Hsu-pu, on the Yang-tse estuary, protecting the flourishing port later to be known as Shanghai. Second in importance was still the base of Ting-hai, set up to defend the capital Hangchow.'

In 1129 trebuchets throwing gunpowder bombs had been decreed standard equipment on all vessels. The treadmill-operated paddle-wheel craft proved invaluable in pitched battles on the Yang-tze, because they were easy to manoeuvre: some were stern-wheelers, others had as many as eleven wheels a side. Armour plating was introduced at the beginning of the thirteenth century. See Needham (6), pp. 476–7.

61.2 EGYPT: Duyvendak (2), p. 32.

61.2 'THOSE WHO . . . EVER GREATER': Part of a translation from *Li-tai T'ung Chien Chi Lan*, or *Essentials of the Comprehensive Mirror of History*, compiled in the eighteenth century, and quoted in Needham (6), pp. 487–8. From an examination of historical sources covering all the expeditions of Cheng Ho, Mills (1), p. 2, has ascertained that representatives of sixty-seven overseas states, including seven kings, came bearing tributed to render homage to the emperor.

61.3 SUNG REGULATION OF TRADE: Filesi (1), p. 9. The level of imports of luxury items had increased steadily during the Two Sungs, a network of informers on the look-out for illegal transactions conspicuously failing to assist the imperial customs officials in their task of protecting the coinage. Only in the Ming period did porcelain, whose manufacture had attained to unknown levels of quality and quantity, supersede all other commodities as the media of overseas trade. Another item of export at the end of the Southern Sung dynasty was tea, originally a medicinal preparation in China but a favourite beverage from the T'ang. Trade in tea was brisk in South-east Asia.

61.3 REPLENISHING THE COURT'S SUPPLY OF LUXURIES: 'If I may say so,' remarks Duyvendak (2), p. 27, 'he [Cheng Ho] went a-shopping for the ladies in the Imperial harem.' It should be recalled that Tamerlane (Timur Lang) had just devastated West Asia and closed all overland routes of commerce. An interesting suggestion in Needham (6), pp. 530–3 is that that both the Portuguese and the Chinese expeditions may have had the search for new drugs as a central motive. In Arabia seeds were amongst the items taken in exchange by Cheng Ho. There was certainly interest in new medicines in Europe and China at this period afflicted by outbreaks of plague, and from South America knowledge of cocaine and quinine was obtained by the Spaniards.

61.4 CHINESE POLICY: Commenting on relations with Africa, which were similar to those with all countries in the southern and western oceans, Filesi (1), p. 72, writes: 'In contrast to the conduct of Egyptians, Phoenicians, Arabs and Persians, before Cheng Ho's expeditions, and to the subsequent policies of Portuguese, British, French, Germans and Italians, the Chinese confined themselves to appearing on the coast of East Africa, without any aim of exerting direct influence on the life and destinies of the local populations. They were neither conquerors nor emigrants in search of new homes, but only able navigators and merchants who made known to remote countries the illustrious name and gracious commands of the Son of Heaven.'

62.3 SIZE OF CHENG HO'S 'TREASURE SHIPS': They could have even had a burden of 2,500 tonnes and a displacement of 3,100 tonnes. For a full discussion of the available evidence see Needham (6), pp. 481–2. Talking of European shipping Brudel (1), p. 317, remarks: 'Very small ships of thirty, forty and fifty tonnes were sailing the seas until the last days of sail. The use of iron made the construction of larger hulls possible only about 1840. A hull of 200 tonnes had until then been the general rule, one of 500 an exception, one of 1,000 or 2,000 an object of curiosity.'

63.1 THE MARITIME EXPEDITIONS: On the first voyage (1405–7) Cheng Ho visited Java, Sumatra, Malacca, Ceylon and Calicut: his fleet comprised 317 ships, including 62 'treasure ships', and carried 27,870 men. The second and less important expedition (1407–9) was connected with the investiture of a new king of Calicut. Cheng Ho did not accompany this fleet of 249 ships, which added to the imperial ports of call Cochin and other coastal cities in southern Indian as well as Thailand. The third expedition (1409–11) sailed with 30,000 troops in 48 ships, visiting Champa, Java, Malacca, Sumatra and Ceylon. On his third voyage and the fourth expedition (1413–15) Cheng Ho's fleet of 63 ships with 28,650 men made for Champa, Malaya, Java, Malacca, Sumatra, Ceylon, the Maldive Islands, Cochin, Calicut, Bengal, and Hormuz in the Persian Gulf. The fifth expedition (1417–19) was ordered to take back safely the ambassadors of nineteen kings, two of whom had been sent from the Zinj Empire. Cheng Ho repeated the visits of his previous voyage, with the exception of Bengal, and for the first time called at La-sa and Aden on the Arabian coast as well as the African ports of Mogadishu, Brava and Malinda. In the meantime the Pacific squadrons also touched on the Ryukyu Islands and Brunei. The sixth expedition (1421–3), the last to sail in the reign of Emperor Ming Yung-lo, visited thirty-six states, returning to all the ports of call during the fifth voyage. The final expedition, the seventh (1431–3), carried 27,550 men and extended Chinese influence in Arabia, where Jidda was visited, and along the East African coast, squadrons of the fleet going far to the south of Malindi.

64.1 THE MAGNANIMITY OF EMPEROR MING YUNG-LO: Needham (6), pp. 514–15. According to João de Barros, whose *Decadas* was the official history of Portugal in Asia, the Pope was empowered to distribute to the faithful all lands in the possession of followers of alien laws. 'If the soul be so condemned', he asked, 'what right has the body to the privileges of our laws?' 'Cruelties', wrote Whiteway (1), p. 22, 'were not confined to the baser sort, but were deliberately adopted as a line of terrorising policy by Vasco da Gama, Almeida and Albuquerque, to take no mean examples.

Da Gama tortured helpless fishermen; Almeida tore out the eyes of a Nair who had come in with a safe-conduct because he suspected a design on his own life; Albuquerque cut off the noses of the women and the hands of the men who fell into his power on the Arabian coast. To follow the example of Almeida and sail into an Indian harbour with the corpses of unfortunates, often not fighting-men, dangling from the yards, was to proclaim oneself a determined fellow. So deeply had the degraded teaching sunk into the minds of the Portuguese that there is every reason to believe that horrible as the cruelties were which Vasco da Gama committed on his second visit to Calicut in 1502, Correa, the historian, deliberately exaggerated them, not to excite pity, but to invest his hero with fresh glories.' *Lendas da India* by Gaspar Correa, first published 1856–61. Not only did the Portuguese burn the cities of Zinj, previously without defence-works, but their slaving activities marked them off as unusual adventurers. Between 1486 and 1641 no less than 1,389,000 slaves were transported from Angola to the New World, where they were used as cheap labour on agricultural plantations. See Davidson (1).

64.2 GALLE INSCRIPTION: Tr. Needham (6), pp. 522; slightly adapted. In 1911 the stele was unearthed by road engineers within the town of Galle. The common list of presents means that the same gifts were awarded to each of the three main religions of Ceylon.

65.1 CHINESE RELIGION: See Cotterell (1). Of interest is the recent translation of Marcel Granet's (1) renowned study.

65.2 THE CHINESE GOVERNOR OF PALEBANG: *Ying-yai sheng-lan chiao-chu*, p. 17; tr. Mills (1), p. 100. Ma Huan, a Chinese interpreter who accompanied Cheng Ho on three expeditions, completed his book about 1433 and it was published some time before 1460. About Palembang, then known as Old Haven to the Ming, he remarks 'ships from every place come here; they first reach the Fresh Water estuary and then enter P'eng-chia strait; they tie up their ships to the shore, where there are many brick towers; then they use boats to enter the estuary, and so they reach the capital'. A prosperous Chinese community existed, emigrants from Canton and Chang-chou, but trading activities were interrupted by one Ch'en Tsu-i, possibly a bandit from Kuangtung. It was this pirate chief, a Chinese not a native of Sumatra, whom Cheng Ho sent back to the Empire for execution. After the death of Shih Chin-ch'ing, the governor installed by the emperor, 'his position did not descend to his son', Ma Huan notes with surprise; 'it was his daughter Shih Erh-chieh who became ruler, and in every case rewards, punishments, degradations, and promotions all depended on her decision'.

65.2 THE MALACCA NAVAL BASE: *Ying-yai sheng-lan chiao-chu*, p. 25; tr. Mills (1), pp. 113–14. 'Wherever the treasure-ships of the Central Country arrived there, they at once erected a line of stockading, like a city-wall, and set up towers for the watch-drums at four gates; at night they had patrols of police carrying bells; inside, again, they erected a second stockade, like a small city-wall, within which they constructed warehouses and granaries; and all the money and provisions were stored in them. The ships which had gone to various countries returned to this place and assembled; they marshalled foreign goods and loaded them in the ships; then waited till the south wind was perfectly favourable. In the . . . fifth moon they put to sea and returned home.'

65.3 THE RUN DOWN OF THE CHINESE NAVY: The Ming fleet, the natural culmination of a seafaring tradition dating from the T'ang period, was deliberately broken up. There were only 140 warships left out of the main imperial fleet of 400 by 1474. At the beginning of the sixteenth century one squadron had dropped from 100 ships to 10. Regulations of 1500 and 1551 declared that either building or going to sea in a two-masted junk was a capital offence. The 1592–8 war in Korea against the Japanese gave the navy a temporary respite, but under the Ch'ing emperors this arm was allowed to wither away through desuetude.

66.2 SUNG FOCUS OF SCIENTIFIC ACHIEVEMENT: Needham (1), p. 134 and pp. 145–7. The completion of the monumental series *Science and Civilisation in China* can be expected to shed new light on the later slackening of pace in Chinese technical progress, but as yet few historians have charted the relations of science and society in Europe, not to mention China.

67.2 'THE MIND . . . THE HEAVENLY POOL': *Yang-ming hsien-seng chi-yao*, ch. 3; tr. Fung (1), p. 197; see also, Needham (2), pp. 506–10, and Chan (1), p. 157.

68.2 'INK PAINTING . . . THE BRUSH': Sherman (1), pp. 16–17.

68.3 'LI CH'ENG . . . OF PAINTING': Tr. Sirén (6), p. 165.

69.3 CHIN PING MEI: The comment and extract from ch. XXXVIII of the novel; Lu Hsun (1), pp. 234–6.

70.2 LO KUAN-CHUNG: The dates of this prolific author are uncertain, though he appears to have been active during the later half of the fourteenth century. *The Romance of the Three Kingdoms* is almost as widely known as *Pilgrimage to the West*. The authorship of *All Men are Brothers*, the title of Pearl S. Buck's rendering of *Shui Hu Chuan*, or *The Tale of the Marsh Edge*, has been disputed. However, all of Lo Kuan-chang's historical romances have been re-edited and revised to an unknown extent: no original versions survive.

71.1 'IN THE LONG HISTORY . . . CHINESE DESIGNS': Garner (1), p. 1.

71.3 IMPERIAL ORDERS: See Hobson (1).

3 THE FOUNDING OF THE CH'ING DYNASTY

74.3 TAIWAN: Named Formosa, 'the beautiful', by the Portuguese, the island came under Dutch control from 1624 till 1661, when Cheng Ch'eng-kung took possession on behalf of the fallen Ming. The significance of this episode in seventeenth-century history is the ease with which Cheng challenged the Dutch ships. Subsequent decline in the naval capability of China was hastened by the Ch'ing dynasty as a matter of deliberate policy. In return for assistance over the capture of Taiwan the Dutch were given trading rights in four mainland ports.

75.2 'THOUGH THE COUNCIL . . . STAGING AREAS': (*Ta-Ch'ing Sheng-tsu Jen Huang-ti*) *Shih lu*, 599, 43–6; tr. Spence (1), p. 38; slightly adapted. Keng Ching-chung and Shang

Chih-hsin were the other Chinese military leaders who shared power in South China with Wu San-kuei.

76.3 HAN-LIN ACADEMY: During the T'ang reorganization of higher education an Imperial Academy, the Han-lin or 'Forest of Pencils', was added to the Imperial University in 754. With a membership of around five hundred scholars, the Han-Lin Academy gradually assumed precedence over all other educational institutions. Its members compiled and edited the *Yung-lo Encyclopedia* (1407) as well as the *K'ang Hsi Dictionary* (1716). The quotation about Emperor Ch'ing K'ang Hsi comes from Martin (1), p. 44; slightly adapted.

79.3 'ON APPOINTING CH'EN . . . GOVERNOR': Spence (1), p. 52.

80.2 'WHEN ONE IS . . . RETURN': *Ibid.*, p. 8.

80.5 CHARLES THOMAS MAILLARD DE TOURNAN, Patriarch of Antioch, was appointed by Pope Clement XI to investigate the causes of disharmony between the missionaries, particularly in China. When as legate he issued an edict forbidding participation in Confucian ceremonies under pain of interdict and excommunication, most of the missionaries remained steadfast to the interpretations of Matteo Ricci and appealed to Rome. In 1720 a second legate, George Ambrose de Mezzabarba, Patriarch of Alexandria, arrived to enforce the will of the Holy See and end Jesuit accommodation of Chinese traditions. Emperor Ch'ing K'ang-hsi was displeased with Papal insistence on doctrine and no progress was made on the issue. Finally in 1742 the bull *Ex quo singulari* ruled against any compromise: the Jesuits were obliged to submit and the Catholic faith in China went into decline.

82.2 'EVERY COUNTRY . . . OTHERWISE': Spence (1), p. 80–1. Joachim Bouvet, a French Jesuit, came to China in 1687–8 and served as a surveyor. Mariani was a member of the Sacred Congregation of the Propaganda, set up in 1597 by Clement VIII. Asked to consider the facts of the controversy over Confucian rites in 1642, the Congregation reached a decision hostile to the Jesuits. When Bouvet and Mariani were chosen to accompany the gifts of Emperor Ch'ing K'ang-hsi to the Pope, so fierce was the struggle between them for precedence that as a result neither could be sent.

83.2 PERSECUTION OF CHRISTIANITY: Provincial officials initiated action against missionaries, who successfully appealed to Emperor Ch'ing K'ang-hsi in 1691. The Jesuits used their contacts in the court to obtain a favourable ruling from the Board of Rites and in 1692 an edict was issued declaring that Christianity was not a 'false sect' but a faith entitled to respect like Confucianism, Taoism and Buddhism. In 1717, however, officials in Kiangnan memorialized the throne advocating stricter controls, the result being the introduction of passes for missionaries approved by the authorities. Deportation awaited those lacking such credentials. Both Emperor Ch'ing Yung-cheng and Emperor Ch'ing Ch'ien-lung remained cold towards Catholicism, the wrangling between the missionaries themselves only giving support to the assault by the Confucian *shih*.

84.2 VIETNAM: Periods of Vietnamese independence correspond with those of weakness in China. During the T'ang Empire there was a Chinese administration in Annam for two hundred and fifty years. Then the culture of China, in one of its most brilliant epochs, made a profound impression on the Vietnamese people, whose own distinct heritage has only become apparent through their historical southward movement, away from the Chinese border. After the Two Sungs it was usual policy to accept a Vietnamese acknowledgment of Chinese suzerainty as adequate respect, though Emperor Ming Yung-lo annexed Annam from 1407 to 1427. Left more to themselves, the Vietnamese could march south in 1471 against Champa, recently a dependency of Cambodia. The struggle for control of what is now the southern provinces of Vietnam, originally the homeland of the Chams, was fought out between the Cambodians and the Vietnamese until the end of the seventeenth century. The Tay Son rebellion (1772–1802) started in the Mekong delta and for many years it was extremely successful. A popular movement against the Confucian model of the state, as expressed in the domination of the northern provinces, its strong nationalist tendencies have encouraged comparisons with the T'ai P'ing rebellion in China (1851–64).

86.1 'COASTAL DEFENCE . . .': See Fitzgerald (4), ch. 6.

88.2 'WHITE LOTUS': Chu Yuan-chang was probably a member of the 'White Lotus', a popular organization dedicated to the expulsion of the Mongols. During the Ch'ing dynasty a number of insurrections were organized by the secret society: in 1774 and the major rising of 1794–1803, after which its members were hounded by the authorities. Other secret societies took the lead in the nineteenth century, though the 'White Lotus' was behind the 'Black Banner' peasant rising of 1861–3 in Shantung and Honan. See Chesneaux (1), ch. 2.

90.1 THE HOPPO: This was an English corruption of the Chinese name of the government department in which he served, the *Hu Pu*, the Board of Revenue.

90.2 TRADE IN FAVOUR OF CHINA: Lord Macartney calculated in 1792 that the balance of trade was in favour of Great Britain partly through the illicit traffic in opium, then running at £250,000 or 2,500 chests. Only in 1783, when a shortage of bullion occurred, did the East India Company itself sell opium at Canton. Within their territories in India the British had assumed a monopoly on the sale of the drug in 1773 and later in 1797 assumed a monopoly of its manufacture. Revenue from these monopolies formed a substantial part of the receipts of the East India Company.

Edicts against the importation of opium were issued by the Ch'ing emperors between 1729 and 1797, when a total ban was imposed, perhaps in recognition of the spread of the habit beyond the province of Kwantung. The weakness of Chinese naval forces made smuggling opium an easy operation. In China the use of opium hardly preceded the Ch'ing dynasty. The Spaniards introduced the smoking of tobacco sometime during the seventeenth century and soon afterwards tobacco mixed with opium appeared, probably from Dutch territories in Formosa and Java. Once established in China, opium was smoked alone. The first shipment of opium in quantity to China was made by the Portuguese from Goa.

90.2 LORD MACARTNEY (1737–1806): He had a distinguished public career. In 1764 he was sent as envoy-extraordinary to the Court of Catherine the Great at St Petersburg. A treaty of commerce was arranged but hopes of an alliance were dashed by the Russian insistence upon support against the Ottoman Turks. In 1769 he was Chief Secretary for Ireland; then, after serving as Governor of Grenada, in 1780 he took up the appointment of Governor of Madras, the first person to be selected from outside the ranks of the East India Company; but five years later he declined to succeed Warren Hastings as Governor-General of Bengal. His 'pecuniary moderation' was appreciated by the East India Company, which granted him an annuity of £1,500 for life. Remarkable for the time was his unwillingness to enrich himself by public office. The last public position he held was that of Governor of Cape Colony, whence he returned in 1798 owing to ill-health.

91.2 'THAT THE NEWS . . . COASTS': Cranmer-Byng (1), p. 63.

91.2 TIENTSIN: Lord Macartney was told the population of the city exceeded 700,000. Equally astonishing were the numbers of different kinds of vessels he observed, though their weakness away from the coastline did not escape his notice. *Ibid.*, p. 81.

92.1 'WE HAVE INDEED . . . OCCURS': *Ibid.*, pp. 87–8.

92.2 'THE COMMANDING . . . ATTAINED': *Ibid.*, p. 124.

92.3 PARK OF THE SUMMER RESIDENCE: Lancelot Brown (1716–83) was the greatest landscape gardener of eighteenth-century England. 'For in the course of a few hours', Lord Macartney wrote, 'I enjoyed such vicissitudes of rural delight, as I did not conceive could be felt out of England, being at different moments enchanted by scenes perfectly similar to those I had known there, to the magnificence of Stowe, the soft beauties of Woburn or the fairy-land of Painshill.' *Ibid.*, p. 126.

92.3 'THE SAME JEALOUSY . . . CONFIDENCE': *Ibid.*, p. 129.

93.2 'THE CELESTIAL EMPIRE . . . MANUFACTURES': *Ibid.*, p. 340.

94.4 'HOW ARE . . . CAN': *Ibid.*, p. 164.

94.5 THE VIEW OF FATHER AMIOT: *Ibid.*, p. 151.

95.1 'TO CONVEY . . . INFRINGE THEM': *Ibid.*, p. 168.

95.2 FINAL ENTRIES ON EMPIRE: *Ibid.*, pp. 212–13.

4 THE CELESTIAL EMPIRE

97.2 'TALKED . . . SERIOUS, SIR': 10 April 1778. Boswell (1), vol. 3, p. 292. Also see Fan Tsen-Chung (1).

97.5 'REMARKABLE . . . WEALTH': Gallagher (1), pp. 55–6. This is a translation of Nicolas Trigault's *De Christiano Expeditione apud Sinas suscepta ab Soc Jesu ex P. Matthieu Ricci ejusdem Soc. Commentarus . . .*, Amsterdam, 1615. Trigault, a missionary for a number of years in China, translated Ricci's diary and papers into Latin. In the preface he stresses that the difference between his book and earlier travel books is the careful observation of the Jesuits as well as their acquisition of the Chinese language. Besides providing a balanced account of China at the beginning of the seventeenth century, Ricci's writings inaugurated a bitter theological dispute between the Jesuits and the Dominicans and the Franciscans, the latter orders insisting that there was no scope for toleration of non-Christian practices, however moral, because the heathen were damned. Leibniz took a prominent part in defending the Jesuit tolerance of Confucian rites, whilst Voltaire took the view that the dispute was a supreme example of Christian intolerance. The Jesuits were able to admit the excellence of Neo-Confucian ethics because they held that the existence of God and moral obligation could be established by reason, but that scripture, revealed truth, was necessary for salvation. See Hudson (1), ch. x, and Rowbotham (1), ch. XVIII.

99.1 'HIS SELF-MASTERY . . . OF THEM': *Ibid.*, p. 30.

99.2 '. . . EMPIRICAL GEOMETRY': From the preface to *Novissima Sinica*. Quoted in Dawson (1), p. 189.

99.2 'SPACE . . . THE CHINESE TEXTS': Needham (2), p. 502. See also Cotterell (1), pp. 196–9.

102.2 FRANÇOIS QUESNAY (1694–1774): The leader of the philosophical school known as the *Physiocrates*, was an advocate of '*depotisme éclairé*, a notion he fully developed in *Le despotisme de la Chine* (1767). Though the ceremonial ploughing undertaken by Louis XV in 1756 was the only public manifestation of his sympathy for physiocratic ideas, it reveals the interest in Chinese tradition at the French court, a place frequented by Jesuit missionaries. See Reichwein (1), p. 106.

102.2 PÈRE DU HALDE: This priest was responsible for the publication of a mass of material collected by the Jesuit missionaries. He attempted to engage the general reader as well as signify the achievements of the mission. An atlas of maps accompanied the *Description de la Chine*. See Du Halde (1).

102.2 PEPYS AND KIRCHER: Rowbotham (1), p. 279.

105.1 ROCOCO: It was in interior decoration and furniture that the Rococo style reached its apotheosis. Thomas Chippendale (1718–79) was greatly influenced by the Chinese fashion, the designs for many of his cabinets being taken from Du Halde's book. A design similar to the Beaufort bedstead appeared as plate XXXII in Chippendale's *The Gentleman and Cabinet-Maker's Director*, which was published in 1754. Of rococo, Brackett (1), p. 54, suggests that 'at root of it lay a desire to escape for a time from the lifeless rigidity and monotonous accuracy which the Palladian school demanded. It was an attempt, feeble perhaps and misguided, of the romantic spirit to blossom in an arid and unsympathetic soil'. For Reichwein (1), ch. III, 'a relaxation of style is characteristic of the Rococo. The restraint of the Louis XIV period having degenerated into rigidity in all forms of life, the death of the king was inevitably followed by the licence of the Regency. The straitjacket in which thought, plastic creation, and human conduct generally had been confined, was burst asunder. The reaction which followed take the form of the Bizarre. . . . The delicate tones of porcelain, the vaporous colours of silk, all the things that gave to the Rococo world its charm and grace, are, as it were, enshrined in the paintings of Watteau. . . . Anyone who has studied closely Chinese landscapes of the Sung period is immediately struck by their affinity with the landscape background' in the *Embarkation of Cythera*, painted in 1717. 'The fantastic forms of his mountains . . . closely resemble the Chinese forms. . . . The use of monochrome colouring for background landscape, such as Watteau loves, is one of the most prominent

characteristics of Chinese landscape painting.' See also Honour (1).

105.1 OLIVER GOLDSMITH: See Dobson (1), p. 38.

105.2 LEOPOLD VON RANKE (1795–1886): A leading German historian of the nineteenth century.

106.1 ECONOMIC DECLINE: Elvin (1) has some pertinent things to say about 'the high-level equilibrium trap' of the late Empire. Of China's retarded technological advance he notes that 'through a number of interlocking causes, the input–output relationships of the late traditional economy had assumed a pattern that was almost incapable of change through internally generated forces', p. 312. Again, 'it was not the size of the eighteenth century British market (tiny compared to that of China) but the speed of its growth that put pressure on the means of production to improve. In eighteenth-century China, the high level of agricultural and water transport techniques, together with near-to-complete resource use and vast scale, made a comparably rapid growth in surplus and *per capita* demand impossible. There is a sense in which, compared with China, western Europe in the early modern age enjoyed many of . . . "the advantages of backwardness",' p. 318.

106.1 'ENCOURAGED . . . MISERY': Cranmer-Byng (1), p. 226.

106.1 'THE GOVERNMENT . . . CHINESE': *Ibid.*, p. 236.

107.2 K'ANG-HSI ON RIGHTS OF TENANTS: Elvin (1), pp. 247–8.

107.3 INDIA AND JAPAN: 'Chinese rural society in the nineteenth century and early twentieth century was thus one of the most fluid in the world, lacking any of the status or caste restraints which typified pre-modern Japan or India. The Communist land-reform documents of the 1930s . . . give proof of this. According to a Communist party ruling, it took only three years to establish "landlord" or "rich peasant" status; and there are a number of references to the problems of dealing with those who had been landlords for only a short time, and of categorizing characters like a certain Chou Tsung-jen who had risen in the space of twenty years from a hired labourer to a landlord and moneylender,' *ibid.*, pp. 258–9.

107.4 SECRET SOCIETIES AND 1911: Chesneaux (1), p. 139.

108.1 'THE TRIAD': 'From 1911 onwards, however, the Triad entered a new phase and its activities became more and more gangster-like. It is too simple to explain this degeneration . . . by saying that the historical mission of the Triad had been accomplished with the fall of the Manchus in 1911, and that from then on the society found itself in a political vacuum.

'The fact is that, from the nineteenth century onwards, the criminal and political aspects of its activities were inextricably linked. They represented two facets of the same sociological reality, provoked by the sheer severity of the imperial order. But in modern times, and especially since the Republican revolution, the political function has been assumed by other organisations: political parties, trade unions, and various professional and cultural bodies. The Triad was therefore forced to fall back on its criminal activities. From then on it became much more than before: an instrument in the hands of politicians and intriguers.

'The spread of its criminal activities, especially in the great ports – Shanghai, Singapore, Hong Kong – grew with modern developments. Capitalist activity, in particular by concentrating in these ports immigrant communities of both and other nationalities, helped to speed up the process.' *Ibid.*, p. 34.

108.3 'THE RECRUITMENT . . . FIRE-RAISERS': *Ibid.*, p. 60. The extract comes from a letter of February 1875 in which Father Leboucq described characteristics of the 'White Lotus' he had observed in Hopei. 'If a wife's admission is earlier than the husband's', he continues, 'she is from then on mistress of the house in everything concerning domestic management.'

108.4 THE BOXERS AND OTHER SOCIETIES: Originally an offshoot of the 'White Lotus', the 'Righteous Harmony Fists' were primarily concerned with the containment of foreign penetration of China. But in 1898–9, for obscure reasons, but probably as a result of encouragement from the court, the Boxers allied themselves to the Ch'ing dynasty, in spite of its Manchu origins, and appealed to the Chinese to rally in its defence against foreign aggression. Other secret societies did not respond to the call and fighting occurred between members of the 'White Lotus' and the Boxers.

109.1 'ANYONE . . . TERMS ARE': Elvin (1), p. 269.

109.3 'IN THE REGION . . . SELLING DEAR': *Ibid.*, p. 267. A picul equals sixty kilograms.

110.1 CAPITALISM IN THE LATE EMPIRE: See Balazs (1), pp. 39–54.

110.3 'NO INDEPENDENT . . . OF WORLD CONQUEST?': Baudel (1), pp. 410–11.

110.4 ZAITON AND ALEXANDRIA: Marsden (1), bk. II, ch. LXXVII.

111.1 CHINA AND EXPANSIONISM: See Needham (9), 'Western Misconceptions about East Asia', pp. 163–72.

111.2 MONEY AND OFFICES: Ho Ping-ti (2), pp. 40–3: The author relates an interesting anecdote. According to the tale Emperor T'ang T'ai-tsung (627–50), after seeing an august procession of newly qualified scholars, the successful candidates in the imperial examinations, remarked with gratification: 'The world's men of unusual ambitions have been trapped in my bag!' Whatever the truth of this late T'ang story, it suggests that informed people had come to believe that such had been the real purpose of the early T'ang state making the examination system permanent.

111.2 'WHATEVER . . . HIS POWER': Cranmer-Byng (1), p. 237.

111.4 JOSEPH CASTIGLIONE (1688–1766): His pleasure pavilions at the Summer Residence were accompanied by fountains erected by a French Jesuit who was familiar with the water-works at Versailles. The *Yuan-ming-yuan* was the only departure made by the Ch'ing dynasty from the architectural tradition inherited from the Ming.

113.2 'ONCE AT KUANG-LING . . . DETAILS': Tr. Whitfield (1), p. 108; slightly adapted. Kuan T'ung (*c.* 907–50) was noted for his delight in autumn and winter landscapes: his brushwork, according to contemporary witness, was 'swift' and carefree – to some critics even careless.

113.4 BUDDHIST PAINTERS: Two other notable monk-artists were Shih-t'ao (1641–*c.* 1710) and Shih-ch'i (active 1650–75). Whilst the latter spent his days in a monastery at Nanking, ending his life as its abbot, the former, a lineal descendant of the Ming house, travelled widely and felt a profound intimacy with the natural world, which he attempted to recreate in his landscapes as well as his designs for gardens. Both painters, however, were outsiders, their compositions largely overlooked by the scholar-painters and those at work in the Ch'ing court.

113.6 K'ANG HSI PORCELAIN: 'The K'ang Hsi "blue and white" reached a technical excellence that has never been surpassed. The porcelain, pure white and of fine texture, is covered with a glaze of slightly bluish or greenish tint and the decoration, at its best, is in a pure blue of great luminosity. Although the European potters were never able to approach the quality of Chinese "blue and white", some of the copies of Chinese "blue and white" in delftware are surprisingly good, in view of the differences of material,' Garner (1), pp. 43–4.

115.1 'ALTHOUGH CH'ING ART . . . DETERIORATION': Liang Ch'i-ch'ao (1), p. 118. Born in Kwangtung in 1873, Liang studied under K'ang Yu-wei and later followed his teacher in politics. Exiled from 1898 until the establishment of the Republic in 1912, he returned to China and held several ministries in Peking. His book on the Ch'ing intellectual experience was written at a time of revived interest in Chinese civilization. A personal stimulus was the futility of destruction involved in the First World War, a conflict he came to view as a direct result of Western materialistic civilization. Thus, the enthusiastic reformer, the advocate of progress on Western lines, turned to teaching and a re-assessment of the enduring qualities of China. Though he died in 1929, his writings exerted considerable influence on the succeeding generation.

115.2 SPECIAL EXAMINATIONS: Such periodic devices were used to attract fresh talent to the official class. The governor of Hangchow sent Yuan Mei to Peking for the examination with money and a servant. Of two hundred candidates only fifteen passed. See Waley (11), a first-rate biography of the poet.

116.3 'MORNING AFTER . . . MY RESPECTS': Tr. Waley (11), pp. 39–40.

116.4 MANCHU CENSORSHIP: 'More than at any previous time in Chinese history the writer of books of any kind was under suspicion. Quite apart from the question of orthodox political views there was that of philosophical orthodoxy. The whole educational and examination system was based on the Neo-Confucian interpretation of the classics, and any criticism of this interpretation could be made a case for impeachment (*k'o*), *ibid.*, p. 65.

117.2 'AS FOR . . . WOULD NOT LIKE': *Ibid.*, p. 202.

118.2 THE DREAM OF THE RED CHAMBER: There has been uncertainty about its authorship ever since publication. Opinion today accepts that the first eighty chapters were written by Ts'ao Hsueh-ch'in, an impoverished *shih*, whilst the final chapters were added by Kao Ou, possibly on lines indicated by the author.

118.4 'RESOLUTE MEN . . . DUST': Liang Ch'i-ch'ao (1), p. 85.

118.5 K'ANG YU-WEI'S TEACHING: Liang Ch'i-ch'ao (2), ch. III, notes that 'in teaching his students, Mr Kang took as the matter Confucian, Buddhist, Sung, and Ming scholarship; he took as the method history and Western studies. He taught solely by fostering a spirit of determination, by expanding upon essentials, by aiming at knowledge in a broad way.'

119.2 K'ANG YU-WEI AND THE REPUBLIC: Despite his distaste for republicanism, K'ang Yu-wei did not fight the Republican Government under Dr Sun Yat-sen. Indeed, he sought to aid the provisional president against the ambitions of Yuan Shih-k'ai, whom K'ang Yu-wei held responsible for the *coup d'état* against the reform movement of 1898 as well as the murder of Emperor Ch'ing Kuang-hsu in 1908. He steadfastly refused offers of ministerial office made by Yuan Shih-Kai.

119.3 'THE MEN . . . HOLDING OFFICE': K'ang Yu-wei (1), p. 39. *The Ta T'ung Shu* contains a number of strikingly modern ideas, such as an end to any moral ban on the practice of homosexuality. Because the world was still in the 'Age of Disorder' and he felt his notions to be far in advance of the times, K'ang Yu-wei did not lecture on the One World and allowed only selected students to peruse the manuscript. He sought real equality and individual independence, by the abolition of nationality, class, property, race, sexual discrimination and so forth. His vision of mankind as one people, a new physical amalgamation hastened by 'rules . . . formulated to encourage mixed marriages', is spoilt somewhat, because of his assumption that 'yellow and white' peoples are superior and the world's ultimate ideal. This was, of course, the result of his background: the Chinese scholar impressed by late nineteenth-century Western civilization.

5 WESTERN IMPERIALISM AND THE COLLAPSE OF THE CHINESE EMPIRE

121.2 LORD PALMERSTON ON OPIUM: *Hansard* (1840), 53, p. 940.

121.2 'A WAR . . . NOT READ OF': *Ibid.* (1840), 53, p. 818.

121.2 OPIUM ONLY A COMMODITY: *Ibid.* (1870), 201, p. 516. An impressive example of gobbledegook was the line of argument deployed by Lord Melbourne. He said that because the British Empire had large districts peculiarly fitted for opium production he could not pledge himself to give up the trade, but he did wish the Government were not directly concerned in the opium business. See Williams (1), II, p. 526.

122.2 THE BATTLE OF KOWLOON: Waley (12), pp. 69–70, ingeniously suggests that the first skirmish was accidental. The corrupt units of the Canton Navy may have been attempting to enlarge their bribe for tolerating trade between locals and British ships.

122.3 SIZE OF THE BRITISH FORCE: There were 9,000 fighting men in 1841–2. Casualties were small; at Chinkiang on the Yang-tze, where the stoutest resistance occurred, only 168 men were lost.

122.3 'OPIUM . . . NOT TO BE MISSED': Waley (12), p. 219

125.1 TREATY OF NANKING: In fact, the principles of extra-territoriality and the 'most-favoured-nation' were added in the following year through a supplementary agreement, the Treaty of the Brogue. The United States of America, in the 1844 Treaty of Wang-hsia, had the principle of extra-territoriality extended to include civil as well as criminal cases.

125.3 THE GREAT EXHIBITION: Hobsbawm (1), pp. 32–3, writes: 'If Europe had still lived in an era of the baroque princes, it would have been filled with spectacular masques, processions and operas distributing allegorical representations of economic triumph at the feet of its rulers. In fact the triumphant world of capitalism had its equivalent. The era of its global victory was initiated and punctuated by giant new rituals of self-congratulation, the Great International Exhibitions, each encased in a princely monument to wealth and technical progress – the Crystal Palace in London (1851), the Rotunda ('larger than St Peter's in Rome') in Vienna, each displaying the growing number and variety of manufactures, each attracting native and foreign tourists in astronomic quantities'.

126.2 'I THOUGHT . . . PROVOCATION': Walrond (1), p. 213 and p. 227.

126.3 BURMA: The Chinese formally recognized the annexation in 1886 when an Anglo-Chinese convention was signed.

128.2 'BUT EVERYTHING . . . TO REFUSE THEM': *Ying-yao jih-chi*, entry of 28 June 1877; tr. Frodsham (1), pp. 142–3. Liu Hsi-hung was more conservative in outlook than Kuo Sung-t'ao, the first Chinese minister appointed to the Court of St James. The two *shih* were at odds with each other, even after the appointment of Liu as ambassador to Germany.

128.4 'LET ME . . . THE MANCHUS': Jen (1), pp. 19–20. Upon the painstaking researches of Jen Yu-wen the section entitled 'The T'ai P'ing Revolutionary Movement' is founded.

129.1 T'AI P'ING CASUALTIES: Ho Ping-ti (3), p. 247. 'The T'ai P'ing Rebellion is deservedly called the greatest civil war in world history. In sheer brutality and destruction it has few peers in the annals of history.'

129.1 1911 CENSUS: See Orleans (1), ch. 2.

130.2 'A SWORD . . . AND SISTERS': Hamberg (1), p. 11. This is the earliest and most trustworthy account of the mental illness suffered by Hung Hsiu-ch'uan.

130.2 T'AI P'ING MORAL CODE: Jen (1), p. 66. These precepts were included in orders jointly issued by the Heavenly King and his senior commanders in 1851.

131.1 T'AI P'ING T'IEN KUO: The name T'ai P'ing was derived from an ancient text, the *Kung-yang chuan*, which described the three periods of social development: first, anarchy and decline; second, order and peace; third, eternal peace and prosperity (*t'ai-p'ing shih*). The name T'ien Kuo, 'Heavenly Kingdom', probably derived from the Protestant pamphlets. See Jen (1), p. 65.

132.2 SHAVED HEADS: Before the rebellion started Hung Hsiu-ch'uan used to reply that he was in mourning when questioned about his refusal to shave part of his head and grow a beard, obligatory Manchu customs. In fact, the T'ai P'ings were known as 'the Hairy Ones' because they let all of their hair grow, unlike the rest of the population.

132.3 'TSENG KUO-FAN ... THE EMPIRE': Tr. Jen (1), p. 242; slightly adapted. Tseng Kuo-fan was on home leave because of his mother's death. It was customary to retire from office for a period of one to three years. He had been pressed into raising the 'Hsiang Army' by the governor of Hunan, who was alarmed at T'ai P'ing advances.

134.2 'SCHOLARS, PEASANTS ... CLANDESTINELY': Tr. Jen (1), p. 148. Indeed, the generally illiterate T'ai P'ings, much in need of assistance in the preparation of reports, orders and letters, accorded those *shih* who agreed to act as scribes profound respect, addressing them as 'masters'. The survival of so many scholars in the provinces overrun by the rebels must be partly attributed to the awe felt by the *nung* for the written word.

134.3 'CULTIVATING ... WARMLY DRESSED': Tr. Jen (1), p. 144.

134.4 FOREIGN SETTLEMENTS: There were three large areas outside the city of Shanghai leased to Britain, France and the United States for commercial and residential purposes. They were each called Concessions or Settlements. The British and American Concessions merged in 1863 into what later became known as the International Settlement.

134.5 'WE BELIEVE ... T'AI P'INGS': *Shanghai Times*, 15 March 1862. See Jen (1), p. 451.

138.2 HAI-KUO T'U-CHIH: See Hughes (1), pp. 201–2.

139.3 'COTTON ... USEFUL ARTICLE': From pp. 80–90 of the Report on Trade for 1866 by the Commissioner of Customs at Tientsin. Quoted in Rhoads Murphey, 'The Treaty Ports and China's Modernization'; Elvin and Skinner (1), pp. 27–8.

139.4 PER CAPITA COMPARISON: *Ibid.*, p. 46. A traveller, Robert Fortune wrote in 1847: 'In no country in the world is there less real poverty and want than China,' p. 40.

140.1 ROCK BOTTOM: *Ibid.*, p. 47.

140.2 SHANGHAI AND LONDON: *Ibid.*, p. 40.

140.4 'CHINAMEN ... BY THE THOUSANDS': *Bankers Magazine*, v (Boston 1850–1), p. 11. See Hobsbawm (1), p. 63.

149.1 THE KAISER'S ORDERS: Li (1), p. 430.

149.2 STUDENT STATISTICS: Hughes (1), p. 168.

6 THE REPUBLIC

150.1 'GO SLOWLY ... AND SEE': Ch'en (1), p. 85.

153.1 'THE ELECTION ... PROCEEDINGS': Woodward (1), p. 266; slightly adapted.

153.3 'NOT KNOW ... OUR PEOPLE': Liang Ch'i-ch'ao, *Ho-chi*, essays, 33, pp. 108–9; tr. Ch'en (1), p. 193.

153.3 TWENTY-ONE DEMANDS: The main Japanese demands were (i) the transformation of Tsing-tao into a Japanese sphere of influence covering all of Shantung; (ii) extensive commercial, industrial and residential rights in Manchuria and Inner Mongolia; (iii) extended leases for Dairen and Port Arthur on the Liao-tung peninsula; (iv) partial control of the important iron and steel plants in the Yang-tze Valley; (v) China's agreement 'not to cede or lease to any other Power any harbour or bay or any island'; (vi) the employment of Japanese as political, financial and military advisers in the central government; (vii) the right of Japanese to own

land in China; (viii) joint control of Chinese police forces; (ix) the granting of rights to Japan for the construction of railways; and (x) oversight of Chinese borrowing of foreign capital for economic development.

154.1 'WHAT LAW ... CONSCIENCE: Pai Chiao (ed.), *Yuan Shih-k'ai yu Chung-hua min-kuo*, Shanghai, 1936, p. 366; tr. Ch'en (1), p. 191.

154.2 'THERE ARE ... HIM': Tawney (1), p. 77.

157.3 YANG-TZE RIVER FLOTILLA: The size of the Royal Navy was revealed in 1920 to the Shanghai Chamber of Commerce by Vice-Admiral Sir Arthur Duff. A decade later the military presence was six battalions. See Endicott (1), ch. 1.

158.1 WANHSIEN BOMBARDMENT: Remer (1), pp. 100–1.

158.2 EARLY BRITISH VIEWS OF CHIANG KAI-SHEK: The desire of the Generalissimo to become 'virtual dictator and unchallenged head of party, Government and State' was appreciated by the Foreign Office. Even Sir Miles Lampson, perhaps the most sympathetic British minister Chiang Kai-shek encountered, said on one occasion that he was establishing 'something like a fascist dictatorship'. Endicott (1), p. 15.

158.2 OPIUM TRAFFIC: British consuls on the Yang-tze River reported that the Generalissimo connived to have the lion's share of the traffic in opium. The proceeds were 're-mitted direct to General Chiang's Field Headquarters at Nan-ch'ang'. *Ibid.*, p. 21.

160.3 'FROM ... THEIR PUPIL?': Mao (1), IV, pp. 412–13.

160.4 'JOINT COLONY ... EXPLOITATION': Manifesto, 1922, quoted in Gittings (1), p. 32.

160.5 'I FELT ... CHINA': Snow (1), p. 176. For an insight of Chairman Mao's mind in 1936, after the Long March, readers could not do better than consult *Red Star Over China*. It records the personal interviews enjoyed by the young American reporter.

161.2 MAO TSE-TUNG REBUKED: Ch'en (2), p. 139.

161.3 'THE RUTHLESS ... SOCIETY': Mao (1), II, p. 308.

162.3 'WE SAY ... DEFEAT': Mao (1), I, pp. 161–2.

162.4 POISON GAS: Snow (1), p. 425.

163.1 'CRUELTY ... OF YUAN SHIH-K'AI': *Ibid.*, p. 427. The National Salvation Movement, a left-wing organization, co-ordinated widespread anti-Japanese agitation during 1936. At Tokyo's request, the Nationalist police arrested its leaders, all prominent citizens, and suppressed fourteen popular magazines. They even tolerated the landing of Japanese marines at Tsing-tao in order to quell patriotic strikes against Japanese aggression.

164.1 'THE END ... IN CHINA!': *Ibid.*, p. 427.

165.2 'THE RICHEST ... BURNED TO DEATH': Mao (1), II, p. 186. In conversation with Mao Tse-tung, P'eng Teh-huai, a leading 'Red Army' official, told Snow (1), p. 313: 'The main reason for partisan warfare in China is economic bankruptcy, and especially rural bankruptcy. Imperialism, landlordism, and militaristic wars have combined to destroy the basis of rural economy, and it cannot be restored without eliminating its chief enemies. Enormous taxes, together with Japanese invasion, both military and economic, have accel-erated the rate of this peasant bankruptcy, aided by the land-lords. The gentry's exploitation of power in the villages makes life difficult for the majority of the peasants. There is widespread unemployment. There is a readiness among the poor classes to fight for change.'

168.2 'THE FIRST . . . MILLIONS': Mao (2), pp. 67–8.

169.1 'NOT . . . OR GROUP': Gittings (1), p. 116.

170.1 GI MISBEHAVIOUR: 'The one abiding sentiment that almost all American enlisted personnel and most of the officers shared was contempt and dislike for China. . . . They believed the Chinese were corrupt, inefficient, and unreliable'. They nick-named them 'slope-headed bastards' or 'slopies', White and Jacoby (1), pp. 154–8.

170.2 'I STILL . . . THAT': Melby (1), p. 56.

170.4 'WHEN . . . KILLINGS': Gittings (1), p. 130.

171.1 'OUR PRINCIPLE . . . PARTY': Mao (1), II, p. 272.

171.1 'THE VAST . . . WHAT': Melby (1), p. 47.

172.1 'IF CHINA . . . LIFE': See de Francis (1), p. 241.

172.2 'FACTORY WORKERS . . . PRACTICES': Quoted by Hsia (1), p. 9.

172.2 LANGUAGE: Ch'ien Hsuan-t'ung wrote that the Chinese 'language is absolutely unfit for the new era of the twentieth century. Let me boldly repeat my manifesto: to the end that China may not perish and may become a civilized nation of the twentieth century, the basic task is to abolish Confucianism and annihilate Taoism. But the destruction of the Chinese written language, which has served as the repository of Confucian morality and Taoist superstition, is a prerequisite for the accomplishment of this task.' *Ibid.*, p. 10.

173.2 'THE GREATEST . . . ARMY': Mao (1), pp. 668–9.

174.2 'AS FOR . . . NOTHING': Lu Hsun (2), p. 112.

174.4 'THE LAND . . . LAND-OWNERSHIP': Sun Yat-sen (1), Part III.

175.2 HUANG PIN-HUANG: For an excellent discussion of his position see Sullivan (3), ch. 2.

7 THE PEOPLE'S REPUBLIC

177.1 US $60,000: Melby (1), p. 268.

177.3 'THE UNFORTUNATE . . . COULD NOT': From Dean Acheson's 'Letter of Transmittal' accompanying *United States Relations with China, With Special Reference to the Period 1944–9*. See Gittings (1), ch. 6. Discussion of the international situation in the final chapters leans upon Gittings' excellent and up-to-date study of China's foreign relations.

180.1 'THE CHINESE . . . COUNTRY': Quoted in Gittings (1), p. 138.

181.1 'HE LOOKED UPON . . . CORNERS': Deutscher (1), p. 84.

181.3 FULTON SPEECH: Delivered on 5 March 1946, it contained the famous sentence: 'From Stettin in the Baltic to Trieste in the Adriatic, an iron curtain has descended across the Continent.' Though he was out of power, Churchill's call for an Anglo–American alliance against the Soviet Union was influential. The Cold War and the wrath of Senator Joseph McCarthy ensued. By April 1950 the American document, *National Security Council Paper No. 68*, could admit that the new military posture 'means virtual abandonment by the United States of trying to distinguish between national and global security'.

181.3 'AT THAT . . . III': In *Survey of China Mainland Press*, Hong Kong, No. 4060. The Soviet Union did not explode its first nuclear device until September 1949.

181.3 ATOM BOMB A PAPER TIGER: Extract from Mao Tse-tung's interview in August 1946, quoted by Schram (1), p. 404.

181.3 GENERAL MACARTHUR: The UN forces were commanded by a man who had publicly proclaimed his admiration of Chiang Kai-shek and his detestation of the People's Republic. The advance into North Vietnam was an abandonment of the original purpose of intervention: the destruction of the North replaced as an aim the preservation of the South. Peking was apprehensive that fighting would spill over to Manchuria, and until his dismissal in April 1951 MacArthur did his utmost to precipitate a war between China and the United States. See Ambrose (1), pp. 211–13.

184.1 'CERTAIN PEOPLE . . . FOR IT': Extract from *On the Correct Handling of Contradictions Among the People*, Peking, 1957, quoted by Schram (1), p. 307.

185.2 'WHILE WE . . . ECONOMIC BASE': *Ibid.*, pp. 307–8.

187.1 'THAT WHICH . . . MARXISM': *Ibid.*, p. 309.

187.3 'THE PRESENT . . . RELATIONSHIPS': Liu (1), p. 53.

188.1 INCREASED IRRIGATION: In 1949 China had 20 million hectares of irrigated land. The Great Leap Forward aimed to increase the total to 130 million hectares or 89 per cent of the crop land: by the middle 1960s this target was surpassed. See Buchanan (1), p. 194.

189.1 'CHINA . . . HEMISPHERE': Dumont (1), p. 254; tr. and discussion Buchanan (1), p. 235.

190.3 'IT IS NOT . . . DESTINY': Lattimore (3), p. 28.

190.3 LAO-TZU: See Bynner (1).

190.4 'FRAUGHT . . . NOTHING ELSE': Quoted in Ch'en (3), pp. 21–2.

191.1 'WE MUST . . . TRADITION': Quoted in *Chinese Education*, Peking, Spring 1968, Vol. 1, No. 1, p. 37.

192.2 'BUT ONLY . . . EDUCATION': Karol (1), p. 317. Reported conversation with Chen Chun.

192.4 'COMRADE . . . THE COUNTRY': From the foreword to *Quotations from Chairman Mao Tse-tung*, Peking, 1966.

192.5 'ALL COMMUNES . . . AFFAIRS': Extract from *Resolution on the Problems Raised by the Socialist Education Movement in Rural Areas*, Peking, 1965, quoted by Karol (2), p. 133.

197.1 MAO'S FAMILY: Mao Tse-tung never lived with his first wife, to whom he was betrothed in traditional fashion as a child. His second wife was killed by the Kuomintang in 1930. He sent his third wife to Moscow for medical treatment shortly after the Long March. In 1938 he married Ch'iang Ching, the Shanghai actress; his colleagues insisted that their acquiescence depended on her playing no part in politics. Of Mao Tse-tung's children little is known. Some children were left with *nung* during the Long March. One son was killed during the Korean War. Another son is an engineer. By the marriage with Ch'iang Ching he had two daughters.

197.2 INTERROGATION OF CHOU EN-LAI: See Karol (2), p. 282. On 15 September 1966, Chou En-lai had told a mass rally of revolutionary students and teachers that 'the factories and the countryside cannot take holidays like the educational institutions and hold up production to make the revolution. Student revolutionaries must respect the great mass of workers and peasants, trust them, and be convinced that they are perfectly capable of guiding the revolution to its goal.' The speech appeared in the *Peking Review*, No. 39, 23 September 1966. Two years after the firing of the British Chancellory Chou En-lai personally apologized for the incident.

198.1 'WE ARE . . . THE PAST': Quoted in Karol (2), p. 290.

198.1 'IT IS . . . COUNTRYSIDE': The *nung* would not merely teach these townees to cultivate the land, but also give them 'a profound class education'. *Peking Review*, No. 52, 1968, pp. 6–7. Quoted and discussed by Schram (1), p. 110.

198.1 'WE WERE . . . IDEOLOGY': Quoted in Karol (2), p. 329). The student was at Tsinghua University, one of the foremost centres of Red Guard activity in Peking.

198.3 CHOU EN-LAI'S SUCCESSOR: Interesting article by Victor Zorza entitled 'Stormy finale to the great brawl of China', *The Guardian*, London, 9 February 1976.

199.1 'FORCE IS . . . UNDERSTAND': Truman (1), Vol. 2, p. 342.

199.1 'ALMOST GENERALLY . . . MAINLAND': *Keesing's Contemporary Archives*, London, Vol. 10, p. 14118.

199.1 'THE GREATER . . . HOSTILITY': Fitzgerald (6), p. 95.

203.3 SINO–INDIAN BORDER: For a glimpse of the great intrigues of nineteenth-century Britain and Russia in Central Asia, see Skrine and Nightingale (1).

8 CHINA, THE MODERN MIRACLE

204.1 'IN PLACE OF . . . AWARENESS': Kato (1), pp. 22–3.

204.1 'A POLITICAL . . . REVOLUTION': Lattimore (3), p. 7.

207.2 'MAO TSE-TUNG . . . DOING SO': Quoted in Schram (1), p. 111.

207.2 'WHAT MAY . . . MATERIALISM': Needham (9), p. 66. See also Needham (2), p. 455 and Cotterell (1), p. 199.

208.3 'TODAY'S CHINA . . . APPLIED': Quoted in Schram (1), p. 112.

210.1 'IN THE . . . BOURGEOISIE': From 'Chairman Mao's Latest Directive', *Peking Review*, No. 16, 1968.

210.2 THE YANG CH'ENG-WU AFFAIR: See Karol (2), pp. 316–26.

210.3 'CHAIRMAN MAO . . . SICKNESS': The view of cadres in 1972. *Ibid.*, p. 415.

211.2 'IT IS . . . VERDICTS': Reported in 'Mao attacks Teng in move to split pragmatists', *The Guardian*, London, 11 March 1976. This article points out that the *People's Daily* carried 'brand-new quotations from Mao, and such new 'sayings' have been a feature of all major campaigns in China in the past. They are 'literally' verbal weapons of great power which the Chairman puts in the hands of his supporters at the appropriate moment.' Chairman Mao's comment is unmistakably a backhand swipe at Chou En-lai's rehabilitation of Teng Hsiao-ping.

211.3 CHENG CH'IAO: See De Francis (1), p. 10.

211.3 'THE WRITTEN . . . LANGUAGES': Quoted in 'Language Reform in China' by H. C. Mills, *Far Eastern Quarterly*, 15, 1955–6.

214.1 'IT IS . . . ARTISTIC': From 'Current Tasks of Reforming the Written Language', pp. 9–14, in Chou En-lai, Wu Yu-chang and Li Chin-hsi, *Reform of the Chinese Written Language*, Peking, 1958.

214.2 IMPORTANCE OF ADULT EDUCATION: See Chen (1), pp. 10–11, and 75–8.

214.2 CHAOYANG AGRICULTURAL COLLEGE: Reported in 'Movable campus makes for the grass roots', *The Times Educational Supplement*, London, 4 April 1975. See also Chen (1), pp. 287–91.

214.2 'THE METHOD . . . THEM': Quoted in Ch'en (3), pp. 21–2.

215.1 'A DEBT OF BLOOD AND TEARS': See Chen (1).

215.3 'IT IS . . . PERSISTS': Kato (1), p. 31.

215.4 RETAIL PRICE INDEX: Reported in 'How Mao thought China out of the red', *The Guardian*, London, 11 September 1974.

215.6 'THERE CAN . . . WEST': Galbraith (1), pp. 118–20. He accepts as likely a ten to eleven per cent annual rate of increase in Chinese industrial and agricultural output.

217.2 YEAR 2000: Reported 'Peking strives for take-off', *The Guardian*, London, 24 January 1975.

218.1 ANTI-URBAN TEMPER AND TREATY PORTS: See Rhoads Murphey, 'The Treaty Ports and China's Modernization'; Elvin and Skinner (1), pp. 68–70.

218.3 SHANGHAI . . . A YEAR: Extract 'The Rebirth of Shanghai', *The Sunday Times*, London, 14 April 1975. Originally a paper delivered at a United Nations conference on exploding cities.

221.2 'A PLACE . . . HARVESTING': Richman (1), p. 61.

221.2 'I THINK . . . STRONG?': Quoted in Schram (1), p. 351.

221.3 'SEPARATE ALL . . . CHARACTER': Mao (1), II, pp. 380–418.

222.1 'THE DEMANDS . . . ENFORCE IT': Quoted by Scott (1), pp. 14–15.

222.2 ANCIENT INHABITANTS: See Cheng Te-K'un (3), pp. 5–6, 7–8 and 11–13 respectively.

223.2 CH'IN SHIH HUANG-TI: The discovery of the buried army of Ch'in, as yet not fully excavated and reported, will compel a reassessment of early Chinese art. Previously, little had survived from the Ch'in Empire. Peking Radio's association of Lin Piao with the enemies of Ch'in Shih Huang-ti was reported by John Gittings in *The Guardian*, London, 13 July 1974.

225.2 'WHILE WE . . . MATERIALISM': Mao Tse-tung, 'On Contradiction', 1937. Quoted in the *Little Red Book*, p. 222.

225.4 'THE CHINESE . . . THEIR OWN': Quoted in Schram (1), p. 374.

226.2 POPULATION: For a balanced treatment of Chinese population figures see Orleans (1), ch. 6. He points out the proportion of Chinese to the total population of the globe is, slowly but surely, decreasing.

EPILOGUE

228.1 HUA KUO-FENG: One month after the death of Mao Tse-tung the elevation of Hua Kuo-feng was announced on big character posters in Peking. They read: 'Resolutely support the resolution concerning the appointment of Comrade Hua Kuo-feng as chairman of the Central Committee and chairman of the Military Affairs Commission.' The latter appointment is a key one, since it is the formal link between the Party and the People's Liberation Army. It was also announced at the same time that Hua Kuo-feng would be in charge of all Chairman Mao's writings – the ideological fount itself.

No ideologue himself, the new chairman was given the special responsibility of sorting out the aftermath of Lin Piao's fall, a difficult task he undertook at the request of Mao Tse-tung. After the dismissal of Teng Hsiao-ping he found himself acting Prime Minister. Now, as the successor of Mao Tse-tung, Hua Kuo-feng's rise to power appears swift, and the important first step was probably his election to the Central Committee at the close of the Cultural Revolution. Previously he had been a little known party secretary in a county of Hunan. Hua Kuo-feng is considered to be inclined neither to the 'ultra-Left' nor the 'capitalist roaders'.

Bibliography

All references made in the notes to the text are given in full here. Numbers follow on from those used in *The Early Civilization of China*. Each entry comprises the name of the author, the title of the book or article, and relevant bibliographical details with dates. Entries are presented alphabetically.

Ambrose, S. E. (1), *Rise to Globalism*, London, 1971.

Balazs, E. (1), *Chinese Civilization and Bureaucracy*, trans. H. M. Wright, New Haven, 1964.

Boswell, J. (1), *The Life of Samuel Johnson*, London, 1811.

Brackett, O. (1), *Thomas Chippendale, a Study of his Life, Work and Influence*, London, 1924.

Braudel, F. (1), *Capitalism and Material Life, 1400–1800*, trans. K. Kochan, London, 1973.

Buchanan, K. (1), *The Transformation of the Chinese Earth: Perspectives on Modern China*, London, 1970.

Buchanan, K. (2), *The Chinese People and the Chinese Earth*, London, 1966.

Bynner, Witter (1) (trans.), *The Way of Life according to Lao Tzu*, New York, 1962.

Carl, K. A. (1), *With the Empress Dowager of China*, London, 1906.

Chan, Wing-Tsit (1) (trans.), *Instructions for Practical Living and other Neo-Confucian Writings of Wang Yang-ming*, New York and London, 1963.

Chen, T. Hsi-en (1), *The Maoist Educational Revolution*, New York, 1974.

Ch'en, J. (1), *Yuan Shih-k'ai*, Stanford, 1972; originally published as *Yuan Shih-k'ai (1859–1916): Brutus Assumes the Purple*, London and Stanford, 1961.

Ch'en, J. (2), *Mao and the Chinese Revolution*, Oxford, 1965.

Ch'en, J. (3), *Mao Papers*, London, 1970.

Cheng Te-K'un (3), *Archaeology in China*, supplement to 1: *New Light on Prehistoric China*, Cambridge, 1963.

Chesneaux, J. (1), *Secret Societies in China in the Nineteenth and Twentieth Centuries*, trans. G. Nettle, London, 1971.

Chi Ch'ao-ting (1), *Key Economic Areas in Chinese History, as revealed in the Development of Public Works for Water-Control*, London, 1936; New York, 1970.

Contag, V. (1), *Chinese Masters of the Seventeenth Century*, London, 1969.

Cotterell, Y. Y. and A. (1), *The Early Civilization of China*, London, 1975.

Cranmer-Byng, J. L. (1) (ed.), *An Embassy to China; being the journal kept by Lord Macartney during his embassy to Emperor Ch'ien-lung, 1793–1794*, London, 1962.

Cronin, V. (1), *The Wise Men from the West*, London, 1955.

Dardess, J. W. (1), *Conquerors and Confucians. Aspects of Political Change in Late Yuan China*, New York and London, 1973.

Davidson, B. (1), *Old Africa Rediscovered*, London, 1959.

Dawson, R. (1), *The Chinese Chameleon. An Analysis of European Conceptions of Chinese Civilization*, Oxford, 1967.

De Francis, J. (1), *Nationalism and Language Reform in China*, Princeton, 1950.

Deutscher, I. (1), *The Unfinished Revolution: Russia, 1917–67*, Oxford, 1967.

Dobson, A. (1) (ed.), *The Citizen of the World by O. Goldsmith*, London, 1934.

Du Halde, J. P. (1), *Description géographique, historique, chronologique et physique de l'empire de la Chine et de la Tartarie chinoise*, Paris, 1735.

Dumont, R. (1), *La Chine surpeuplée: Tiers-monde affamé*, Paris, 1965.

Duyvendak, J. J. L. (2), *China's Discovery of Africa*, London, 1949.

Elvin, M. (1), *The Pattern of the Chinese Past*, London, 1973.

Elvin, M. and Skinner, G. W. (1), *The Chinese City Between Two Worlds*, Stanford, 1974.

Endicott, S. L. (1), *Diplomacy and Enterprise. British China Policy 1933–37*, British Columbia and Manchester, 1975.

Fan Tsen-Chung (1), 'Dr Johnson and Chinese Culture', *Nine Dragon Screen, being reprints of addresses and papers presented to the China Society 1909–45*, London, 1965.

Filesi, T. (1), *China and Africa in the Middle Ages*, trans. D. L. Morrison, London, 1972.

Fitzgerald, C. P. (4), *The Southern Expansion of the Chinese People; Southern Fields and Southern Ocean*, London, 1972.

Fitzgerald, C. P. (5), *A Concise History of East Asia*, Hong Kong, 1966.

Fitzgerald, C. P. (6), *China and South-east Asia since 1945*, London, 1973.

Fitzgerald, C. P. (7), *Flood Tide in China*, London, 1958.

Fitzgerald, C. P. (8), *The Chinese View of Their Place in the World*, London, 1964.

Frodsham, J. D. (1) (trans.), *The First Chinese Embassy to the West. The Journals of Kuo Sung-t'ao, Liu Hsi-Hung and Chang Te-yi*, Oxford, 1974.

Fung Yu-Lan (1), *The Spirit of Chinese Philosophy*, trans. E. R. Hughes, London, 1947.

Galbraith, J. K. (1), *A China Passage*, London, 1973.

Gallagher, L. J. (1) (trans.), *China in the Sixteenth Century: The Journals of Matthew Ricci: 1583–1610*, New York, 1953.

Garner, Sir Harry (1), *Oriental Blue and White*, London, 1954.

Gittings, J. (1), *The World and China, 1922–1972*, London, 1974.

Goodrich, L. C. (1), *China*, Berkeley, 1946.

Goodrich, L. C. (2), *A Short History of the Chinese People*, New York, 1943.

Granet, M. (1), *The Religion of the Chinese People*, trans. M. Freedman, Oxford, 1975.

Hamberg, T. (1), 'The Visions of Hung-siu-tshuen, and Origin of the Kwang-si Insurrection', *China Mail*, Hong Kong, 1854.

Herrmann, A. (1), *An Historical Atlas of China*, Edinburgh, 1966; based on *Historical and Commercial Atlas of China*, Harvard–Yenching Institute, Monograph Series 1, 1935.

Ho Ping-Ti (2), *The Ladder of Success in Imperial China: Aspects of Social Mobility, 1368–1911*, New York, 1960.

Ho Ping-Ti (3), *Studies in the Population of China, 1368–1953*, Cambridge, Massachusetts, 1959.

Hobsbawm, E. J. (1), *The Age of Capital*, London, 1975.

Hobson, R. L. (1), *Wares of the Ming Dynasty*, London, 1925.

Honour, H. (1), *Chinoiserie. A Vision of Cathay*, London, 1961.

Hsia, C. T. (1), *A History of Modern Chinese Fiction*, New Haven, 1971.

Hucker, C. O. (1), *The Traditional Chinese State in Ming Times (1368–1644)*, Tucson, 1961.

Hudson, G. F. (1), *Europe and China; a Survey of their Relations from Earliest Times to 1800*, 1931.

Hughes, E. R, (1), *The Invasion of China by the Western World*, London, 1937.

Jen Yu-wen (1), *The Taiping Revolutionary Movement*, New Haven and London, 1973.

K'ang Yu-wei (1), *The One-World Philosophy of K'ang Yu-wei (Ta T'ung Shu)*, trans. L. G. Thompson, London, 1958.

Karol, K. S. (1), *China: The Other Communism*, New York, 1967.

Karol, K. S. (2), *The Second Chinese Revolution*, trans. M. Jones, London, 1975.

Kato, S. (1), *The Japan–China Phenomenon. Conflict or Compatibility?* London, 1974.

Kiermann, F. A. and Fairbank, J. K. (1) (ed.), *Chinese Ways in Warfare*, Cambridge, Massachusetts, 1974.

Lattimore, O. (1), *Inner Asian Frontiers of China*, Oxford and New York, 1940; American Geographical Society Research Monograph Series 21.

Lattimore, O. (3), *History and Revolution in China*, Lund, 1970; Scandinavian Institute of Asian Studies Monograph Series 3.

Lawton, T. (1), *Chinese Figure Painting*, Washington, 1973.

Lee, Sherman, E. (1), *The Colours of Ink. Chinese Paintings and Related Ceramics from the Cleveland Museum of Art*, New York, 1974.

Lewis, J. W. (1), *Leadership in Communist China*, Ithaca, New York, 1963.

Li, Dun, J. (1), *The Ageless Chinese*, New York, 1965.

Liang Ch'i-ch'ao (1), *Intellectual Trends in the Ch'ing Period (Ch'ing-tai hsueh-shu kai-lun)*, trans. I. C. Y. Hsu, Cambridge, Massachusetts, 1959.

Liang Ch'i-ch'ao (2), *Biography of K'ang Yu-wei*, Shanghai, 1907 and 1908.

Liu Shao-chi (1), 'Report on the Work of the Central Committee', *Second Session of the Eighth National Congress of the Communist Party of China*, Peking, 1958.

Lo Jung-Pang (1), 'The emergence of China as a sea power during the late Sung and early Yuan periods', *Far Eastern Quarterly* XIV, 4 August 1955, pp. 489–504.

Lu Hsun (1), *A Brief History of Chinese Fiction*, Peking, 1964.

Lu Hsun (2), *Selected Stories*, Peking, 1972.

Macnair, H. F. (1) (ed.), *China*, Berkeley, 1946.

Mao Tse-tung (1), *Selected Works*, Peking, 1960–1.

Mao Tse-tung (2), *On the Correct Handling of Contradictions Among the People*, Peking, 1957.

Marsden, W. (1) (trans.), *The Travels of Marco Polo*, London, 1908.

Martin, W. P. (1), *Hanlin Papers*, Shanghai, 1880.

Mason, G. M. (1), *Western Concepts of China and the Chinese, 1840–1876*, New York, 1939.

Melby, J. F. (1), *The Mandate of Heaven. Record of a Civil War, China 1945–49*, London, 1969.

de Mendoza, J. G. (1), *Historia de las Cosas mos notables, Ritos y Costumbres del Gran Reyno de la China, sabidas assi por los libros de los mesmos Chinas, como por relacion de religiosos y oltras personas que an estado en el dicho Reyno*, Rome, 1585. English translation by Robert Parke, London, 1588; (ed.) G. T. Staunton, London, 1853; Hakluyt Society Publication, 1, 14–15.

Mills, J. V. G. (1) (trans. and ed.), *Ma Huan, Ying-yai Sheng-lan. The Overall Survey of the Ocean's Shores, 1433*. Cambridge, 1970; Hakluyt Society, Extra Series 42.

Needham, J. (1), *Science and Civilisation in China, 1: Introductory Orientations*, Cambridge, 1954.

Needham, J. (2), *Science and Civilisation in China, 2: History of Scientific Thought*, Cambridge, 1956.

Needham, J. (6), *Science and Civilisation in China, 4: Physics and Physical Technology, III: Civil Engineering and Nautics*, Cambridge, 1971.

Needham, J. (8), *The Grand Titration: Science and Society in East and West*, London, 1969.

Needham, J. (9), *Within the Four Seas: The Dialogue of East and West*, London, 1969.

Orleans, L. A. (1), *Every Fifth Child: The Population of China*, London, 1972.

Parry, J. H. (1), *The Age of Reconnaissance*, London, 1963.

Reichwein, A. (1), *China and Europe: intellectual and artistic contacts in the eighteenth century*, London, 1925.

Remer, C. F. (1), *A Study of Chinese Boycotts*, London, 1933.

Richman, B. (1), 'Capitalists and Managers in Communist China', *Harvard Business Review*, January–February, 1967.

Robinson, J. (1), *The Cultural Revolution in China*, Harmondsworth, 1969.

Rowbotham, A. H. (1), *Missionary and Mandarin*, Berkeley, 1942.

Schram, S. R. (1), *The Political Thought of Mao Tse-tung*, New York, 1963; Harmondsworth, 1969.

Scott, A. C. (1), *Literature and the Arts in Twentieth-Century China*, London, 1963.

Sirén, O. (2), *The Walls and Gates of Peking*, London, 1924.

Sirén, O. (3), *The Imperial Palaces of Peking*, 3 vols., Paris and Brussels, 1927.

Sirén, O. (5), *A History of Early Chinese Art*, 4 vols., London, 1929. Vol. 1, Prehistoric and Pre-Han; Vol. 2, Han; Vol. 3, Sculpture; Vol. 4, Architecture.

Sirén, O. (6), *The Chinese on the Art of Painting: Translations and Comments*, New York, 1963.

Sirén, O. (7), *China and the Gardens of Europe*, New York, 1950.

Skrine, C. P. and Nightingale, P. (1), *Macartney at Kashgar: New Light on British, Chinese and Russian Activities in Sinkiang, 1890–1918*, London, 1973.

Snow, E. (1), *Red Star Over China*, London, 1937.

Snow, E. (2), *Scorched Earth*, London, 1941.

Spence, J. D. (1) (trans.), *Emperor of China. Self-portrait of K'ang-hsi*, London, 1974.

Sullivan, M. (3), *Chinese Art in the Twentieth Century*, London, 1959.

Sullivan, M. (4), *The Meeting of Eastern and Western Art, from the Sixteenth Century to the Present Day*, London, 1973.

Sun Yat-sen (1), *Three Principles of the People*, trans. F. W. Price, New York, 1943.

Tawney, R. H. (1), *Land and Labour in China*, London, 1932.

Tregear, R. T. (1), *A Geography of China*, London, 1965.

Tregear, R. T. (2), *An Economic Geography of China*, London, 1970.

Truman, H. S. (1), *Memoirs*, Vol. 1, London, 1955; Vol. 2, London, 1956.

Waley, A. (11), *Yuan Mei: Eighteenth-Century Chinese Poet*, London, 1956.

Waley, A. (12), *The Opium War Through Chinese Eyes*, London, 1958.

Waller, D. J. (1), *The Government and Politics of Communist China*, London, 1970.

Walrond, T. (1) (ed.), *Letters and Journals of James, Eighth Earl of Elgin*, London, 1872.

White, T. H. and Jacoby, A. (1), *Thunder out of China*, London, 1947.

Whiteway, R. S. (1), *The Rise of Portuguese Power in India, 1497–1550*, London, 1899.

Whitfield, R. (1), *In Pursuit of Antiquity. Chinese Paintings of the Ming and Ch'ing Dynasties from the Collection of Mr and Mrs Earl Morse*, Princeton, 1969.

Williams, S. W. (1), *The Middle Kingdom*, New York, 1848.

Woodward, H. G. W. (1), *The Truth About the Chinese Republic*, London, 1925.

Worsley, P. (1), *Inside China*, London, 1975.

Index